**Sista,
Speak!**

SONJA L. LANEHART

Sista, Speak!

BLACK WOMEN
KINFOLK
TALK ABOUT
LANGUAGE
AND LITERACY

 University of Texas Press, Austin

Requests for permission to reproduce material
from this work should be sent to
Permissions, University of Texas Press,
P.O. Box 7819, Austin, TX 78713-7819.

♾The paper used in this book meets the minimum
requirements of ANSI/NISO Z39.48-1992 (R1997)
(Permanence of Paper).

Library of Congress Cataloging-in-Publication Data

Lanehart, Sonja L.
    Sista, speak! : Black women kinfolk talk about
language and literacy / Sonja L. Lanehart.—1st ed.
        p.   cm.
    Includes bibliographical references and index.
    ISBN 0-292-74728-4 (cloth : alk. paper)—
    ISBN 0-292-74729-2 (pbk. : alk. paper)
    1. African American women—Social conditions.
2. African American women—Education.   3. Literacy—Social aspects—United States.   4. African
American women—Biography.   5. African Americans—Race identity.   6. African Americans—
Languages.   7. Language and culture—United
States.   I.   Title.

E185.86 .L353   2002
305.48'896073—dc21
                                        2001052225

CONTENTS

For
    my awesome God,
who blesses me in spite of myself.

For
    my family,
especially Granny, Mom, Nanny, Aunie, Dad, Sis,
    and my husband, Paul,
who believed in me even when I did not,
    and for Uncle Ellis,
who would have been proud too.

For
    Maya, Grace, Reia, and Deidra,
who helped me come to believe what filmmaker Julie Dash
    knew:

    "In my world, Black women can do anything."

For
    all the other teachers I have had,
both in and out of school,
    both sentient beings and sentient texts,
who helped me come to know and embrace what
    Johnnetta B. Cole articulated so well:

    "I need to keep thinking and analyzing,
    and have that transformed onto a piece of paper [because]
    if we as African-American women
    don't write our own books,
    then other folks will continue to define us."

————————————————————————————————— •

ACKNOWLEDGMENTS

I felt sort of like Ross Perot throughout my time in higher education: "The American people asked me to be here to fight for them and so that's why I got into the race." In my case it was my family who asked me to fight. I had to do something that I didn't fully understand or realize when I decided to go to college and on to graduate school to earn a Ph.D. I had a mission: to earn those degrees along with my family. Most of my family made it through high school, but no further. All of them wanted me to get my education no matter what. All of them made it through with me except one. We lost him not long ago in a tragic accident. When I told my mom that he would miss graduation—so close to realizing our goal—she reminded me that he would miss a lot of things, but he had been there for a lot too.

Many people in my family, people who are important to me, struggle with literacy. The concept has lost most of the meaning I thought it had when it was first introduced to me in graduate school. But many people in my family know what it means to them: To read, write, and comprehend. To feel secure in *your* knowledge and understanding. To express your feelings, opinions, convictions, hopes, desires, dreams, fears, frustrations, and anxieties in a meaningful and insightful way. To be respected for your words and thoughts, which can easily be conveyed in the way you talk, and for the very act of writing with self-assurance.

It is a popular saying in this country that Americans must take care of our own; we cannot help others until we help our own, our home. We must cut foreign aid and help the needy we have right here in this free, democratic, capitalist society they call a Superpower. To an extent, I agree with the essence of that rhetoric. Before I can help others, I have to help "Home." That means bringing my mother and others into this world of literacy they so desperately want to be a part of and feel so hopeless and helpless about. Like many others, they have stories to tell and voices to use, but they have limited means to express themselves if they are not literate—or so they believe. I have come to realize that it does not matter what I believe, and it does not matter that I feel they are capable of so much unless they believe it themselves. I must do something. I hope this book is one way I can do something, but I know I have more to do— as we all do.

I would like to thank my husband, Paul, for being the friend he is. He read every draft, encouraged me when I did not think I could finish, lived with me through my many impossible days, gave me good advice, and took on more than his share of household responsibilities so that I could complete this book.

In addition to my family, others have been of great support and inspiration to me. In particular, I thank Geneva Smitherman, John Baugh, Marcyliena Morgan, Arthur Spears, Walter Edwards, Michele Foster, Salikoko Mufwene, John Rickford, Walt Wolfram, William Kretzschmar, and Barbara McCaskill for their counsel, mentoring, and friendship.

I thank Alisea Williams McLeod for her conversations and shared reflections, which were always challenging and enlightening.

I thank Richard Bailey for insisting that I do what I wanted to do and not what I thought I should do.

I thank Jay Robinson for showing me that I could read, and think, and write for pleasure and engagement, and for helping me to learn what Barbara Smith, a book publisher and sociologist, revealed in *Proud Sisters:* "Writing travels so much farther than you could ever go. Something that was part of me gets to go places that I may never see" (p. 48).

I thank Thomas Cable, Gary Underwood, and James Duban, my early advisors at the University of Texas, for the encouragement, good counsel, support, and friendship they offered to a first-generation doctoral-student-to-be. They were all greatly instrumental in my pursuing both a career in academia and goals in other areas of my life because they taught me and convinced me that I could.

I thank Claire Ellen Weinstein and Bruce Smith for providing me with insights about learning, and knowing, and living.

I thank Juanita Johnson-Bailey and Shirley Brice Heath for reading all parts of earlier versions of the book and providing helpful feedback.

I thank Theresa May, assistant director and editor-in-chief of the University of Texas Press, for her wonderful faith and advice, and the reviewers for their editorial improvements.

Also, I would like to extend my gratitude to the Center for Humanities and Arts, directed by Betty Jean Craig, at the University of Georgia and to the Ford Foundation, with its very supportive postdoctoral fellowship, staff, and annual conference, for awarding me research funding to complete *Sista, Speak!* Their financial support was most welcome.

Though it would have been difficult to do any of this without my family and the others named, it would have been impossible to do any of it without the help and grace of God.

Sista, Speak!

INTRODUCTION

From the very beginning I saw myself as writing . . . for those who would care about . . . women not only because of their unique individualities, but also because of what they represent: black women/writers struggling against unfavorable odds to create their personalities and artistic selves.

—Gloria T. Hull, in Johnson, *Proud Sisters*

● ● ●

STORIES TO BE TOLD AND NOT FORGOTTEN

Maya, Grace, Reia, Deidra, Sonja: all African American women in one family—my family—whose stories have spoken to me for as long as I can remember. They were purposely chosen for this study because I want to share their stories with others, who I know have mothers, grand-mothers, sisters, and daughters just like mine. As sociolinguist Gwendolyn Etter-Lewis notes, "The notion that African American women are an invisible group on the sidelines that easily can be combined with other groups is a convenient fiction that conceals their power and importance. They have played major roles in all of American culture and continue to do so in spite of resistance and a variety of formidable barriers" (*My Soul Is My Own*, p. xvii). So, although these African American women do not speak for all African American women, they can certainly speak to many of them as well as to other people.

I present their stories as narratives. Their narratives are important because they are stories to be told and not forgotten. That, of course, is the way I see them, because these are women who are mothers, sisters, daughters—others—whose stories are too often untold and unreflected upon. The narratives allow you to see each woman as she wants you to see her. The women tell their own stories because the stories are theirs to tell. They appear independently of one another, but, as you know, all of our stories are interdependent. That interdependence resonates with a clear

●

voice because we are not alone. It is important for us to realize that if we do not already, and *Sista, Speak!* should help to solidify that message.

As Etter-Lewis notes, African American women are conspicuously absent from major studies in most disciplines. Additionally, as scholar Paula Giddings notes, despite the range and significance of the history of African American women, we are often perceived as token women in Black texts and as token Blacks in feminist ones. We need our own texts, because the paucity of investigations of African American women's speech demands that we be rendered visible in our own right, as scholar Margaret Andersen notes, instead of invisible in the various studies that concentrate only on the experiences and perspectives of dominant groups to the detriment of the recognition of African American women's contributions and worth to society.

Sista, Speak! tells the stories of five African American women in the same family across three generations. The stories illustrate the themes of language, literacy, identity, ideologies, education, and sociohistorical context—issues that touch all of our lives. They reaffirm what I know to be true—that African American English is not "bad" English, and, as pointed out by linguist Rosina Lippi-Green, that there is no such thing as "standard" English. This is a powerful myth that most Americans believe is as right and as real as rain, but it is no less a myth. Its partner in crime is the literacy myth, coined and explicated by literacy scholar Harvey Graff.

In probing these mythical concepts, I found no less than three intersections between the rhetorical ideologies of literacy and "standard" English. I call those three intersections the "Ideology of Opportunity," the "Ideology of Progress," and the "Ideology of Emancipation." I discuss these ideologies in more detail below because they affect these women's lives (and those of others) in different but significant ways. Their stories are laced with references to these ideologies and show the power they have on individual lives and across generations of a family.

WHO HAS THE ARMY AND THE NAVY?: MYTHS, MAYHEM, AND METAPHORS

Good poetry and successful revolution change our lives. And you cannot compose a good poem or wage a revolution without changing consciousness. And you cannot alter consciousness unless you attack the language that you share with your enemies and invent a language that you share with your allies.

—June Jordan, in Johnson, *Proud Sisters*

What came first—language or grammars? Okay, that's easy. Language came first. Since humans verbally communicated long before grammars were first written, it is an unavoidable conclusion that the grammatical structures of a language develop at a time when there are no grammarians. Okay, now a harder question. What came first: schooling (i.e., an institutional entity) or literacy? I propose that literacy came first. Literacy and "standard" English can be used as a means of control—they are political. Both tend to belong to those in power and to those who are able to determine what is acceptable. In their view (i.e., that of those who have power), it is dangerous to have the masses constructing society. It is safer and more suitable for those in power to direct how society is to be structured, which thus ensures that those in power will stay in power. One can control who gets in and who stays out by controlling who reads, what they read, and how they read as well as how they talk—all by establishing the rules in favor of the elites.

Proponents of the Ideology of Opportunity espouse the societal benefits of literacy and "standard" English through opportunity—in other words, opportunities galore knock at the door of the literate and "standard" English speaker but not of those who adhere to neither. This ideology purports: (1) better educational opportunities; (2) greater success in school; (3) diminished social barriers because of conformity to the prestigious norm (White, middle-class, Eurocentric, etc.); and (4) better job opportunities because one fits the "cookie cutter" pattern of the presentable employee. This ideology is problematic because it does not account for all the other things that make the possibility of being gainfully employed at one's skill level more complex than that—like race, ethnicity, and gender.

Linguist James Sledd acknowledges in his polemical essay "Bi-Dialectalism: The Linguistics of White Supremacy" (p. 320) that since linguistic prejudice can keep one from moving up, it is taught that people who want to be decision-makers had better talk and write like the people who make decisions. Our society does not quite work that way. As scholar J. Elspeth Stuckey indicates, "Lives are defined by language if language is a tool of oppression. . . . What Vološinov knew of language is surely true of literacy: the society that fixes the worth of speakers fixes the worth of their words also" (*The Violence of Literacy,* p. 92). Hence, the rules would only change and the people would still be the same. I am not going to deny that in a literate society being literate can be advantageous. According to Stuckey, the achievement of literacy is made important in such a society not only because it is a social construction but also because it is a social restriction and a system of oppression for those who are not literate. However, being literate or speaking "standard" English does not necessarily deliver on all the promises the ideology declares.

I am often reminded of Sledd's comment in 1972, still true today, about the futility of learning "standard" English for those who are not the ones making the decisions about what "standard" English is:

> In the U.S.A., we are being told, everybody wants approval—not approval for doing anything worth approving, but approval for doing whatever happens to be approved. Because approval goes to upward mobility, everybody should be upwardly mobile; and because upward mobility is impossible for underdogs who have not learned middle-dog barking, we must teach it to them for use in their excursions into the middle-dog world. There is no possibility either that the present middle class can be brought to tolerate lower-class English or that upward mobility, as a national aspiration, will be questioned. Those are the pillars on which the state is built. (p. 325)

We must stop blaming those whose language is different and start looking at the people and the system that criticize them for being different. It is not acceptable to say that corporate America wants people who can write and speak "standard" English or to say that success comes only to those who speak "standard" English. We need to break out of the mindset that says that because that is the way things are we have to go along to get along. Tradition does not make something right. If it is broken, it should be fixed. If the social or economic structure is unjust and perpetuates exclusion based on language, race, gender, or social status, then the structure has to change, not the people who have done nothing wrong except to physically and culturally exist as different from a supposed norm.

Literacy researchers such as Graff and Carl Kaestle and his associates have shown that one does not necessarily have better educational opportunities, better success in society, diminished social barriers, or better job opportunities just because one is literate. There is not a causal relationship between literacy and opportunity. It is more likely that race, gender, ethnicity, social status (or class), and religious background are better determinants of opportunity than literacy. For example, in Graff's study of nineteenth-century Canada, being Black or Irish Catholic and literate did not mean nearly as much as being White, English Protestant, and illiterate. In fact, for those who were oppressed and the targets of the schooling and literacy campaigns at the time, schooling and literacy mostly served to further oppress those already being oppressed and to further heighten social and economic stratification. The situation was and is similar to that of the United States. There are many instances today among the oppressed and disempowered in which they are in school but not of it. In other words, they are allowed into schools because of state laws, but they are not really part of schools that are based on middle-class (and mostly Eurocentric) life.

According to scholar Katherine Bassard, in her essay "Gender and Genre: Black Women's Autobiography and the Ideology of Literacy," literacy, equated with freedom and economic advancement, is an ideological construct and thus a product of culture and social formation. The middle class will not tolerate nonstandard English or differing cultures and their values and beliefs (or alternative conceptions) about literacy. Hence, as Sledd notes, even "compassionate, liberal educators, knowing the ways of society, will change the color of a student's vowels because they cannot change the color of their students' skins" (p. 325).

The Ideology of Progress claims that those who are literate or those who speak "standard" English will: (1) overcome the adversities and shortcomings of a deprived or deficient culture that does not use "standard" English or value literacy, and (2) develop greater cognitive and logical abilities that will facilitate abstract thought. The Ideology of Progress is firmly entrenched in our society. It concerns me because of its cultural and racial biases as well as the lack of insight into what language means to its users and what literacy is and is not.

The Ideology of Progress is seen to be ethnocentric and racist when the research and reasons for the research are probed. Psychologists Martin Deutsch, Irwin Katz, and Arthur Jensen were clearly in search of a way to distinguish intellectually between races (yet another social construction). Literacy scholars Jack Goody and Ian Watt unduly privilege the alphabet over other forms of writing as well as privileging the mental capacities of those who are "alphabetically" literate. Educator Eleanor

Wilson Orr believes that "for students whose first language is BEV [Black English Vernacular, now referred to most often as African American Vernacular English], then, language can be a barrier to success in mathematics and science" (*Twice as Less*, p. 9). She also believes the grammar of "standard" English has been shaped by what is true mathematically. Orr concludes then that linguistic systems like African American English are inferior because they are not capable of certain abstract and logical functions inherent in "standard" English. As a result, African Americans who speak African American English will perform poorly in math and science. Linguist John Baugh, in his review of Orr's book, states, "Her conclusions regarding linguistic differences between BEV and standard English, as well as the cognitive assertions that grow out of her linguistic impressions, tend to be uninformed and somewhat naive" (p. 395).

Linguist William Labov has shown in his seminal studies of urban Black youths in the 1960s and 1970s that nonstandard English (which is typically spoken by people of color and those of lower socioeconomic status groups) is just as logical and just as viable a means of communication as "standard" English. Labov has shown that the problem does not lie with the speakers of nonstandard English, but with the failure of educational institutions to recognize and build on the existing verbal abilities, linguistic systems, and cultures of those who speak nonstandard English and with the bias against such varieties of English in the social system. The language of the child did not then (i.e., at the time of Labov's research) and does not now need to be replaced; it needs to be acknowledged in a positive way.

In 1971 a resolution was brought to the Linguistic Society of America that called to public attention the linguistic evidence against Deutsch's, Katz's, and Jensen's point of view, stating that no natural language has been shown to be superior to another for the expression of logical thought. The referendum was passed and was endorsed again at the annual meeting two years later. As linguists James and Lesley Milroy indicate in *Authority in Language,* though middle-class language is seen as superior in every respect—as more abstract, and more flexible, detailed, and subtle—this is clearly not the case. Each child's language has quantity, quality, and potential for use in intellectual contexts despite its differences from "standard" English or the ingrained expectations that the language of an African American child, or other nonnative speaker of "standard" English, is deprived or deficient. In Ralph Wiley's *Why Black*

People Tend to Shout, which contains his *signifyin* piece, "Why Black People Have No Culture," he states: "Black people have no culture because most of it is out on loan to white people. With no interest" (quoted in Geneva Smitherman's *Black Talk,* pp. 21–22).

Psychologists Sylvia Scribner and Michael Cole, in *The Psychology of Literacy,* also countered the Ideology of Progress with their research on the Vai in Liberia. The Vai have three different literacy environments: English literacy, which is taught in a formal school setting; Vai script literacy (a syllabic system), which is taught informally among peers and family; and Arabic literacy, which is taught in a formal, disciplined setting. A Vai may practice from none to all the literacies. Scribner and Cole found that neither Vai script literacy nor Arabic alphabetic literacy was associated with "higher order intellectual skills" as measured by typical school-based tests, nor did either enhance the use of taxonomic skills or contribute to syllogistic reasoning. English literacy was associated with certain types of decontextualization and abstract reasoning; however, this was not a lasting attribute. The residue of English literacy was seen in verbal explanation tasks (i.e., talking about tasks). Hence, English literacy taught in formal school settings served the needs of English literacy in formal school settings. The alphabet has no special power despite those who stand behind its tyranny.

The Ideology of Emancipation purports: (1) autonomy; (2) empowerment due to the development of critical thinking; and (3) emancipation (real or symbolic) because of the control one will be able to achieve as a shareholder in what can constitute or lead to real power. In this view, literacy is empowering, transformative, emancipatory, and self-enlightening. It inspires confidence. It is emancipatory through revolution. This ideological perspective intrigues me the most because it seems to require a transactional view between the individual (or group) and society. To accept this view of literacy is to define literacy beyond the ability to read and write on some arbitrary hierarchical level, unlike the Ideologies of Opportunity and Progress.

My concern with this ideology is the claim that critical literacy makes everything right with the individual and the world. As Stuckey notes, it paints a romanticized or spiritualized view of literacy. If everyone were critically literate, the world would be a much better place for all humankind, as noted by literacy scholar Johan Galtung in "Literacy, Education, and Schooling—For What?":

What would happen if the whole world became literate? Answer: not so very much, for the world is by and large structured in such a way that it is capable of absorbing the impact. But if the whole world consisted of literate, autonomous, critical, constructive people, capable of translating ideas into action, individually or collectively—the world would change.   (p. 93)

This ideology sees the good in literacy and the possibility that literacy really is the key to all that is better. But, as Stuckey notes, literacy is more than self-fulfillment. Literacy is also social and political and economic in nature. Society wields its literacy more powerfully than does the individual, and a fight against the literate bureaucracy is more than, say, a fight against City Hall. Literacy neither imprisons nor frees people; it merely embodies the enormous complexities of how and why some people live comfortably and others do not.

But there are and have been other limits to the literacy-as-freedom ideology, as Bassard calls it in her 1992 essay:

Their [i.e., nineteenth-century African American women autobiographers'] views about themselves as writers and the purposes of their written texts reflect a broad range of positions vis-à-vis literacy, and even language itself. These women are keenly aware of the limits of the literacy-as-freedom ideology, due to their multiply marginalized position in the social order, and they express everything from mild tension to outright suspicion of the power of the Written Word to provide freedom, economic security, and a restructuring of social formations of power. . . . Though literacy was often used as a means to freedom, it could not entirely constitute freedom.   (p. 120)

The same power is espoused to language standardization. All will be right with the individual and the world if the standard variety of a language is the only one there is. The United States is guilty of pandering a mythology of a standard language and all the goodies that come with it. Reality and the limits of the possibilities are lacking.

We (i.e., those not born into the mainstream and not easily accepted into it) have been told that if we acquire a second dialect, we will have two linguistic systems to call upon in oral or written communication. However, Labov and his associates (i.e., Wendell Harris, Sharon Ash, and John Myhill) have shown that "underlying grammatical patterns of standard English are apparently learned through 'meaning' and intensive interaction with those who already use standard English grammar, not simply by exposure in the mass media or in schools" (Labov and Harris 1983, p. 22). Consequently, "blacks who move in white circles show a major shift in their grammar in the direction of the white norm, but the same is not true for whites who move in black circles" (Ash and Myhill 1983, p. 16). According to literacy scholar Marcia Farr in her essay "Language, Culture, and Writing," "although such whites can learn to 'sound black' by using black pronunciation and vocabulary, they do not acquire BEV [Black English Vernacular] grammar. Such asymmetry is not surprising, of course, considering the social, political, and economic value of standard English, as opposed to BEV, in the mainstream society" (p. 212). A similar statement could be made about the differing uses of literacy in African American communities and the importance of the "Oral Tradition" in those communities when compared with the views of mainstream communities about the "efficacy" of those differing uses and the value of anything "oral."

A slightly altered Ideology of Emancipation, one without the godlike qualities, still conveys the belief that literacy does not involve simply the ability to read and/or write. Literacy is a social construction. As literacy scholar Carolyn Marvin indicates, while literacy may be said to begin with the introduction of writing systems, it is not the same thing as writing. If a person is able only to read the words on a page or write letters on a page that form words, that person is not literate. Just as reading is not holding a text and writing is not moving a pencil or punching a keyboard, literacy is not simply the ability to read and write. For this ideology, literacy is more than the sum of its parts.

Each of these three ideologies is problematic, though certainly the Ideology of Emancipation, especially with the amendment I suggest above, is not as problematic as the other two because it is essentially free of bias based on differences from a supposed norm (e.g., that writing is better than speech or "standard" English is better than nonstandard English). However, the three overlap to some extent, and, in this case, there is still the implication for the Ideology of Emancipation that some people (the literate) are better or better off than others (the nonliterate). Although that may be true to some extent in the First World, I am not convinced that it is intrinsically so. Though I cannot deny that being literate in a society that values literacy or that speaking "standard" English in a society that values "standard" English (even though it has yet to determine what "standard" English is) can be beneficial, none of the ideologies can deliver on all the promises proclaimed. Society is too complex to allow us to believe that all one has to do is be literate and speak "standard" English and all will be well.

THE LAY OF THE LAND

Guided by my heritage of a love of beauty and a respect for strength—in search of my mother's garden I found my own.

—Alice Walker, in Johnson, *Proud Sisters*

As you have probably noticed by now, my name is among those of the five women examined in this book. My decision to include my story with the others, to make this a self-study of sorts, was based not only on the reasons given at the beginning of this introduction, but also on the fact that it could not have been any other way. This book arose from my desire to answer questions that have bothered me since I was a child. I had noticed things about language, about literacy, about African Americans, about women—about being in this world in all those ways and more—that I needed, was compelled, to know more about. I also wanted to understand, accept, reveal, and share the existence and experiences of these women because I knew I was not alone and because these experiences are not unique. I knew I could not do their lives justice without including myself because I was very much a part of them. I knew that even though I did not randomly choose the people I wanted to study, I did not need to. I have seen my story and that of these women acted out in other people's lives. Our stories are not unique, but I think isolation can make us think they are. You are getting the chance to look at me looking at my life and that of the women who have had the greatest impact on it. As such, you also get to see me and my role in the lives of others. That view was truly eye-opening for me because I saw I was not always the person I thought I was even though I knew I was not the person I used to be.

In reading this book you will see a blueprint for what I think we all need to do at some point in our lives. We need to study ourselves, get a good look at ourselves, in order to unmask who we are within ourselves and in the context of our interactions with those who help to make us who we are. I know some could say that I am too close to the subject to see it objectively. They might be right if there were such a thing as objectivity. Who we are and how we come to be influences how we do what we do and why we see what we think we see. We cannot separate ourselves from our sociocultural and sociohistorical contexts. Though this approach—collecting data about myself, performing the same tasks as the other participants, and analyzing and reporting on my own data—may be unique in this type of study and not without its critics, I think both you and I see the participants and my analysis of them without pretense. We are our mothers' daughters, warts and all.

Part One begins with an introductory narrative that presents how I came to do this study[1] (see the notes section for a detailed discussion about the methodology for the study) and why it was important to me. Each subsequent narrative in Part One is that of one of the five participants. The narratives are arranged in the same sequence: background, education, language, literacy, and goals and possible selves. The analyses of the narratives in Part Two proceed for the most part in reverse order: goals, possible selves (with respect to literacy and language), language, literacy, ideologies (with respect to language and uses of literacy), and education, with background integrated in each. As such, there is a familiarity in the structure of each narrative though each is distinctly individual. Also, keep in mind that these areas overlap in meaningful ways, especially with respect to attitudes, ideologies, and behavior.

To explore these issues of language and uses of literacy as integral parts of identity and culture, I present the data from the five participants in the form of self-narratives, a unique and valuable format for sociolinguistic research since much of the data is presented as the text as opposed to being subordinated to analysis or methodology. All the words of the narratives are by the participants except those enclosed by square brackets and in the same font as the rest of the text (i.e., Stone Serif). The contrasting font (i.e., Stone Sans Italic) always represents the actual speech or writing of the participants except names of people and places that might further compromise confidentiality.

In part because of this construction, some editing was necessary to maintain the integrity of ideas while providing a coherent narrative. Since each narrative is pieced from transcriptions of the participant's speech and writings,[2] there may seem to be inconsistencies in punctuation and spelling. This is partly due to the speech transcriptions' being limited by a punctuation system meant for writing and not speech as well as a spelling system that does not necessarily reflect the way words are really said. So, how you hear the narratives in your mind may not be how they were produced. However, I did alter the spelling of some words transcribed from speech to make an alternate representation of the word appropriate (e.g., "achieveded" instead of "achieved" to show redupli-cation of the past tense -*ed* marker). Moreover, some inconsistencies in punctuation and spelling occur because I wanted to faithfully reflect the actual writing of the participants, which includes lack of any punctua-tion in some places as well as lack of capitalization or inappropriate punc-tuation. In those cases where such might be problematic, I included ap-propriate punctuation. Otherwise, the mechanics represented reflect that of the participants (of course that will not always be easy to determine since their speech and writing are intermixed throughout the narratives; however, misspelled words and problematic punctuation are good signs that the source of the narrative was writing). Despite these modifica-tions, I do hope the essence of each person's voice is heard and that there is little if any cognitive dissonance because of the construction of the narratives.

The analyses in Part Two fill in the gaps and details, and further con-nect components of the women's language and literacy identities. Part Two concludes with an update on the lives of the women and a discus-sion of the significance of the narratives and data and what they have to tell us. The combination of the narratives and the analyses implicitly il-lustrates the relationship between the participants' beliefs and behavior by its context. What the participants chose to share depicts what they considered important to include as a necessary locus for understand-ing the relationship between language and literacy, beliefs and behavior, and identity in their sociocultural and historical contexts or ecological spheres. The better you understand where each woman has come from, the better you understand why those overlaps are meaningful and in what ways they contribute to how and who each woman is.

> Things like that gave me my first glimmering of the universal female gospel that all good traits and leanings come from the mother's side.
> —Zora Neale Hurston, in Johnson, *Proud Sisters*

THE NARRATIVES
Peculiar to Your Mind

Darlene trying to teach me how to talk. She say
US not so hot. A dead country give-away. You
say US where most folks say WE, she say, and
peoples think you dumb. Colored peoples think
you a hick and white folks be amuse. What I
care? I ast. I'm happy. But she say I feel more
happier talking like she talk. . . . Every time I say
something the way I say it, she correct me until
I say it some other way. Pretty soon it feel like I
can't think. My mind run up on a thought, git
confuse, run back and sort of lay down. You
sure this worth it? I ast. She say Yeah. Bring me
a bunch of books. Whitefolks all over them,
talking bout apples and dogs. What I care bout
dogs? I think. Darlene keep trying. Think how
much better Shug feel with you educated, she
say. She won't be shame to take you anywhere.
Shug not shame no how, I say. But she don't
believe this the truth. Sugar, she say one day
when Shug home, don't you think it be nice if
Celie could talk proper. Shug say, She can talk in
sign language for all I care. . . . But I let Darlene
worry on. Sometimes I think bout the apples
and the dogs, sometimes I don't. Look like to
me only a fool would want you to talk in a way
that feel peculiar to your mind.
　　　　—Celie, in Alice Walker's *The Color Purple*

Part
One

And we done learned that anything coming from beyond the bridge gotta be viewed real, real careful. Look what happened when Reema's boy—the one with the pear-shaped head—came hauling himself back from one of those fancy colleges mainside, dragging his notebooks and tape recorder and a funny way of curling up his lip and clicking his teeth, all excited and determined to put Willow Springs on the map. We was polite enough—Reema always was a little addle-brained—so you couldn't blame the boy for not remembering that part of Willow Springs's problems was that it got put on some maps right after the War Between the States. And then when he went around asking us about 18 & 23, there weren't nothing to do but take pity on him as he rattled on about "ethnography," "unique speech patterns," "cultural preservation," and whatever else he seemed to be getting so much pleasure out of while talking into his little gray machine. He was all over the place —What 18 & 23 mean? What 18 & 23 mean? And we all told him the God-honest truth: it was just our way of saying something. Winky was awful, though, he even spit tobacco juice for him. Sat on his porch all day, chewing up the boy's Red Devil premium and spitting so the machine could pick it up. There was enough fun in that to take us through the fall and winter when he had hauled himself back over The Sound to wherever he was getting what was supposed to be passing for an education. And he sent everybody he'd talked to copies of the book he wrote, bound all nice with our name and his signed on the first page. We couldn't hold Reema down, she was so proud. It's a good thing she didn't read it. None of us made it much through the introduction, but that said it all: you see, he had come to the conclusion after "extensive field work" (ain't never picked a boll of cotton or head of lettuce in his life— Reema spoiled him silly), but he done still made it to the conclusion that 18 & 23 wasn't 18 & 23 at all—was really 81 & 32, which just so happened to be the lines of longitude and latitude marking off where Willow Springs sits on the map. And we were just so damned dumb that we turned the whole thing around.

Not that he called it being dumb, mind you, called it "asserting

our cultural identity," "inverting hostile social and political parame-
ter." 'Cause, see, being we was brought here as slaves, we had no
choice but to look at everything upside-down. And then being
that we was isolated off here on this island, everybody else in the
country went on learning good English and calling things what they
really was—in the dictionary and all that—while we kept on calling
things ass-backwards. And he thought that was just so wonderful
and marvelous, etcetera, etcetera. . . . The people who ran the type
of schools that could turn our children into raving lunatics—and
then put his picture on the back of the book so we couldn't even
deny it was him—didn't mean us a speck of good.

If the boy wanted to know what 18 & 23 meant, why didn't he
just ask? When he was running around sticking that machine in
everybody's face, we was sitting right here—every one of us—and
him being one of Reema's, we woulda obliged him. . . . Naw, he
didn't really want to know what 18 & 23 meant, or he woulda
asked. . . . But on second thought, someone who didn't know how
to ask wouldn't know how to listen.   —Gloria Naylor, *Mama Day*

● ● ●

I remember Mrs. Foudy drilling me in second grade on how to speak
"good" English. I could not use "ain't" and double negatives or use "be"
in the "wrong" place. I used my precious grammar book to conduct
classes out of my garage for neighborhood children. By teaching others,
I was able to practice using "good" English. I still have this book stored
in a box at home.

My teacher had a profound effect on my desire to learn all that I could
about "correct" pronunciation and "correct" English. I would go with
my mother through stores reciting a variety of paradigms to instill this
"correct" English. I would constantly correct the way my parents or others in my family spoke. This fervor for speaking "correct" English lasted
for several years. I even entered college as a speech pathology major (as
if varieties of a language are pathologies to be cured) in order to further
my progress in speaking "correct" English as well as teaching others to
do the same. My family still expects this of me. However, after a year in
college, I decided not to be a speech pathologist but a mathematician. I

was intrigued by algebra and calculus. I derived joy from the logic of the arguments, the analytical thinking, and the formulation of complex series of thoughts necessary to thrive in math. The structures of the arguments were like grammatical English sentences. While I was pursuing math, I decided to seek a dual degree in English as well. The combination of logical "sentences" in math and the literature of English was a remarkable integration of my studies in language.

While working as an undergraduate researcher in training in educational psychology, I began to discover how to optimize my efforts in reading, studying, and learning in general. I developed my learning strategies and sought more information about the nature of learning and motivation that provided another dimension to my approach to studying language. For example, I could make even better connections between math and the English language that helped fuel my interests in English language and linguistics as well as other related languages. The readings in Latin further encouraged my interest in language because I could better see how one could use language and how a sentence was more than just words written on a page. When I read parts of Vergil's *Aeneid* in Latin, I was amazed at how language could be so beautifully expressed. For instance, when Vergil spoke of the festival of the wine god, he was able to arrange the words in such a way as to resemble a state of drunkenness. I now understood poet Richard Hugo's assertion that "once language exists only to convey information it is dying." Language is—and has to be—dynamic, fluid, everchanging.

In the midst of my "correct" English crusade as an undergraduate student, I began studying varieties of English. I became deeply interested in the different dialects and accents of English because they showed the diversity in language. Nowadays I do not go around stores practicing paradigms for parts of speech in order to instill "good" English. I realize the English language consists of many varieties and no one variety is inherently inferior or superior to any other—each is simply different. I also learned a bit more about language besides what is assumed to be "correct" and "incorrect."

Although I diligently pursued English language and linguistics during my undergraduate years, it was not until graduate school that I was exposed to issues in literacy and, as a result, made connections between language and uses of literacy. This evolution to studying language and uses of literacy helped me to look at and understand more of what was and had been going on around me. I began to consider my own language and literacy development and community. This trek involved several stages that included moving from a focus on myself to a focus on family and community as well as both in a larger concept of community. This book is a result of that continuing journey.

I have noticed that various members of my family, for instance, are able to demonstrate a particular range of abilities in different socially determined and linguistic situations. And although they are able to style shift, their attitudes regarding their ability to do so or simply their behavior in those varying situations seems to be related to their attitudes and beliefs about language, literacy, and what they believe to be "good" English. They clearly value "good" English, but they do so in different and sometimes conflicting ways.

My mother and father have similar attitudes and beliefs about language and literacy, but their behavior differs. My sister, who is almost two-and-a-half years my senior, has different attitudes, beliefs, and behavior compared to my parents and me. On a language continuum, my sister is considered to be more on the end that is not esteemed (i.e., basilect); I am more on the end that is highly esteemed (i.e., acrolect), and my parents are somewhere in the middle (i.e., mesolect). I am the one who talks "proper," "correct," "good," "White." My position is highly esteemed for what is perceived to be the limitlessness of my possible accomplishments and accolades. At the same time, I am sometimes not so highly esteemed for the very same thing.

For example, sometimes when I am interacting with a predominantly African American group (not including my family), I feel uncomfortable, partly because of my assumptions about how some African Americans may view my speech and partly because I know I lost part of my identity as an African American in my goal (or obsession?) to speak "correct" English. As innocent or as practical—depending on your point of view—as that may seem, I was not able to embark on that journey of assimilation without paying a price. Often lost, ignored, or buried in the quest for admiration and acceptance outside of one's (cultural) community are the trials, tribulations, and consequences of that quest. So, even though I am African American, there are some African American groups I do not fit in with. In choosing at earlier points in my life to disidentify with the language I saw as African American as well as other aspects of African American culture, I chose to identify with what I believed to be the "White" way—but I was wrong. As writer Alice Walker notes in *You Can't Keep a*

Good Woman Down, "any direction that is away from ourselves is the wrong direction."

Not long after relating the story of an incident that occurred during my elementary school years in a paper for a graduate class and my reaction to that story at the time of the class (excerpted in chapter 6), I read an essay entitled "Strangers in the Village" by David Mura. In it he expressed what I had been feeling for quite some time, something that had been growing amorphously but which was beginning to take a coherent and speakable form. The feeling has not gone away or been cured, and it may never. But being able to speak and write about it has made it easier to cope with.

> What I am trying to do in both my writing and my life is to replace self-hatred and self-negation with anger and grief over my lost selves, over the ways my cultural heritage has been denied to me, over the ways that people in America would assume either that I am not American, or conversely, that I am just like them; over the ways my education and the values of European culture have denied that other cultures exist. I know more about Europe at the time when my grandfather came to America than I know about Meiji Japan. I know Shakespeare and Donne, Sophocles and Homer better than I know Zeami, Basho or Lady Murasaki. This is not to say I regret what I know, but I do regret what I don't know. And the argument that the culture of America is derived from Europe will not wipe away this regret.
>
> (p. 17)

I cannot change the choices I made or the experiences I had—I do not want to. They are who I am and part of who I become. That does not mean I am content with all my choices and experiences, but I can use them to make a difference in the lives of others and necessary and inevitable changes in myself—including how I can envision my "possible selves," a construct coined by social psychologist Hazel Markus in "Possible Selves":

> Possible selves represent individuals' ideas of what they might become, what they would like to become, and what they are afraid of becoming, and thus provide a conceptual link between cognition and motivation. . . . An individual is free to create any variety of possible

selves, yet the pool of possible selves derives from the categories made salient by the individual's particular sociocultural and historical context and . . . by the individual's immediate social experiences. Possible selves thus have the potential to reveal the inventive and constructive nature of the self but they also reflect the extent to which the self is socially determined and constrained.   (p. 954)

Given my past experiences and realities, I decided to embark upon a quest with a familial group and familiar issues. *Sista, Speak!* presents and examines the language, literacy, and uses of identity of five working-class and middle-class African American women across three generations of my family. All the women were born and raised in the South. I focus on the matriarch, Maya; Maya's fourth-oldest child, Grace; Maya's eighth and youngest child, Reia; and Grace's two children, Deidra and Sonja. They are three generations of women who are mothers, daughters, and sisters. These women have had a significant impact on my life because they contributed to the views I have about language and uses of literacy. I have a unique relationship with each one. They are family, a community of women with different lives, different dreams, and different realities, as you will begin to see from the brief introduction by each woman below.

M A Y A

[I] *was bone 1920 May twenty. My mother and father died when I was nine years old and ten years old. And they left me then to my sisters and brothers to raise me up. So they raised me up from one to the other one until I got to be* [a] *teenager.*

And then when I got to be thirteen, I went to work in a restaurant. Thirteen years old. Then from that on I worked for families in the homes because I didn't get a education. And I just worked for families, different families in homes. [I] *always would work because I know work, I'd have money if I work.*

And so that's what I did for my living after I growed up and got married when I was the age of seventeen years old—an then started having childern. And the marriage didn't work out. Worked out for a while but it didn't work out that long. But I still was stuck with a couple of children after the divorce. And I went on to work and working and working. And then I was grown up then.

I'm retired from working on jobs, but I'm not retired in this house.
I still wakes up every morning and do what I used to do on those jobs.
I haven't retired from that really.

Maya, my grandmother, was the youngest of thirteen children—nine boys and four girls. They all grew up on a farm in the segregated, Jim Crow South. From her parents' families she knew only one uncle on her mother's side. Her mother, Sarah, suffered with asthma. Sarah had been married once before and had two sons, Samuel and Charles, with her first husband, Hiram Tibbs. Sarah had eleven sons and daughters with her second husband, Peter Johnson. Peter died at the age of 55 when he was hit by a car, and about four months after Sarah died of a stroke at around the age of 50. When her father, Peter, died, there were only two children still at home, Chet and Maya. It was up to them to decide with whom they wanted to live. Chet chose to live with his second-oldest sister, Vashti, and Maya chose to live with her favorite brother, Matthew. Matthew's wife wasn't very kind to Maya, often starving her. Although she finally told Matthew about the mistreatment, she later left to live with other siblings. Not until after Maya had her first child did she finally decide to live with Vashti, the same sister her brother Chet had chosen to live with. Vashti became much like a mother to Maya, and they remained close till the day she died in April 1990. Vashti was never able to have children, and she fell in love with Maya's second child, Gloria, so Maya allowed Vashti and her husband, Joseph, to raise Gloria. (Coincidentally, Joseph's brother married Kate, Vashti's sister.)

Maya was the baby of the family and never knew or saw some of her siblings. Samuel died of cancer about thirty-five years ago. (Although he and Maya lived within two houses of one another at one point as adults, they had little contact. However, one of Samuel's daughters, Etta, who is older than Maya, is still alive and gets along well with Maya.) Three of Maya's brothers died of tuberculosis while still teenagers. Chet, an alcoholic, died of liver cancer. Her twin brothers died while they were still children. Another older brother died young as well without having any children. Her oldest sister, Caroline, died young without having any children. Her third oldest sister, Kate, died more than thirty years ago. She had ten children. When Vashti died in 1990 at the age of 84, Maya was deeply hurt by that since she was closer to her than any of her sisters and brothers. She is the only one left now; her last living sibling, Charles, died March in 1998 at the ripe old age of 100. Maya has the least

amount of education of all the participants, and she had the most difficult life of all the participants. Yet, of all, Maya is most comfortable with
who she is and where she is in life.

Maya married three times and has eight children by four different
men. An interesting thing about Maya's children is that she seems to
have had them in two sets of four. Ruth and Gloria have the same father
and were born to Maya's first husband, Herman. Mavis and Grace had different fathers, to whom Maya was never married. Grace was the baby of
the family for several years. The youngest four children—Felicia, Johnny,
Marcus, and Reia—all have the same father, John, but Maya did not
marry him until after she had married and divorced another man she
never had children with. She is still living in the home she moved into
almost thirty years ago.

One thing I remember about Maya while I was growing up was her de-
termination. She read the Bible daily despite her limited literacy abilities.
I recall her struggles with words, how she would sound out a word and
then go on to either conquer it on her own or ask for help. She recognized her limits as well as her possibilities. When she would know the
answer, she would make sure you knew it as well. And whatever the situation, she would hold her head up high. I can say without a doubt that
Maya is the most resilient woman I have ever known.

GRACE

*I was born on January 21, 1946, to Mr. Josiah Smith and Ms. Maya
Johnson (my mother and father were not married). I don't know what
time of day I was born, but it was during the day. I was born in Tiberius
and grew up there in a small house in South Tiberius on Nelson Street. I
was delivered by Ms. Dehlia, a midwife. We called her Ms. Dear (don't
ask me why).*

*I think my father and mother separated when I was about 2 or
3 years old. My father was good to me; he loved me very much and
supported me as much as he could. I visited him in the summers when
I was out of school. I remember when I was 4 or 5 years old he would
always come and get me and take me to visit his parents. My grandmother's name was Grace Smith (my father named me after my grandmother) and my grandfather's name was King Jones. They owned their
own home and lived good during those days.*

In 1964 I married Eddie. From that marriage I had a daughter born

June 13, 1964. I named her Deidra. I went back to school after having Deidra and got my High School Diploma. I had another daughter born to Jesse & Grace on November 4, 1966. I named her Sonja.

In January or February of 1967, I enrolled in Vocational Guidance School. When I was in Vocational Guidance school I worked at the VA Hospital for 2 years learning clerical work and I was getting payed while training. I also took classes at school in Math, Typing & General office work. I graduated from Vocational Guidance School in 1968 with a certificate in General office work. In 1969 I went to work for DSN until 1971. In 1972 I started working for Farpoint and still there hoping to retire in year 2000.

Grace, my mother, is a central figure in this study partly because I have had the most interactions with her on the subject of language and uses of literacy and partly because she is most concerned about these issues. She often asks me questions about language use and literacy. She admires me on the one hand, but denounces me on the other: she appreciates my ability to speak what she perceives as "good" English, but she admonishes me for using that same "good" English around those who do not use it. Likewise, she admires my vocabulary and often asks me to pronounce and define words, but she scolds me if I do not adjust my vocabulary to better fit my audience. She does not hold attitudes and beliefs similar to mine about language and uses of literacy, nor does she want to be as "limited" in her linguistic styles as she believes me to be. She wants to be competent in my linguistic styles, but she does not want to be like some of the people she envisions in those linguistic styles— pretentious, snippety, mechanical, haughty, White. In other words, she does not want to forget where she came from and she would like to visit there from time to time without being perceived as out of touch.

One thing that continues to stand out in my mind about my mother is how she tries to "talk proper" in phone conversations with someone she does not know, such as a telemarketer or even someone who has dialed the wrong number. She answers the phone with a "hello" that is different from her everyday speech just because she cannot be sure who is on the other end of the line. That she changes her voice is one thing, but what she is trying to imitate is something else. I mean, that is what I remember—the voice. For her, talking "proper" sounds White. The way she changes her voice seems to mimic what she associates with sounding White.

REIA

I was born in Merchant at the most honorable Charity Hospital [July
1960]. [My] *mother was forty and* [my] *father was forty-one when* [I]
was born. [My] *parents lived together for seven years. They separated
when* [I] *was only four months.* [My] *father worked for a freight company as a truck driver and* [my] *mother worked in private homes. They
both had only 3rd grade education. After* [my] *father left,* [my] *mother
had to seek AFDC for assistance to supplement her income.* [My] *father
gave money for the children on special occasions such as Christmas.*
[My] *relationship with* [my] *mother was an affectionate and close one.*
[My] *mother and father reunited when* [I] *was twelve and got married
several months later.*

*One of the best decisions I ever made was to seek employment after
high school. Instead of immediately going into college, I began working
for a bank. Although I never thought of this as a permanent job, nevertheless, it provided for economic independence. After working at the
bank for two years, I decided to enroll in a two-year junior college. The
area that interest me the most was Architectural Drafting. I did quite
well in the program and had every intention to continue this course of
study, but circumstances interfered and changed my direction.*

*Between this time and the next two years, I had the opportunity to
minister to a friend in a very special way. In this process, I discovered
a side of myself that I did not know existed. I realized the compassion
in me to help people who were hurting and needed to be loved. This
brought about an interest in reading materials that were related to the
social sciences. The subject of psychology fascinated me and I acquired
a hunger to know more about this field of study.*

*At twenty-three I entered college, this time knowing exactly what
direction I wanted to pursue. I completed a four-year psychology
program in three-and-one-half years. Much searching preceded this
career choice. It took me nearly six years to find my niche, but when
I found it I never questioned it. I have never regretted majoring in
psychology and I am looking forward to the ministry God has for me
in this area. My present desire is for my profession to be my ministry
and for my ministry to be my profession.*

Reia, my aunt, is Maya's youngest daughter. Her relationship with
Maya is unlike that of any of her siblings in terms of her closeness and

comfort level with both Maya and John. Her oldest sister, Ruth, is almost like a second mother to her. As is true with many of the youngest children in a family, she is largely responsible for the welfare of her elderly parents. Reia has received the most education of any of her siblings even though her sister Felicia was her inspiration and the first to go to college (Felicia received a bachelor's degree in accounting). Out of all her siblings, she sounds the most Southern. Though her grammar may have Southern features, it is truly her accent that is distinctly Southern. That is what I hear when I think of and remember Reia—her old-fashioned Southern charm.

DEIDRA

My Name is Deidra E. Gaultney. I reside in Tiberius. I was born in Harlow at Indepentance Hospital in 1964. My parents are Grace Richardson and Eddie Gaultney Jr. I am dark skinned with brown eyes, black hair; I weight 135 pounds and I am 5'1.

Coming up as a child my grandparents raised me. When I was two years old my mother and Father divoced and they both remarried. My mother moved to picard with her husband and my youngest Sister. My Father remained in Tiberius.

When I was growing up i realize that i had a problem. I have a literacy problem. I notice it when i was in Junior high School when all the another children was pasting and i wasn't. the[y] knew things that i could have never know[n] at that time of my life, like Reading, Writing, and Spelling. at First i just did what any another child would do, and that was just going to school. As I got older i realize my literacy. I went through school just getting buy.

Upon entering college I sta[r]ted off majoring in Nursing and then changed to Social Work and back to Nursing. I was undecided about my major because of me lacking skills In Reading and Writing.

All throughtout my college years I was angry with myself for not being at the academic level I s[h]ould have been. It was So hard for me to comprehend because of my lack of reading and writing skills. Most of all what I wanted to major in at college required a great deal of reading and writing skills which I knew I wasn't good in. I wasn't getting any where in college because of my literacy so i stop going to college. I have Two good jobs that I thank God for.

Deidra, my sister, has great dilemmas with her language and uses of literacy as well as with her family situation (she was raised by her paternal grandparents, Joe and Stella, and not our mother, Grace). Her family situation only seems to have exacerbated her language and literacy problems. Looking from the outside in, she seemed to have gotten everything material she wanted as a child. I begrudged her that at the time because I felt I usually did not get what I wanted. From that experience, I learned you don't always get what you want—and that can be a good thing.

Deidra is uncomfortable in situations where talking "proper" might be expected, such as a job interview. When she moved in with Grace and Jesse (i.e., her stepfather and my father) several years ago, just as I was going away to college, she made an effort to try to change her style of speech. Grace constantly made her aware of her "problems" and she constantly "corrected" her. Grace still corrects Deidra if she hears her say something "wrong." When Deidra was in the process of moving back home to Tiberius after having lived with Grace and Jesse in Picard for a few years, one of the things Grace kept telling her was, "Don't go back there and start talking like those people again. I don't want to hear you talking any old kind of way again." What she was saying was, "Don't speak African American English." She wanted—wants—her to talk "proper." Deidra speaks African American English.[1]

SONJA

I was born in Picard at 5:29 in the morning on November 4, 1966. I forget the name of the hospital. My mom has told me on more than one occasion how she really wanted me to be born in Picard. I lived there all my life until I moved away to attend graduate school.

My parents are from Tiberius. My mom went to Roosevelt High School and my dad went to Jefferson High School—those were the two high schools for Blacks then. My mom married my dad when she was 20 years old I think. That's when she had me. We were a middle class family.

Mrs. Foudy was the best teacher I ever had in elementary school. She taught me a lot of what I know about reading and writing. I think she must have been a phonics person, but I forgive her for that (ha ha). Actually, despite my aversion for "Hooked on Phonics" and my intrigue with whole language, I still say she was the best teacher I had in elementary school because I actually remember learning in her class.

She was an elderly lady who had a profound impact on my language development.

My mom says I have been in school all of my life. I guess that's why I was so prescriptive about language until I got to my latter years in college. I've had a complete turnaround.

I have thought about education quite a bit since I've been at the University. I do believe education is important. It took a while for me to understand that. It has taken a while for me to understand quite a few things—and there will always be more for as long as I live. But I also realize that education has its limits; it is not a cure-all. There are educated bigots and racists and child molesters and spouse abusers and murderers and a whole lot more. I've sat in class with some of the inhumane offenders. I think I am the better for it. I have a lot of work to do in my life it would seem.

Reading has helped me a great deal over the last few years—probably because I actually did some. I have learned a great deal with much more to go from reading and it has contributed greatly to my view of many things and my desire to have the conversations (both verbally and in writing) that I choose to have. I have come a long way from the girl who hardly ever finished a book. I am quite pleased with my literacy practices at this point in my life.

I do a lot of writing, especially since graduate school. I'm still not 100% comfortable with writing. It's hard sometimes to produce a written work. The process can be excruciating. But overall, I like to write. I think I have the potential to be a good writer.

I don't think I went to the best schools or that I even made the most out of the education I have had, but I've done good for myself. I will be the first person in my family to achieve a Ph.D. I look forward to sharing that moment with my family when I walk across the stage and am officially recognized with my Ph.D.

I am told I speak "proper" English. Even though I can speak African American English and often do in certain situations, it is usually not associated with me—especially by my non-Black husband. He teases me when I talk to a family member because he says I "try to sound Black"—but I don't. He does not associate my speech with others in my family just as others in my family don't associate my speech much with theirs. Yet I do possess several characteristics of African American English in my speech. They are most likely evident when I am talking to my family (or sometimes other African Americans). I enjoy high prestige in my family so I am allowed to talk "bad" (i.e., use nonstandard language) without censure even though I have some of the same African American English characteristics as my sister. I, however, am never corrected. My family seems to have a mental scale that rates some language characteristics as "bad" but acceptable and others as "bad" and unacceptable. It would seem I use the former and not the latter.

I don't remember when or how my language changed, but I know my schooling was influential as well as my acceptance of the indoctrination of schooling. I went to an integrated school when I was in the fourth grade because my parents had me bussed to a magnet school. Most of the students were White. The other African American students were bussed in just like me. We moved when I was in the sixth grade from an all-Black, working-class neighborhood to a more integrated, middle-class neighborhood and, as a result, a more integrated, ethnically diverse school. By the time I reached high school, the school I went to was still fairly ethnically mixed but with African Americans as the majority. When I decided to go to college I went to a predominantly White university. My mother often tells me how she regrets sending me to that university. She says that at the same time she says how proud of me she is.

I struggle with how people look at me when I talk as if I'm not what they expected of an African American. I struggle with my mom's attitudes and beliefs about "good" language and "bad" language. I agonize when she expects me to "correct" her when she talks or when she asks me to help her write a memo or letter because she believes in me more than she believes in herself. That is why I believe there is a relationship between confidence and literacy, confidence and language. Our perceptions of our language (and literacy) are integrated with our perceptions of our selves. Because of that, when we talk about language and literacy we should also talk about identity and goals[2] and possible selves (a subset of goals) since they are at stake—or at risk.

I have long since moved beyond my prescriptivist views of language into ones more appreciative and maybe even romanticized. However, before I could continue in that evolution I had to take one long look back at where I had been for so long. I came to realize that earlier in my life I had chosen what was peculiar to my mind. Like most people, I bought into the rhetoric that "standard" English is good and everything else is bad. Since I grew up speaking African American English, I heard that message constantly and with conviction. I was ashamed of my language. As I have indicated, I took steps to eliminate the "problem"—or so I thought.

Suffice it to say, as noted by scholar William O'Barr, each of us could write a linguistic and literacy autobiography, and our divergent stories would be united by tales of early awareness that provoked us to seek ways of comprehending language and literacy as we have known them. I share the stories of five African American women expressed in their language and I examine their ideological perspectives about language and literacy (i.e., the language and literacy experiences that shaped their views of themselves and their worlds). These African American women read their worlds, as critical literacy educator Paulo Freire would say, and talk that talk, as sociolinguist Geneva Smitherman would say. In the process, we perhaps get a better view of how our experiences and cultures and ecologies shape our views of ourselves and our world and where both can and cannot (or maybe should and should not) go.

MAYA
It Doesn't Bother Me

She was looking at the other people in the bar. She liked Alaska. She liked the way the people looked as if they had come, that very month, from someplace else. . . . Irene had sat beside a Native Alaskan woman who talked of the failing eyesight of Alaskans, who were reading print, over long periods, for the first time. "Native Alaskans always took perfect vision for granted," the woman had said. "Then comes this reading. This television. This shopping where everything is labeled with words for more reading. Every-body needs glasses now to see anything at all." She was wearing huge aviator glasses with purple lenses. She yanked them off and blinked at the audience. It was a long pause, during which she dropped the assertive stance of her statement and seemed, some-where inside herself, to fold. "There's a basic distrust maybe," she continued softly, "about acquiring knowledge in a way that can make you blind. This has to be behind many of our older people's reading problems." Irene didn't doubt it for a moment.

—Alice Walker, *You Can't Keep a Good Woman Down*

• • •

I don't know to much about my prantes because they both died when I was just [a] child. I can't really just vision my parents in my mind like I can my brother. It's scarcely in my mind; I know my mama had a mole [just like I have]. She had a mole. That's where the moles come from. And she had to be a kinda tall lady too, not fat, but maybe she wasn't skinny either. Now my daddy, he was kinda short I think and so that's why I'm short. Some took on the mother side and some took on the daddy side. So that's the way I picture 'em. I know she was kinda tall and he wadn't too tall him. I can remember that. But most likely my childhood, I had a pretty nice childhood. Pretty good without a mother and father. I stayed with my brothers and sisters like that. And they were very nice to me.

But still in all when I stopped going to school I was only thirteen. Well they didn't try to make me go. I just went on and did kinda what I wanted to do in that line. And then I just went on to work at thirteen and made my little money. And they'd let me spend my little money on myself and do what I wanted with it. But I knew that after that, after I had gotten grown, really grown, I made a mistake by not going to school and finishing and getting a education. So that's why I had to work all my life doing domestic work and stuff like that.

[I think I'm uneducated and I will continue to be uneducated] *cause I sure don't have any money to go and get any more. I just think I'll be uneducated. I can read and write, but I wished I coulda had more education, I just put it like that, than what I have. Cause sometime things'll run into you* [where] *you need a education and you don't have it. And a lot of times I wished I had gotten a education. But now I don't worry about it really now. But it's still in my mind. I would love to be educated. It doesn't bother me; not now. I like myself. I ain't gone lose no sleep over it. Not a one second of sleep over it. I don't think I'm a failure. I don't think that. I mighta been a failure on some things but I achieved a lot a things too. Achieveded a lot a things. I think* [I will always have confidence in myself] *if I keep this mind I have now. If I keep this mind I sure would.*

EDUCATION: *I Coulda Had a Better Job*

The school I went to just had one teacher and one roof. It was just a one-room [schoolhouse]. *Everybody was in one school up there. It was a small school. We had the different grades, but we were all in one room together. It had higher grades, lower grades, but this one teacher, all I remember, would teach the kids. It probably wasn't a whole bunch of kids either. Maybe* [10–15 kids] *or more. It was a church house. That's what it was.*

I had some [friends back home]. *Like in that day you might have your special friend girl or something like this to be with. I guess I had about maybe three or four. We didn't walk to school together. Sometime maybe a few would walk to school together. But look like it was more me and my brother Chet. I think he was three or four years older than me. School had to be about it seemed like to me about a couple miles. A mile and a half or something. It was something like that I'm pretty sure. I can't tell you just how many minutes it would take us to walk there, but it was a good little stretch.*

I didn't go very high in school. The onlies thing I remember 'bout when I was going to school [is that] *we had a man teacher. It was one. Black man. And I guess he did* [encourage me], *but I was kinda young and like kids don't pay attention. But I guess he would say encouraging words. But by me being so young and everything,* [I don't really remember too well]. *It been so long. That been sixty some year. All I know he would teach the lesson* [and] *teach the school.*

I was interested in school, but I didn't go to school no more than the third grade I think. About the third grade. Reading. That was my best subject. I'm sure it wasn't the spelling. I didn't like geography. I didn't like arithmetic. I didn't do so well in that. I did more better in reading. I was a pretty good reader. I could read good and I could spell good. Now I wasn't dumb in reading. It's because back there, you was gon start in a primer book they call it. Now he was gon let you read that whole book over and over until you really know what you reading or whatever. And see, after you done learned that one then he was gon promote you to another grade.

I was ok in the grades that I was in, but I wasn't like a 'A' student. I wasn't like that. I say maybe like a 'C' or something. But I quit school and went to work. And seem like to me I was about thirteen or something like that. See back there though, I might have been promoted to the fourth grade, but that's where I didn't go back to school. I stopped school and went to work. Now I know I was thirteen. I don't think I went at all when I was thirteen. When the school start back again, I didn't go back. So I mighta been twelve the last time that I attend school.

[I don't think that because I was Black or because I was a woman that that affected my education.] *Like I say, I just stop going to school. It's just the individual. It's like I said. After my parents died and I was staying with my brothers and sisters, from one to the other, I guess it was something about my parents dying. See I probably would have been more educated and everything else if they woulda lived. I was staying from here to yonder. I would stay with one a while and the other'n a while. And well my mind just got off a school and I just went on to work. Course they didn't make me go to work, but the other girls was working, my brother's wife nieces. See we were all together raised, kinda coming up together. They were older than me. And so they was working. I imagine they woulda been going to school too at they age I guess. But they were working and so I decide I wanta work, see, and they didn't put any pressure on me to go to school, get your education. But I wasn't nothing but a kid and so it didn't make me no difference. That's the way I was thinking. See I didn't know the value then. And so that's how that was.*

I have wished that I woulda got an education. I had wished that I

*woulda got a education or went to school—in a higher grade anyway.
I thought about that. I would have more of a education. I could* [have
gotten] *better jobs and I coulda helped my children out when they came
along* [and] *when they was going to school better.* [If] *I know like now, I
wouldn'ta never dropped out.* [Education] *is* [important]. *I really think
that. I wished a many day for an education. I sure have. Since I gotten
grown.*

[I went to an adult education program for] *a little while. It was helpful. I
learnt more there almost look like than I did when I was going to school.
That's the truth. Because I was older and understood better and I was
more interested, you see.*

Many times I wished I woulda got a education. [Dropping out of
school] *was the wrong thing. I realize that was the wrong thing. Because
I coulda had a better job and I'da been a educated person. I really and
truly in the past just wished I went on through and got an education.
Cause I could get better jobs. But as I didn't, I didn't worry about it. But
it have cross my mind.*

I don't know [the contribution my parents, brothers, and sisters made to
my education or language and literacy development]. *I can't really answer
that cause I don't know how they felt. I don't know if they was interested
in getting a education or what—although they sent me to school. They
would help me with my reading* [and] *they would help me with my school-
work for my work the next day at school or something, I guess.*

[I contributed to the language and literacy development of my
children.] *I'd try to tell 'em far as I knew. I know it was 'this' and 'that';
I know it wasn't 'dat' and 'dis.' And I knew a few things about the
language.* [I helped them with reading and writing as] *far as I could.* [I
would] *read stories, books. And like when they had they homework or
whatever, and it wadn't too high a grade, well I help 'em with that.*

I might've helped the older one [i.e., Ruth, Gloria, Mavis, and Grace]
*maybe more because the younger generation, they kinda fast today with
education. They know more in the beginning. But I helped with the last
ones* [i.e., Felicia, Johnny, Marcus, and Reia]. *I remember helping them
when they was in the lower grades. But now when they got up to like fifth
grade or something like that, I couldn't help 'em. I help them as far as I
knew. Maybe like the third, fourth grade. And I don't know if I know too
much about Math. They call it Math now, but we used to call it Arithmetic.
I didn't know too much about that, but I'd help 'em maybe to third grade,
maybe fourth and like that, far as I knew.*

If you got a high school education, it should prepare you for college.
[I think schools should prepare everyone for college—even if they're not going to college.] *I think everybody should* [go to college], *but I know everybody don't want to. I think they should get an education, everybody, if they can. Just like I say, I wish I had got a education—good education. But I don't have it and I don't let it just worry me so.*

L A N G U A G E : *I Don't Be Saying I Be Saying Everything Right*

[People who speak standard English] *use and spell words properly for one thing.* [Speaking standard English is] *important. It's very educated to me. At least some education anyway. It's very important to speak well and know what time to use different words and where to use them.*

[I think I speak mostly like Black people speak], *definite. Some Black people. I want to speak better. If anything I'd want to speak better. I wouldn't want to be any worser. Or stay like I am or something I guess. I think* [I will continue to speak the way I do even though I don't want to] *because if I don't* [do] *anything about it, I'm gonna be speaking* [the same way]. *But I would love to speak better though. If I had the opportunity I would at least like to speak my words, some of the words that I don't know about, where to put 'em in the right place. I would like that now. I think I'd take a chance on somebody teaching me on that. But I would like to be able to speak better English. I'm speaking now but I don't know really what words to use in some. . . It ain't gone get better unlessen I do something to make it better, help myself. I'ma try* [to do something].

In some way [I talk differently to White people than I do to Black people]. *I try to use my words better with White people. With my own color I get a li'l slacker. You know how that is.*

[I try to talk to all White people] *about the same, I think. Cause I know they was educated more and I try to talk the same, saying things that I thought was a li'l more proper than 'dis' and 'dat.' Now maybe sometime with my own color I might. . . . But I don't hardly say that now. That was when I was younger. I don't want to say no 'dis' and 'dat' now.*

Well I might would try to be a little aware [of how I talk to] *a* [Black] *person that I don't know than the person that I know. You know how you get comfortable with somebody you know. And somebody you don't know you try to do not too bad; try to use your language as far as you can. I think I do that more with somebody I don't know. But like somebody I know, I gets a li'l slacker with them.*

I'm really conscious of [my] *talking like maybe* [with] *somebody I never seen before and they might have a real nice accent of talking. I be trying to help myself. I don't be saying I be saying everything right either. Sometime I don't know how to use the word, the real right word in the real language. But I do be trying to help myself.*

[I make fun of the way some people speak.] *I have to say something about some people. I know I don't use good language, but some people is worser than me. They say 'dat' and 'dis' and all kind of stuff like that. I don't really make fun of 'em but I be saying, "Now that's not right." You know, what I know right, and they say it wrong. I guess it just the same way some people with me. And I be saying, "They shoulda said it such and such a way." But I don't tell 'em.* [I will do that with people in my family], *but I tell them.*

Like if them kids or something will say, "Dey did dat," or "Dey did dis," well I might say, "Not 'dey.'" "'They', not 'dey.'" Cause you know how Black people talk back there? Alright let's say for instance like some of them kids might say, "She told me to do 'dis' or 'dat'," to me like in a flat way. Or well I'll put it like this: Like you say, "Well has she ever seen or have you ever seen so and so and so?" You know, [you] *would use a flat word like 'dat' or 'dis' and I might would say, "Not 'dis,' but 'that.'" Somebody say 'dis' I say, "Not 'dis.' Say 'that.'"* [I do that with adults] *if it's adult that I know like that but I don't if* [it's] *somebody I don't really know and they say that. I be knowing it's wrong but I don't fool with 'em. I just let 'em go 'head on.*

LITERACY: *It's What the Individual Really Wants*

I do read. [Being able to read is important to me and my life.] *I really love to read my Bible, the word of God. And that's really one thing I do a lot. The most reading I do is the Bible. I read other things besides the Bible,* [but] *I don't read too much more than the Bible. The Bible is practically everyday, most times. Because like when I pray in the morning, well then I'll read my Bible. I just been got into a habit of reading when I pray most times. I read my Bible most every morning after I pray. I reads in the Old sometime but mostly I read in the New Testament like Matthew, Corinthians. That's a part of me now. See this become a part of me doing this. If I don't do it I don't feel right. I've done it so much. Cause when I finish praying, that's the next thing I do is read my Bible. So I reads that on a daily basis.*

Some of them words I might read but I got to get to understand it, so I think on words and get the things out of the word of God and what it's all about and everything like that. I ask God to open up my understanding to His word and I understands the Bible pretty good, the words that I read. That's the main thing is understanding; to get understanding if you're reading.

I wished I hada read more in my life and that would make me a better reader. I'd like to be more better in reading. Cause it's kinda a company keeper too really. There's a comfortable reading you get into it. If I read more and things like that, I know I would get a little better in it. Get interested and read and understand what I read. I would like to but that doesn't say that I'll get to it.

[Being able to write is] not really [important to me and my life]. I don't write anything, but when I'm going to the store—write a list out, what I want, and writing like that. But just sitting there writing letters, I don't do that hardly. Writing, I don't do very much of that at all. Because I don't write letters. Somebody always writes for me. I can write though, some. I write like a check or something like that. I don't hardly write everyday, the course of a day. I read but I don't write. But every once in a while I might write a little something, like in church. Now I do a little writing in church because I put the scripture down like [when] the pastor get up and you know how preachers maybe take they text from this chapter or maybe go to another chapter? Now that, I be writing that down. But just say here at the house sitting down writing, [I don't do that] because I don't write letters anymore. It might be a little something that I just write down from the Bible. Most of my writing is gon be from the Bible. That's the most writing I do. And make a grocery list out or something like that.

But just writing, I don't hardly ever just do that because I don't have to mail anybody. We talks on the phone. See that's what I do in this day. I use the phone mostly. I shoulda kept writing cause it would help me. But since I stopped writing, some things I lose by stop writing—like constant writing and spelling. And see I can't spell too good. But when I used to write and everything, I was pretty good.

I used to write letters. I didn't read and write as much as I did when I was going to school, but that's how people used to get in contact with each other, by mail. See we didn't have phones. We used to have to write letters to each other. You know like your family or whoever. Like we call now? We used to had to write. So that kept me up pretty good in writing, in that time. And I just fell back when I got to play with telephones and all *this stuff. Since this phone deal, I just start calling, talking on the phone. But I used to write, years ago. Sure did. I still can write. I jot things down and stuff like that and maybe write a little something if I want to keep up with it. I do that now.* [The writing I do now] *is enough for me.*

No indeed [I don't enjoy writing]. *I don't be just feeling like writing. I would love to be a good writer. I been wanting that for years and years and years back. I would like to enjoy writing to a certain extent. I wouldn't say I wouldn't like to enjoy it cause if I could write very well and every-thing, it would be a pleasure for me. I would enjoy it. But now since I got this old and everything, I don't worry about that. I wouldn't worry about that at all. And you see what did it though? I'ma tell you. This telephone. I used to write way more than I do now. But see stead of writing letters to people like people used to do, I don't do that. See that's what messed me up. It's the phones. Now when I want to talk to somebody, I just call 'em.*

[The difference between a good reader and a poor reader is] *just lacking of an education, some education. I think it's the person. If they go to school and don't learn, I think it's up to the person, I don't say it's the teacher. Because if you go to school and you want to learn and got a mind and determined to learn you can do it. See, so I wouldn't put that on the teacher. So it had to be the individual.*

[The difference between a good writer and a bad writer] *all depends upon the person's desire to want to write. They education goes along all with that. But it's what the individual really wants. You know some people slack in some things and they good in another one. But if you want a education regardless to you might not like a subject, but you got to get that subject. But to pass you got to get this subject whether you like it or not. And like some people want to be educated. You done run across hard things in your education, right? But you was determined to get an educa-tion so you worked at it. Now some people just want the education but they don't want to work. They don't want to do what they was suppose to do to get the education. They lazy on that. "Oh I don't feel like doing this," and just push it aside. But you gotta work at anything for to get anything good. You gotta put some effort forth if you want whatever it is. That's right. You go on a job, you got to work. And you want to work and be pleasing to whoever you working under, right? Or whatever you doing, you want to do it right. Like you teach. You want to do that right huh? You don't want no mess up in that. So it's in a person mind what they really wants in life and they go for it.*

But some people don't go for it but they know what they want. See like

*me, I wanted a education, but seems like it just was impossible. And so
I didn't worry bout it. But right now sometime I think about if I had a
education, I could do this and I could do that. But it doedn't worry me. I
don't let it worry me. So I think this is up to the individual.*

[Being literate is important. In order to succeed or function in this
country, you have to be literate. You have to be able to read and] *write
and know how to spell. You supposed to be able to write a letter* [and]
*sign your name. I think it's very important. I know that's right. But thank
God through the ever good Lord I'm succeeding pretty good. It ain't no big
thing but I'm happy in other words. I am happy* [with who I am]. *I think
I'm very important. I don't think I'm very, but I think I'm important. I'm
important to somebody. A lot of people I'm important to. Now I might not
be important* [to everybody, but] *I don't think any of us is important to
everybody.*

GOALS AND POSSIBLE SELVES:
I Wished I'da Got a Good Education

*I can't remember what I said I wanted to be when I was younger. I know it
wasn't a teacher, that's for sure. I know I didn't think that. I don't really
know what I thought I would be; what I wanted to be. But thank God it's
like it is. Cause I dreamed of a lot of things when I was young. But the
education is the one that kinda hemmed up some of my dreams. I wished
I'da got a good education. I would like to've been educated. A many days I
say I wished I'da got an education. Many days.*

*At least if I'da finished high school, I'd have a better education. I could
use my language right and be able to do more with more education—
write letters and put 'em in the right sentences and whatever. See I don't
know all of that. I don't know all that, how to do that. Because I'm not the
person would want a lot of wealth and a lot of mansion and all that stuff.
I'm comfortable like I am. Whatever in my life, I'm comfortable. I'm not
uncomfortable.*

GRACE
I Always Wondered If My Life Would Have Been Different If

She realized that something was shifting, in her talk with Irene. They were still linked together, but it was not, now, the link of race, which had been tenuous in any case, and had not held up. They were simply two women, choosing to live as they liked in the world. She wondered if Irene felt this. "You were my objective correlative," said Irene. . . . "You see, my great fear in college was that I could hardly avoid becoming an ordinary bourgeois success. I was bright, energetic, attractive, with never a *thought* of failure, no matter *what* sociologists say. Those students who were destined, within ten years, to know the names of the designers of their shoes and luggage, to vacation in Europe once a year and read two best sellers every five— while doing a piss-poor job of teaching our children—scared the hell of out of me. That life, and not the proverbial 'getting pregnant and dropping out of school,' represented 'the fate worse than death.' Your dilemma was obvious. You, even *objectively* speaking, didn't know who you were. What you were going to do next; which 'you' would be the one to survive. At the same time that I condemned you for your lack of commitment to anything I considered *useful*, I used you as the objectification of my own internal dilemma. In the weirdest way, your confusion made mine seem minor by comparison. For example, I understood that episode with Source was a short cut, for you, to the kind of harmonious, multiracial community that you could be happy in, and which I also believed possible to create in America. . . . I was looking toward 'government' for help; you were looking to Source. In both cases, it was the wrong direction— *any* direction that is away from ourselves is the wrong direction."
—Alice Walker, *You Can't Keep a Good Woman Down*

• • •

I don't remember all of my life as a child. I grew up on Lofton Street in South Tiberius (when I was about 4 or 5 we moved across the street from Nelson Street to Lofton Street). I sort of remember some of my life. I was the baby until I was 7 years old. Ruth spoiled me as a child. She was raised by her grandmother until she was 7 years old. She had never seen a baby before me and I was like a doll to her. She kept me clean, kept my hair combed with ribbons in it, she dressed me pretty and she took care of me. I sucked a bottle until I was 5 years old. I was even fixing my own bottle. They really had me spoiled. I remember when I was 5 or 6 years old Ruth and Mavis would take me to a place where people would drink beer and just sit around. Children could go in there too. Music would be playing and Ruth would tell me to dance. I would do a dance called the Turkey Hop and I would get out there and dance. People would start throwing pennies and nickels on the floor where I was dancing and Ruth would get the money and we would spend it. Maya found out because they would take me about once a week. She stopped that. To us we were just having fun. Maya was single and she was out a lot so they were doing everything bad. It was fun to us.

Maya worked for the Grayson's. They had a daughter named Sue who was the same age I was and I would get a lot of her clothes.

I remember I wanted a bike one Christmas when I was about 7 or 8 years old. When I woke up Christmas morning there was a blue and white bike under the tree. I was so happy. I stayed on that bike all day. One of the kids said it wasn't a new bike. I had never paid any attention to that. All I knew was that I had a bike and it was new to me. I told Maya what was said. She said Santa was out of new bikes until next year. That was OK with me.

I started school at 6 years old, almost 7, because of my birthdate. I don't remember the first, second and third grades at all. I kind of remember the fourth grade and the fifth grade. I remember the sixth grade the most because I was smart in History. I could read a chapter and memorize it. I remember reading about De Soto. I memorized that and recited it in front of my class.

My 7th grade English teacher—I wish I could remember her name but I can't—she taught me how to use my teeth and tongue to pronounce words. I learned a lot from her. I wish I would have taken that class for (4) y[ea]rs. I didn't realize the importance of it at that time. that class helped me a lot. if I would practice that now I would talk much better but I forget about it when I talk.

I had 4 good friends in elementary school: Laura, Eloise, Margaret, and another one I can't remember. We did a lot of things together in school. I *think that was the best time of my childhood in school. We took dance classes together at school we learned all the modern dances.*

By that time I began to grow into a teen, Maya started to have more and more children. We were excited over Felicia and maybe Johnny, but when Marcus and Reia came we were upset with her because that was more work for us. By that time Ruth, Gloria and Mavis were old enough to date. They started leaving one by one. Ruth got pregnant at 18 years old. Gloria came to live with us by the age of 14, but she got pregnant at 16 or 17 and then got married to Al. Mavis got pregnant at 14 and then got married to Tony. They stayed together for 2 months—that was all. She said he slapped her and she left because she was not going to stay with a man that would fight her.

When I turned about 13 or 14 years old I was the oldest at home. That's when my life turned around. I was a child responsible for 4 children. That wasn't easy. Maya was single and going out all the time. I was the babysitter. I couldn't have a life of my own. Going to school, cooking and cleaning for 4 children, getting them dressed in the morning, and fixing them breakfast—that was too much for a 14 year old child who was trying to go to school and learn. I didn't have a lot of time for homework. ([In] Elementary [I made] 'A's and 'B's, [in] High School 'C's and 'D's.) I eventually lost interest in school. See, school was not important to Maya. That was just a state law to her, so we had to go. Maya felt if you could cook and clean that was your B.A. and B.S. degree. She felt when you got married that was your Master's degree. Don't get me wrong. I felt she did the best she could do as a single mother with 5 children. Don't get me wrong. I loved my sisters and brothers too. A few years ago she said she thought a many of days to just walk off and leave us. She said she didn't think she was going to make it; it was too much for her. But thank God she didn't. I felt sorry for her then.

I feel I could have gotten a better education if I would have had the time to apply myself and someone to help me understand the importance of education. Maybe I was a slow thinker and I feel if I was in a Private school where they help you better to apply yourself I would have done better. I always wanted to go to the private Catholic school in Tiberius. those kids seem different and they were smart. The school I went to was ok; all the black kids went to Jefferson or Roosevelt schools from Elementary to High School. we didn't have a choice. We walked to school but that wasn't a problem at all.

I blame myself and the school teachers. see I feel teachers should try to find out why children are not doing well in class and counsel you on you[r] grades. Maybe sometimes if they see that a child is having a problem they should try and help by taking up more time with the slower kids instead of leaving them behind. That makes children drop out of school. and during that time it wasn't as bad as it is today. the schools were not over crowded at all. they should have worked more we kids. and I feel a lot of kids from those day's would have done better. We didn't fight or kill the teachers like today. We respected our teachers like we did our Preachers or Parents, but that over with. I have to try and pick up the pieces and go on from there.

Maya fussed so much. Growing up I didn't feel loved at all. I was insecure and I had no self-esteem. She was very abusive to us mentally and physically. When she would get up in the mornings she wanted you up. Maybe that is why I stay in bed so long in the mornings now. I was always a nervous child from the fussing. And sometimes she and Mr. John would fight. That was too much for me. I would go outside and sit on the porch and cry. She tells everybody I was her smartest child in the house. That's because I went on and did what was needed to be done so she wouldn't fuss. I couldn't take that all the time. I didn't have a good teen life at all, not at all. Maya did teach us values of life and morals; thank God for that.

You know, I always wondered if my life would have been different if Maya would have motivated me as far as getting an education and being independent and if I would have learned how to read real good and comprehend good and if she would have taught me how to choose a husband. Mr. John was there most of the time so we did have food and clothing, but he didn't pay any attention to us. It was like we weren't there. But since the incident with Regina when Maya thought something was going on— there were 4 girls at home—teenagers—and maybe he was afraid to talk with us. There is no telling what Maya was saying to him.

In high school my best friend's name was Rebecca Turner. She came from a poor family, worse than my family, so we couldn't help each other. When I turned 18 years old I got married and had a child. That was worse than being at home. That was a different situation. I didn't have all the responsibility with kids, but I got married to the wrong person. I didn't know how to choose a husband. We had nothing in common. He didn't work half the time so his mother supported us most of the time. He stayed in the streets all of the time from Sunday to Sunday. I remember when I went into labor they had to get him out of a club. That marriage ended up in a divorce.

When I left that situation I got married again. That was another bad choice. I married Jesse. He was good to me at first, but after you were born he hit the streets. That destroyed our marriage. Also, Jesse's family treated me real bad.

When I came to Picard, I did bring Deidra with me, but Eddie came and got her. He said he wanted to keep her until you were born. That is how Deidra and I got separated. I loved Deidra very much (I would cry sometimes because I missed her so much).

Later when you were born it took me awhile to get used to you. By that time Jesse was in those streets and I was at home, so I devoted all my time to you and just spoiled you too much. You were so fat and pretty. I would pack you around all the time. Jesse had a car but I didn't (you know how selfish he is). He had to be at work for 7:30 and he could have taken you to the day care, but I had to take you. I walked holding you there everyday and I picked you up in the evenings like I had a car, but my feet were my transportation. I didn't know any better. I was doing what I saw Maya doing. When I got home I would cook, feed you, and bathe you. And when Jesse came home I would fix his plate, put it on the table, and everything. I don't think he knew any better either. I would do, he did nothing. I guess I think about that now and I feel he didn't know how to treat a wife, but he could have tried. He could have thought that I wanted to be treated like I was treating him, but he never did learn—or he just didn't care. Since he didn't have a father at home he only saw his mother working all the time and thought that was the way it was supposed to be: A woman's work was never done and the man's work was done after he got off from his job (he turned the bible around then like he does now).

You know Jesse and Anne [Jesse's second oldest sister] always thought they were better than I was and I thought they were too. I grew up insecure and with low self-esteem. I put them first for years. But one day I woke up and realized I was just as good as they were. They didn't have anymore to offer in life than I had. I would buy things for Jesse sometimes (he was a little better then; he did buy for me sometimes also), but I started fixing myself up and spending my money on myself and feeling good about myself.

I was fortunate enough to get a good job. I thank God for it. I have good benefits and retirement. I got a job which I never, never thought I *would get, but I did it with prayer and faith because I know that God can do anything but fail. See I think sometimes about my childhood and tears come to my eyes thinking about how abusive my mother was, but on the other hand I wouldn't trade her for anyone else. She may not have known anything about reading, writing and math, but she knew everything about the real deal—God almighty—and she taught us about God. She gave us a degree in the Father, the Son, and the Holy Spirit. If we didn't know about Jesus Christ we would not have made it this far in life without getting into some kind of trouble or being dead now because we didn't care; we had nothing. See we had to go to Sunday School every Sunday and church. That is how we survived in this world. I remember when I was looking for a job for 9 months and I was looking daily, Maya told me that if I prayed and had faith in God he would supply all of my needs; He would give me a job—and He did.*

I put an application in with Farpoint in January, 1972. Maya told me that if I just believed in God everything would be OK. I had put in applications everywhere. She said, "You have done your part. If you make one step, He will make two." I prayed that weekend and I didn't go out looking that Monday or Tuesday. On that Wednesday you were at school and I was folding clothes. The phone rang and I said, "Hello." The man on the other end of the phone said, "Is this Grace Richardson?" I said, "Yes." He said, "This is Charles Jones with Farpoint. I wanted to know if you still need a job." I sat there for a minute. I couldn't believe it. When we got off the phone I fell on my knees praying. That is why I know their is a God and that with faith He will supply your needs. So I ended up with a good job. With the help of God you can do anything because He has all power and everything is His. So, if you believe in Him its yours.

I know things happen in life to turn things around like Jesse losing his job. That was bad. But with the help of God we have managed this far. When he had that job he never felt as if I was a part of his responsibility. He felt I should work and take care of myself. I felt when he bought this house that was too much for his salary—and it was. He was used to me making ends meet, but that was a little bit too much for us. Instead of us putting our money together, he would give me so much money for the house note, utilities, etc. I had to come up with the rest of it. That was wrong. He didn't care if I had money left for my personal use like lunch, gas, etc. Now he wishes he had put his money with my money because he is not making that much money now. He feels that if I would be respon- sible for everything then I could be under all that pressure. But now he sees how I used to feel when I had to do everything and didn't know how I was going to make it. What goes around comes around. See all my life I have been put in the position of being responsible for people and everything. I don't have money now I can put my hands on, but God has blessed me and He sees that I have what I need and a lot of things I want. I do have money saved with my job for retirement and I have social security also, thank God, so I won't say that I did too bad in life. It could have been worse. I will be taken care of with or without a husband.

EDUCATION: *I Didn't Have No One to Help Me*

I went to school to learn. I didn't go to school to be petted up or to be spoiled or to get attention. I went there to learn and they did try to teach me. So I feel as a person they treated me like a person and they taught the class and I was there to learn and to do my work and I did. [But] *I have a lotta problems with teachers having pets in school. I've always noticed that teachers, they always pick someone to be the head of the class or someone to do more than other people. They'ah pick the smart one or either to me, when we were growing up, they'ah pick the brightest ones— and they don't really have to be that smart. And I still would say that. If you were pretty and you were bright and you had long hair, that was the teacher's pet. And then to the other students that make them feel bad that they wasn't that important. And that is harmful to children. And you grow with this insecurity in life.*

When I was in sixth grade (I can't remember like first, second, third and fourth that much), I remember it was the four of us—Margaret (the most fair skinned, like a Frenchman like), Eloise and Laura (they were mostly brown skinned) and all of us. It wasn't that I was a pet or anything like that. I was in that group with them. We used to do a lot of dancing and talking and entertaining and talent shows and stuff like that. And most time like that, people do pay attention to you because of that, the things that you do, being active in different things. And I guess because the four of us used to be together all the time, they did pay attention. They treated me like I was a person, but not a particular or special person. They treated me like a person but they didn't take up enough time with me as a person.

I can remember when we were in school they had the majorettes. People paid more attention to the majorettes back then than the cheer- leaders. And now when you was at the pep rallies and stuff like that, oh they enjoyed that. But out on the field nobody even looked at cheer-

leaders then. They just looked at the majorettes. And all the majorettes was bright. All of 'em they picked was bright. They had to pick 'em bright with the nice legs and stuff like that. I remember this one girl got on there and she was darker than me and she should have made lead majorette, but she didn't and everybody was upset because she was dark. They kept Liza and Juanita—I always will remember their names and I always will remember them on the front line. But they never did make the other girl because she was very dark. But she had long hair and stuff. And that's the only way she got on there probably because of her hair. I think it's wrong for them to do that because it make other children grow up very insecure and make them feel that they are less than other people because they don't have no long hair or they are not light skin. And that's very bad.

Now when I was growing up and I was in school, I like darker skinned guys with nice hair. Nice hair; that was me. It wasn't because they were bright or whatever. I'm a hair person. I think I am a hair person. People have different things they like about people. I don't care about a person, how dark they are or this or that. I'm just a hair person. I like nice hair. And to be honest, that's just me. But only thing about that, with little kids and stuff like that, you don't do that because children remembers all that. And it make them feel insecure and stuff like that growing up because they feel less than other people. You can make them feel less than other people and less than a person.

I remember we were in the sixth grade and [the teacher] was a French-man, very very very light skinned, and her husband was too because he taught driver's ed. And there was the four of us in her class. And we would all do things. She would always call on us to do things and stuff like that. And one day we was gonna have a little party and we was gonna go into the store and she was gonna let us go across the street to the store. And she called Laura, Margaret and Eloise I think and she didn't call my name. And I remember saying, "I figured she wasn't gonna let me go." I don't know what I said, but I think about that now because I felt she always included me because of them, because I was with them. But it wasn't that she really cared that much for me like she did them. When it came to making a choice, if it had to be one or two, it would be one of them or two of them; it wasn't me and one of them. I think I was included because of them. And all that—see stuff like that?—has stayed with me.

Like with my male teachers, I had no problem with them. It was just women that would do that to me. It all depend, like I say, what a person like about a person. They always thought I had nice legs and this and that, so men would sorta cater to me in that manner. [That] *could have made somebody else feel bad, I don't know. But, like I say, I guess it all depends on what people like about people.*

During the time when I was going to school, we were not integrated back then. All of my teachers was Black. There was no White teachers at that school. All the Blacks went to school together and all the Whites went to school together. You didn't even see a White person. You walked the streets all day going to school and coming from school. You were not gonna see a White person in that area. Because they had they own area. That's all was out here. Black. No White people lived around us. None. They were like ten, fifteen, twenty miles away and that was a long ways because we didn't have transportation hardly. Ok, just like State University down there. I always thought it was so far and I found out it was bout five miles down the street from us. I didn't even know that it was in the back of my school until we was at Reia graduation and they say that's Roosevelt right back there. And I still haven't gotten over that. All I had to do was look across the fence and that was State University back over there.

But as far as walking there and stuff like that? See I never went past certain streets. And then I'ah tell you another thing. If you went too far, and like at night, you couldn't go really down in there because those White kids, those White students down there, they would do a lot of stuff to you. They'ah kill Blacks and all kinda stuff. You wasn't getting too close to those people. They would do a lot of things because I know one guy, a friend of Jesse's, they took and threw acid in his face, some White guys. That's the kinda stuff they would do if they would come in your part of town. That's what they was coming for. You had your own [area]. *You wasn't going to just walk the street and see White people. You couldn't walk out of your house and walk and see White people, unlessen they was driving a car, going to town or something like that. They wasn't walking out there. Because that was not their area of town. Everybody had their own area of town. And that's the way it was back then when I was growing up.*

And I always felt that Whites got a better education than Blacks. We always got their hand-me-down books and different stuff like that. And being Black—I think they taught different things in their school than they taught in our school. And I still say that.

And I'ma tell you another thing. I was telling that to Reia today. You know when you were talking about Simon did a better job on his test, on the English, than you did and stuff like that? And what I still can't get her to see those tests are not designed for Black people. They're designed for

White people. I don't care how smart you are, they're not designed for you to pass. Now I don't know how you passed it, but I'm telling you. They design things for them. I don't know what goes on in those schools or how they're taught.

And I think a lot has to do with the teachers. I really do. I don't know if Black teachers—I'm sure they probably grew up some of them in the same manner that I did and by them not knowing I'm sure they went through a lot of hard times too and they did the best they could do. I can say my mother did the best she did raising me. I feel they did the best they could do. But I always felt that the other races got a better education than we got for some reason. And I don't know what manner it was, how they were taught or what. But we were always left behind. And I'm sure it's because of race. They will not let you catch up with them. And that's why they didn't want integration I'm sure.

There was a trade school and we were going to senior high. There was a trade school right next door and I didn't even know it. And when you got in eleventh grade you can go to trade school and substitute that for subjects. And a lotta people back then, you see these people who have two-year RN degrees, them older people? That's where they went. And I didn't know that. If I'da known that and had somebody to help me and somebody like a counselor or anybody and I woulda known that, I could've gone right there and I could've gotten a two-year RN degree and still have it, still work a lot of places. And they had beauty school over there and all that. I didn't even know that. Now I look back and I say, "Do you know that's what they were doing over there?" And I didn't know what they were doing. And children was come from different schools and go over there. Cause I say, "Oh, they go to Jefferson; they comes from over there." And I didn't know what it was really. All I knew it was a trade school.

I guess I didn't know too much about anything and no one told me too much about anything. I think I sorta kinda hung maybe with the wrong crowd of people who I felt was more like me and I guess they didn't have anybody to help them either. You have to have guidance and somebody has to kinda help you and tell you a little. Then I think if people kinda say, "Well, you may not be cut out for this or that. Why don't you try so and so and so or whatever?" Like some teachers can talk to you and tell you, "Maybe you're not cut out for a English major. Why don't you try Math? Maybe you're not that. Why don't you try nursing?" or "Why don't you try this and you can take some classes?" I didn't have that kinda guidance and that kinda counseling. I know I wasn't gonna get it from home.

I felt I did more [for my children's education than my mother did for me] *because I understood more than she did toward education. I understood the importance of it maybe, more than she did. At that point in time I realized that education was important and I didn't do a lot that I could have done, but I did what you all needed. I had it there for you if you needed something for school or you needed your books or you needed your paper or you needed your pencil or whatever; it was there. Only thing I can say I did help.*

You were in school when you were two months old. That could've had a big, big effect on you. Because the school I had you in, those people were good to you and they just loved you. I remember that lady she said, "I just love Sonja," she say. And "She's just so smart, and she's just so . . ." And you were fat and she said, "Oh she's just so pretty." And people cater to people like that. So they probably was helping you and teaching you and that's why she couldn't understand why you couldn't get potty trained at a year old. But you wasn't a year old. But see I had [lied about your age]. *I say, "Oooh they could be whipping my child." And I start teaching you at home. You always had story books and you always liked to do stuff like that and we always helped you. You was always interested in stuff like that and we always helped you. So I feel we contributed toward your language, your reading and your writing and stuff like that and Deidra too. I feel like I contribute towards my children, Deidra—because Deidra was with me until she was two years old. Cause I know y'all used to have paper, writing and reading and stuff and we'd just sing. We used to do all that.*

And I go back to when you asked me about my parents and I'll say yes they did [contribute to my language and literacy development], *to the best they could. Because they had to help me, to kinda teach me how to read. They taught me some, my mother, the best that she could. Then I had Ruth 'nem there to help me too. I'm sure they are the ones that taught me how to read in the beginning. So I'll say yes they did help some. Because Maya always could read. She could read like up to fourth grade. She helped. She contribute toward my elementary part.*

They always bought little story books and stuff for to read. I can't remember but I know she did [read to me] *because I saw her do it with the other ones. And I saw her with Mavis. Maya used to try to make her get her homework. Now see I remember all that. See when they were growing up, they were all bout the same size and it wasn't really no li'l children round there. And she used to make 'em get they homework. I remember that. And she used to sit there with Mavis and whip Mavis* cause Mavis couldn't read and spell or something it was. I remember that. And all of us remember that. She say she couldn't understand why Mavis was like that. And so I know if she did it with them, she had to do it with me, and they had to. And I feel with my children, I bought y'all books. I read to you all. You read to me. And I always had books and stuff there for you to read and I always read you story books and bought your books. And see you went to school for one thing at a early age. Yes I did contribute toward helping my children to learn how to read and write and stuff because that's where you learn—at home. They teach your ABCs. I taught you all your ABCs and stuff like that. So yes, I felt that I did contribute toward that at that time.

I didn't get that from school. I didn't have anybody. If I would have and if they were helping the students, I don't know why I didn't know about that trade school was going on over there. I just didn't know. And I think too, I remember I was going to Roosevelt Junior. It was Roosevelt Junior and Roosevelt Senior mixed together and maybe when they build [the] other school down in the bottom as we call it, I moved from by the trade school and I start going to school down there. That's how they did. That was just a junior's high and then they put the senior high down there. And by me not seeing those children going over there anymore because we had moved, I didn't even know what was going on. But look like it should have been some people, like speakers or teachers or somebody come in and tell you, "Hey, you can go . . ." Like if everybody go in the auditorium and they would say, "People who are interested in this, you can take classes here. You can do this." Just like now. They have students working different places when they get in eleventh and twelfth grade, and they place 'em and stuff. Look like they coulda looked at student records to me and seen, "Well maybe they're not good in this, but maybe they'ah do good in a trade school. Maybe they wasn't cut out for college," and tell you stuff like that.

To me, seem like they were more lenient on the female in school than they were on the males because I guess they felt that you was gonna have to be the head of your house and you was gonna need the education. That's how people felt. The male needed more education to me than the female because they looked at females was gonna be home having children, cleaning up, didn't have to go out and work a lot of 'em and the male had to be the head of the house. And to me they were really harder on them and they pushed them more to try to get an education to support their families. They were hard on those boys. I used to see that.

[They pushed them in some of the ways I was saying I didn't get pushed or didn't get helped.] *Because they had all kind of workshop, like woodshop, all kind of stuff for them. Trade and stuff like that. And I think they knew more about trade school than the girls did. Now they taught us home ed —how to sew and how to cook. But boys had other little things that they could do. Cause I really think they felt that they was gonna need that.*

And see what they was teaching 'em? How to be a carpenter and different stuff like that. They wasn't really teaching them college, preparing them for college and stuff. They was preparing them just because they felt this is the furthest you was gonna get anyway. You wasn't gonna get a good job. You probably have certain type jobs. Because that's how they looked at it back then. They felt you wasn't gon have no suit on and going to work unlessen you went to college and got a teacher's degree or something like that. No, it wasn't no White children going [to school] *over there. It's no way.*

I think schools should be preparing students for college. Start in elementary school preparing them, teaching them, making sure that they're advancing. I feel when that student finish high school, if that student is college material—because everyone is not college material—[that student should be prepared to go to college]. *I just don't feel that. So I think you should be taught in school and to work and do the best you can, work as hard as you can to find what field that you are best suited for. Because that's why the world is made up of so many different jobs and everything. Some people are cut out to be garbage men. Some people cut out to be nurses, doctors, lawyers, teachers, preachers, warehouse workers, maintenance people, this and that. And everybody fits in a certain category. And I think everybody should be taught: whatever you do you do it well.*

Education I feel is put there for you to learn, and I think you should. And I think teachers should guide children in that manner to try to find out what is best for each student that they have and try to work with each student. And like I say, everybody's not college material, but I think education should prepare students for college or some kind of business college. There're different kind of colleges. There are the school of performing arts. There are different things that children can do and I think the teacher should recognize things in students. I'ah say education is to prepare a child for the future. For what is suited best for them and in college and stuff like that. To prepare a child for the future. To prepare a person for the future, where they can try and do the best they can so they can try and get a good job so they can support their family and themselves and be independent and try to do the best they can do as far as in school and doing the best they can to get a good education and whatever they feel that they can do. If it's going for a teacher, going for a lawyer, going for a doctor, going for a maintenance man, going for a carpenter, whatever. I guess just to say it in a simple way: preparing children for an education is preparing yourself for your future.

I won't say they didn't [do that for me]. *I think it was part them and part me because I lost interest. I lost interest in school because I didn't have no one to help me. And when you got twenty and thirty children in a classroom and here one, you're trying to help this person, this person showing no interest; well, they just leave you alone. But I feel that they should try to find out why. Why is this child not showing any interest in school? Why are they not doing anything? And I feel back then it was no reason for that. Because they was not overcrowded. And they could call your parent, talk to your parent, or write a letter and ask your parent to come over there or whatever and try to find out what is wrong with this student. Is this a single parent? Do you have a mother at home or a father? What are you doing? Because I feel if somebody say, "Well this child has to come home because I have four kids here that need to be taken care of and I can't do it by myself. I'm a single parent so and so and so." Then I think the teacher would understand and I think you would have more help at school. I'm not saying you should give them separate homework or this or that, but I think you should be allowed to do your work at school and somebody there to help you. And they know that you need to get this work done because you can't do it when you go home because it's nobody to help you or to support you. And I guess I feel that's what teachers are for. Because teachers to me back then we respected them like we respected our mother and our preacher or something. I realize that* [is] *what bothers me—I didn't get a good education and I don't think the education I did get prepared me for college. And I guess when I realized I needed an education, I was married and I had children then.*

I think they do what the purpose of education is but there are students there that need more attention than other students. Some people have five and six children. Each child has a different personality, and everybody's not the same. Some need special attention. So I feel they are doing what they should do in a manner of teaching you. And I know you don't go to school for people to be a mother to you or this or that. But I feel since you are there and they are the teacher, they should recognize when a child is not doing what they should do. It's something wrong. Only thing I would say if you would just make one phone call and ask the parent. Try to find what kind of household this person came from. What is going on there; this child can't do they homework or whatever. Yeah they do what they suppose to do. To teach you. And if you can't catch on and you can't get it, well they just leave you behind. But I don't think they should do that.

If they are slow students, I think they should have some kind of program or something for the[m]. See I say that but I hate to see people separate kids—take them and say, "Well, this a slower child. We gonna put them in a slower class"—because I don't think that's right because then that make kids really not do. I think that's bad. I think you leave 'em all together and you work with this student a little more or try to talk with their parents to get their parents to work with them a little more and try to get them to help that child a little more because you never know what's going on in the people home. Maybe the parents is not helping because they're not interested in education. So I don't like that moving the kids to a slower class. Because kids are slower, some of 'em, and then there are just some kids who just don't know because of some problem. And if you find a child with a problem, you should take it a little further and see what's wrong. I think they should have special classes for kids who seem to be a little different from the other kids as far as catching on and this and that and stuff like that. And I still think that's bad.

But then I think there should be tutors at school too, not to be paid, but to help the slower students so they can keep up in class. Because there are people who can't afford a tutor. And I think it's wrong because you're going to school to get an education to better yourself and I think all that should be there at certain hours, even if it's after class or before or during. You should have a study period for to go to a tutor to help you keep up. They will be surprised at how many children learn how to read, write, catch on and everything. But no, you have to pay for this services, although you going to school and the teachers are there to teach you. And if you a slow child and you can't catch on, you got to pay somebody twenty dollars an hour to tutor you. And I think that's wrong when that's what you going to school for.

And I think they should give you aptitude tests and all kinda stuff. And when your score is low, below a certain level, you think they try to come and try to find out why? They just continue to teach and leave you right behind, and I think it's wrong.

And the teachers, I fault them for a part of that too. Because I think they should have other people, professional people, come in and those

*children who had low scores and stuff like that, give them some other kind
of test to try to find out if these children have some type of Dyslexy or
what they have and try to help them in some kinda way. Because everybody pay tax and I know they have enough money.*

L A N G U A G E : *I Value Standard English More*

*Good English to me is when a person talk and use their words correctly in
making a statement, speech or everyday conversation with others. It can
help you get a better job. People listens when you speak well and they feel
you are competent. I value standard English more* [than Black English]
because of getting jobs and talking to different races of people.

[I don't believe there is one right way to talk] *and you know why? It is a
right way, but I don't think it's one right way. Because I guess I feel things
changes and people always adding and taking away. So there is a right
way, but I think there are other ways you can speak too that it's not
so bad.*

[I think Black English is bad English]. *I believe black english started
doing slavery time. Blacks were not able or aloud to learn how to read or
write the Caucasion english. I feel the blacks who got a chance to live or
work in the white house as maids or buttlers got a chance to hear and pick
up on some words of the Caucasion english. When they talked the blacks
would try and listen and try to pronounce the words but, not knowing
how to spell the word they would half pronounced the word. And when
talking to the other blacks who worked in the fields, trying to help them
learn the english, the word was pronounced wrong. Like they would say
'dhis' for 'this' and 'dhat' for 'that' and that was past on from generations
to generations because of not knowing how to read, write or spell the Caucasion english. I believe if you can't spell a word it is hard to pronounce
the word correctly because you don't know the sound of the letters. Black
English is a beautiful language among blacks and that is as far as I would
take it.*

[Black English is important] *when you are talking to other black people
who can only speak black english and if you are an actress or actor and is
playing a part of speaking black english or just being yourself as a black
person around other blacks that you feel comfortable with.*

[I think I speak Black English]—*in a way. I think I sort of. In a way I do
and in a way I don't. I say it's sorta in between.* [I speak the way I naturally, normally, do] *because I just don't take the time out to try and teach*

myself to speak the way I would like to speak. I don't take the time out to do it. And I guess I've done it for so long and spoke that way and so many other people talk like me. And it frustrates me sometime. It all depend on who I'm talking with. But I've done it for so long. And you keep thinking you getting older and I say, "Oh well, I'm getting older now; I'm not gonna worry about it." But, like I say, I would like to learn how to speak better. And it's me who don't take the time to try and learn how to speak better. It all depends, like I say, on who I'm talking with and what conversation I'm in. It all depends. If a person I feel come and start talking to me and I feel that they are talking correct, I try to talk correct to them and it doesn't matter [if they are a man or woman].

[I talk differently to White people in general than I do to Black people in general] *because I think I feel we talk bad anyway and I always try to talk a little better when I talk with them. I think it's when it's people I know I try to talk a li'l better. People I don't know it really doesn't bother me too much but I try. I would try to think about what I'm saying because I'm thinking they're steadily saying, "Ooh look how she's splitting those verbs. Ooh look what she's saying." I would feel more comfortable talking to Sylvia* [a former White neighbor of Grace and Jesse who visited occasionally even after moving] *than to your professors because I be saying, "I know they beating me down." I know they be saying, "Now where does Sonja get her smartness from. It sure ain't from her." See all that running through your mind.*

I talk differently to Black people I don't know. It's certain ones. [I] *try to talk better than* [when I'm] *talking to Sally and Cassie* [two African American coworkers and long-time close friends of Grace] *and people that I know. It's important to me to use my 'he,' 'she' and 'it'—'he said,' 'she said,' stuff like that. It's important to me to use that. Now when I do that I feel good. Instead of saying 'she do,' you see, saying 'she does' or 'he does' instead of saying 'he do.' See when I know* [I] *said 'he does' or 'she does,' I feel that I'm doing ok then. Whatever else I make mistakes on it doesn't bother me that bad. But when I can say certain things that I feel that it's just norm and common to say, I feel more comfortable. But Gwen* [an African American acquaintance of Grace], *I try to kinda think before I say things. But Gwen speaks bad for a teacher. That's why a lot of children doesn't get a good education and doesn't learn how to speak. That's why I say it come from a lotta the school teachers cause they don't know themselves a lot of 'em.*

[I don't imitate the way people speak]. *Only thing I do if I go to*

Breauton and they talk and it tickles me—[but] *not to make fun of any-*
one. I don't do that. It doesn't matter to me how they speak. But it's just,
like I say, if I go down there and they say that stuff, like talking 'bout,
"That man cut that girl's 'years' off," and stuff like that. But as far as
people saying anything else, no. I'm used to all that. That's just the way
they talk and that's their language and I feel I know what they are saying.
Just like at work, Adrienne is a stone Frenchman and she talks, "Gul, let
me tell yuh." I don't pay any attention. It kinda tickles me. And Bridget is
too. They say these things like 'gu-rl,' you know how Breauton people talk.
But I feel that's how they talk; that's their language and I don't pay atten-
tion to them. And they seem like they're comfortable with it. Just like
Jeanette, she told me, she say, "I'm demontrating this Cappichina." She
say, "The 'artinic.' " I say, "'Artinic'?" I say, "That's 'authentic.'" And
she'll continue to say 'artinic.' Then I be saying, "Now I wonder if she's in
that store saying that." And I kept kinda say[ing]*, "Oh, the 'authentic.'"*
And she's in college. You see? Because everybody cannot talk and every-
body cannot write. You gonna write the way you talk.

　　I don't [like myself that much because of my language and literacy]
because I feel that I don't use my words correctly; I don't talk correctly. It's
ok talking to my family and whatever. But when I'm at work and people
looking at you and judging you by the way you speak . . . I don't feel com-
fortable talking a lotta time and the whole time I'm talking I'm wondering
if I'm saying the right thing. And that kinda keeps me nervous and upset.
It's very important to me to speak right, to speak correctly. I know I might
say some words and I'll say, "That wasn't right." I always beat myself
down when I'm talking. [I started doing this] *a few years* [ago] *because I*
know Lenora is good with writing. She is a good writer now and a lot of
people brings her stuff to write because everybody's is not a good writer.
Some people are and some people are not. She's good in English and she
writes good and I guess I just feel if I would write something to her, she
would know it's wrong and that's why I don't write anything to her.

　　And then some of 'em with degrees they don't even know how to read
nor write that well. I found out that they don't know. Like Lenora was say-
ing, "And Gertrude, she can't even write a sentence." I hear 'em criticize.
You see they criticize so much until it make you afraid. And these are
people with degrees. But everybody are not a good writer nor good reader.
And you might hear her say, "And with her dumb self. She can't even write
a good sentence." And then someone might say, "Well Lenora could you
do this for me," because she's a good writer. Because everybody are not.

As long as my words is spelled right and everything I guess I wouldn't worry about it if I could. I don't want to say 'is' when I should say 'are' and I don't want to say 'are' when I should say 'is.' That's why I ask you a lot of times about stuff like that. But as far as my language and literacy, no I don't feel comfortable around people who I feel criticizes. I hear a lot of that at work and I think that's why I feel so uncomfortable. Now if I talk with Sally or somebody, I don't care. Because we all talk alike.

I know a lotta educated people who know how to speak better and they don't. There are people who talk with me who's educated and they feel comfortable talking with me and they talk worse than me. But if they have to write something on a piece of paper, write a letter or write something or had to make a speech, they would do so much better than me because then they know how to do it. But just in the everyday, they talk just like me. And see I would like to do that: Know how to read and write, even though I may not use it all the time. But I would love to know how.

L I T E R A C Y: I Need to Do Better

[Literacy is] the ability to read and write; to comprehend what you read because understanding what you read is important. You are able to pick up a pen or pencil and write a letter, poetry, school work, policies and procedures for your job, your resume, wheatever you would like to read or write. You can write a book if you desire without being afraid to read or write thinking someone will criticize you.

It's the teaching for one thing [that accounts for the difference between a good reader or writer and a poor reader or writer], whether it come from the parent or the teacher. Somebody teaching and helping you to learn how to read. I was doing fine in elementary school. When I got to junior high, I guess the transition was so different and everything and we were in with the high school students and different stuff like that. I don't know if they was carrying me too fast or what. And I got kinda lost. I think they start moving real fast. In elementary school they take up more time with you and I did ok there. But when I got to the seventh and eighth grade, that's when I noticed [I started having trouble with reading and writing]. It was a big change and a big difference and then I start losing interest.

It could be genetic because some people inherits—like you might say that person is smart just like their mom or their dad. [So I think some people are born to be good readers and some people are born to be poor readers.] I really do. I think some of this stuff is hereditary. But I really think it all come from teaching. You have to be taught how to do these things. It just doesn't come to you so it has to be taught. I still say it's teaching from parents or teachers or whomever.

Reading broodens the mine, opens up your mine of understanding, helps you to understand more about things that is happening in the world and in your environment. Reading open doors to opportunity for you. [I enjoy reading] when I read something that is true or a true story—something that I can relate to, something I have been through—and it is easy to understand because I have lived it in some way or another. My favorite books are true stories on celebrities, entertainers. the reason is because I always wanted to be an entertainer. About five years ago it was "I, Tina," Tina Turner's life story. I enjoyed it. I saw it in a store and I bought it. [But the type of reading I usually do in the course of a day is:] 1. Reading memos. 2. Instructions concerning my job. 3. Reading some of sunday's paper. [I would like to read:] 1. [the] Newspaper Daily; 2. Novels (True Stories); 3. Magazines; [and] 4. Books in General—for instance reading everything that comes accross my desk.

I am not reading enough on a daily basis. I don't feel I am progressing enough at this time. I need to read more books, newspapers, magazines and etc. if I want to learn and accomplish from it.

[My] reading ability [is] not good at all. I don't comprehend well at all. I will read something and I don't understand what it means sometimes. I have to read it over and over. Then I get frustrated and stop. It is hard for me to get an overall pitcure of what I read. I would love to be a good reader. I am not comfortable at all reading out aloud. I get nervous because I am not understanding half of what I am reading so I feel no one else is understanding what I am saying. I am not comfortable at all reading. It irritates me.

I don't understand when I read silently. I understand better when I read by myself a little bit aloud. If I'm around somebody I don't know what I'm reading. I'm just reading, I'm just saying words. I do better when I'm by myself. Look like I hear myself better. But if I read silent I don't hear anything. I hear but I don't remember it. I have to kinda read it where I can hear.

In 1984 I took a reading class. I didn't like the teacher but she taught me the sounds of words and she said I new words I just would read slow. She felt I should practice more to read faster and better.

[I'm being held back from reading more like I should] because of the situation that I'm in and I always feel I don't have time because I always *feel I have too many other things to do. I don't know how to relax. I don't take the time for myself that I should. If I had someone to help me. See it all comes back to help. Somebody helping somebody. I can do what a lot of people do too and just leave everything undone and come sit here and read and read and read. But nothing would get done and I can't do that. Because if I would come here and sit with a book to read two and three hours or whatever, I wouldn't know what I read because I'm not relaxed because I know I have to finish doing what I was doing. If I had someone to help me to keep things in order and stuff like that and I would finish, I could say, "Oooh, I'ma sit here and read this book for an hour." But I just can't throw everything aside. And that is one of my problems that I have. I need to learn how to relax and stop worrying about other people and helping other people and doing for other people and try to help myself.*

I think maybe I always wanted to be accepted because maybe I felt that I wasn't never loved the way I wanted to be loved. And you feel people need you and stuff. I think that's the way you feel people care about you. And if I can get that out of my mind and stop worrying myself about that. . . . Now I've gotten to the point I need time to myself, to help myself now, and I don't need this in my life anymore. I need to try to help myself regardless to how old I am. I still feel I need to do better. And if I would take time to read more, I would be a better reader. If I would take time to write more, I'd be a better writer. But just to pick up a pen and write, that's not easy for me to do unlessen I'm just writing stuff that happened in my life and stuff. And a lot of stuff I wouldn't even want people to see so I wouldn't know if it's correct or not. Because I would like to write where I could say, "Here, read this for me." Punctuations and stuff like that is hard for me to do and get my sentences and stuff right. I'm the type person, I can't do but one thing at a time. I can cook and keep the house clean or I can let everything else go and I can read. I can't do it. Some people can do this and do that and some drive themselves half crazy. I don't wanta be like that. I see 'em do it at work. Crazy as a bat. I'ah be too confused.

[I didn't have a problem reading "I, Tina"] because with her book I have lived some of her life. So it wasn't hard to comprehend. I already knew because I had lived a lot of her life already. I didn't go through all that she went through. But she lived a everyday common life like everybody else. It's nothing to comprehend because it's already there, you already know, and you can just about say what's gon happen on the next line. They wasn't using words that you couldn't understand. It was just like I was talking. They wasn't coming here with words that you couldn't under-

stand, big words and stuff. They would just [be] like everyday words that be in a book, that I knew how to write, I knew how to read without having to go to a dictionary [to] see what they mean about this.

See I like just simple reading. Just like Sunday when we were in church and Reia was saying, "I enjoyed church Sunday. I enjoyed that." And I was surprised for her to say that because he spoke on all this stuff. Same thing they hear when they go to their church. When he talked and he a say a word, he gon tell you what he meant to everyday people. People like me, people like Maya could understand. If he say a word like "simplicity" or something, he gon tell you what that was. He said, "Now let me tell you, I meant simple like." You see what I'm saying? Like people using these words and you don't know what they're saying, I think that's wrong because you have all different type of people sitting in your audience and you shouldn't do that. And if you gonna use a word, you explain it like he did so everybody can know.

Writing is important. Knowing how to write gives you the opportunity to express yourself in whatever the situation may be, like writing letters, memos, books, poetry, feeling out a job application or just to write a good paragraph.

[The type of writing I usually do in the course of a day is:] 1. Writing out reports for my job/w[hich] is statistics. 2. Filling out immunization cards for patients. 3. Writing messages for my department. I would like to write sometime about things going on in my life; just write even if I have to throw it away. I feel it will help me mentally. [I would like to write:]
1. More at work; 2. Letters; 3. Whatever is on my mine, and what I plan to do in life to better myself; 4. Things that distrub me—write it down and get it off my mine—Writing when I am stressed out or angry to help clear my mine and throw it away. I don't write enough at all. I need to write more if I want to learn to get in school. I need to do much better and much more reading & writing.

[My] writing ability [is] not good at all. I would love to write but my patience is very short. If something gives me a problem I can't deal with, I stop instead of challenging it. Writing is ok, but it is hard for me to put writing together like in a good sentenance or paragraph. [I] don't feel comfort writing because I am afraid the structure is not put together right. [I] don't enjoy writing, but would love to write if I could get my sentences and paragraphs together the way it should be. Then I would enjoy writing. Some people can write and express themselves so good. I would like to write like that without feeling uncomfortable.

[I don't write as much as I should] *because I feel I'm using the wrong words. That wouldn't bother me if I'm just writing for myself. But to write something to give to somebody? I wouldn't want to just write anything and give to someone to read. If I'm writing for myself and just writing, I still don't know how to punctuate that. I still don't know if my sentence is right. So if I'm getting ready to write something for somebody else, I still don't know. How would that help me knowing where to put my periods and my commas and this and that? See that be my thing. How to end a sentence I guess. Where do my sentences ends and where to start another sentence instead of just writing and not ending a sentence. But I'm just saying if I would go over and over and over I still wouldn't know where to end it. That's why I told you I say, "Well send me my paper back and show me where I should end my* [sentences]." *See I can look at that and I would go over that. See if I had somebody to go over things—like I wrote that to you—and then if you would go over it and you would say, put it like in red, "You need a period here. This starts another sentence," and I can look at that over and over and over. But I need guidance in the beginning. You don't just write without having a comma or period or quotation marks or whatever. And I think if I would write you something every month* [and] *you say, "No, this should be like this," I think I would learn more like that. But I could write for a year. I could write for ten years and never know how to break it down into sentences and stuff where my periods and stuff go. It wouldn't help.*

So if you can understand what you're reading and what you're writing, sure it helps you. And you understand and you comprehend what is going on. It helps. But then there are people like Byron [a relative], *for instance. Somebody like him who is not educated and you look at him and you talk with him, look at the kinda sense he have. He can go on a job interview and clean hisself up and put some false teeth in his mouth and stuff. He'ah get him a job.*

Some people can't read and write, but they got a lotta common sense and that's what help. That takes the place of it. They can figure they way out. They can get a good job. You'll be surprised of people that is illiterate. But they have a lotta common sense and that's how they get over. And a lotta times people don't find out that they are really a illiterate person for a long time. But I'm not saying anybody like that could go and just say they want to be a politician or something like that. You have to have that understanding in another way then. They wouldn't make it like that.

Cause see, I always said if you don't have any common sense, you could forget about the other stuff because that's not gonna help. But one thing I learned. I paid attention to you. You know how I used to tell you you didn't have any common sense? But since you went on and got your education and stuff like that, look like your mind opened up and under-standing and stuff to other things. You have a lot of common sense now. I noticed when you started going to school, you had gotten independent, on your own and stuff like that, start figuring out this or that. It came from your understanding opening up and your mind opening up from reading and learning and stuff like that. Because to me, it will open up your under-standing and your viewpoints on things. And all that plays a part and works together.

Cause one time you was here, I told someone, "You know Sonja tricked me?" I said, "You know I was saying something and she come asking me a question?" And I said, "She ain't have sense like that before." So maybe that can help you out with that common sense. [I used to say you] *didn't have no common sense at all. I said, "Don't you know common sense tells you what to do?" Well reading, writing and understanding and this and that, I think all that plays a part too.*

GOALS AND POSSIBLE SELVES:
If I Had Someone to Push Me . . .

[I dreamed of becoming] *a nurse, an RN* [when I was young] *because I've always wanted to take care of people. And I just wanted to be an RN.* [One of the things I like about myself is] *having a good heart, helping others, not being selfish. I just felt that I always wanted to take care of people and be there and I always wanted to feel needed and wanted and I thought being a nurse I would always be needed and wanted. And I'm sure that was my reason.*

[I didn't make that dream come true] *because I had no guidance in growing up or anyone to talk to me, to help me to get through school and to tell me the importance of going to college and to try to make something outta myself and get some type of degree. But if I would've had someone to just help me and to make me feel that I was important and I was better than just somebody to cook and clean up and take care of children all the time, see that's what I felt I was cut out for. Because I guess you look at your parents and you see what they do and you feel, "Well, I guess this is the life* [for me]. [This is] *what I'ah be doing." I just felt I would be clean-ing up people house like my mom was cleaning up people house and com-*

ing home cooking, having a house full of children. That's what I thought at that time. Because I couldn't see. I couldn't see any further than that. I couldn't see past that. Because there was no one to help me see past that. Cause I thought that was life and I looked at all of my sisters and stuff and look what they were doing. So I just thought . . .

[But I decided] *I wasn't doing that. What happen? I think by me getting married and being around different people. You see what I'm saying? And then by me being married and had somebody kinda help me—and Stella 'nem wasn't poor people. I remember when I start going to Jefferson and start changing then. I start seeing a little better. That it was a better way for me. Because I move from Maya—from taking care of those children, doing all that work—and I moved to another house where it wasn't children. You see what I'm saying? And I didn't have all that to do. It gave me more time to do other things and to see better. Then I moved from there and then with Jesse and Anne 'nem. And then I start watching them. They had different ideas in life. And you know Anne. You know she has ideas about she gonna be somebody in life this and that. And that's what motivated me a lot. I start looking at other people and things.*

My key moment was when I did finish high school because for me to do that, I thought I had really done something in my life because none of my mother children before me had finished high school. I was the first one. And I was determined. And I was gonna finish—even when I was in high school and I got pregnant and I was in twelfth grade so I had to drop out. But after I had Deidra I went back to school and I finished because I felt that was important to do, to get a high school education. I knew it could help me and I wanted to do something better than they did and I knew I wasn't college material. And that's what I did to better myself in life because I felt that would help me get a job. And at that time that's what you needed. It wasn't a lot of Black people with college education. So if you had a high school education that was very good back then. You could get a job.

But I just hate I didn't get in the trade school. I think that was one thing for me. If I just woulda got into that trade school. I don't worry about if I went to college cause I don't feel that I would have really survived. It'a been too hard. But if I could've gotten into a trade school or something like that. I was more of a person to take the trade school courses. Do the two-year RN or beautician or something like that I felt. Because maybe I didn't want to. Maybe it was me. Maybe I didn't want that challenge. I don't know. I don't know.

I would change everything [about my education if I could]. *I would change the fact that I don't have a college degree. I would get one. It don't necessar*[il]*y have to be a college degree, but I would get a degree. If I could change and go back, I would work as hard as I could to have done better than I did. And I feel if I could change, I would change all of that and I would have been a smart person. Because all I had to do was study and if the answers was in the book, I woulda found it. And I think if I could start over again from the first grade on I could go on through college after that.*

But you need this certain background that I missed. I don't think I can just start off going, talking about take a test and enter into college. I need a lot of other things that I missed. And then it was a lot of subjects we didn't take in school. We didn't have a lot of subjects that a lot of kids had as far as the kids went to private school and the children went to White school. They didn't offer us a lot of that. They offered us reading, writing, math and that was a certain limit—add and subtract and multiplication. And I remember doing some decimals and that was it. They didn't offer us a lot. See because I guess they felt that was enough; that's all you needed to know and that was too much. Oh but if I could change, I would change all that back around. And if I could start over again, I would try to have a open mind and I would just go from first grade all the way.

Macon focused his eyes on his son. "Papa couldn't read, couldn't even sign his name. Had a mark he used. They tricked him. He signed something, I don't know what, and they told him they owned his property. He never read nothing. I tried to teach him, but he said he couldn't remember those little marks from one day to the next. Wrote one work in his life—Pilate's name; copied it out of the Bible. That's what she got folded up in that earring. He should have let me teach him. Everything bad that ever happened to him happened because he couldn't read."

—Toni Morrison, *Song of Solomon*

• • •

It is interesting how I can remember specific events that took place in our house, but I do not remember the house itself, nor do I remember the neighborhood in which we lived. The night we moved from the old neighborhood and the next sunny day in the new one are as clear to me as if it happened yesterday.

It took some time to adjust to leaving familiar territory to begin Head Start. I recall going through the tearful routine every morning for several months. Eventually I started enjoying Head Start and looked forward to going everyday. The first time I experienced the death of an acquaintance was in the first grade. My favorite friend at school was run over by a car while playing in the street one day at home. I could understand a car running over her, but I did not completely understand death. Somehow I did realize a certain finality of death. When I saw her lying in the coffin she looked as though she was asleep and seemed so still and quiet. I did not feel sad, yet I knew that we would not play anymore at recess. I thought about her at recess for a few days, but I do not recall missing her. As I write this paper, I feel that I miss her more now than I did at six years old. During this period of development [i.e., early childhood], my uncle also passed away. I remember questioning in my mind why was my aunt weep-

ing. After the funeral service I walk up to the coffin and touch it. It frightened me and I quickly jerked my hand away.

In primary school, my peer relationships continued to develop. I mixed well with my peers but there were those times when aggressive peers made life a little uncomfortable. I remember the two bullies in third grade who would threaten to beat me up after school if I did not give them paper and pencils. My solution to this problem was to play hooky. I got away with this for three days. My brother found out about my skipping school and told my mother who in turn explained to me that if I played hooky again she would tell my teacher. This hurt more than a spanking or a punishment, because I highly respected my teacher. I did not want my teacher to find out about my transgression so I told my mother why I skipped school. Thankfully, this solved the bully problem. There were a few fights during these tedious years of which I won two out of three. After losing the last fight, I decided to refrain from this behavior. I am surprised that children come out of this critical period unharmed. One of the most disappointing things that happened to me during this period was being told that the Pilsbury dough boy did not exist. I learned this when my mother brought home a can of cinnamon rolls and to my surprise when she popped the can open the dough boy did not jump out. I felt angry with the dough boy because he had deceived me.

It was during [late childhood] that I sta[r]ted developing an interest in God. My nieces and I used to converse about heaven and hell. I would recall the Reverend saying God had a Son. We would wonder what God and His Son looked like and where in the sky did they live. The conversation would always end with a comment on the consequences of being naughty. All bad children would go to hell, and the good children would go to heaven. This brings to mind another important figure in my life who pretty much possessed the characteristics of God. As a matter of fact, I could understand this character more than God because this character was tangible. This is none other than old Saint Nicholas himself. He came to our home every year and left us brand new toys. He was omniscient because he knew when I was naughty or nice. He was magical because he had flying reindeers and little elves. I even knew what kind of clothes he wore and how he looked. If only my mother had taught me that God should be my Santa Claus and not some dead saint, I could have avoided another disappointment. Since I was older, I took the news about Santa Claus much better than the news about the Pilsbury dough boy.

During my adolescent years . . . I do remember the internal and external changes that took place in the physical and emotional aspect. Physically, my body seemed to have been changing week by week. Everything from my head to my feet increased within one summer. When I graduated from the sixth grade, I was a skinny little kid, but by the time I reached the eighth grade my body had fully developed into the figure of a woman. My superiors started calling me a young lady instead of a little girl. At times, I felt self-conscious about the tremendous weight increase. Emotionally, I went through a short period of not knowing if I wanted to be called a young lady or a little girl. At one point, I felt that I wanted to hold on to my childhood and never grow up to be an adult.

In elementary school I was basically a shy kid, but as I approached the middle school years, my social skills became more sophisticated and I began to wean from my shyness. After school I spent considerable amounts of time with my peers. I chose to associate with the less intellectual group even though I was more academically competent. Homework was not the number one item on our list of priorities. My grades in middle school did not reflect my best academic performance because I had to conform to the group's standards. We teased the kids who stayed inside after school and did homework. Instead of studying, we would engage in outside endeavors such as walking, playing games, listening to music, and dancing. In high school, my grades became very important to me and I received a lot of positive reinforcement for my efforts. I was praised by my instructors and peers for my academic achievements and participation in extra-curricular activities. My drama teacher would always tell me that I was talented and pretty. All of this helped me to develop a healthy self-esteem which made my high school years pleasant.

I can recall walking to my Algebra class one day and thinking to myself, "What is the purpose for all of this education?" I thought about how everyone travels through the same life cycle: primary and secondary school, college for at least four years, a job, marriage, possession of material things, children, the empty-nest syndrome, retirement, and death. I said to myself, "There must be more to life than this." At that moment life seemed empty and futile. I sensed that something was definitely missing in the quest for happiness and fulfillment in earthly things.

My first religious experience was at thirteen years of age. One day while watching television, I came across the 700 Club. I can not explain exactly when the feeling came over me but I found myself weeping while the host prayed for viewers who had not received salvation. Several nights later, I experienced the most disturbing dream that I had ever had in my life.

I dreamed about the day Jesus came and I was not yet saved. From this time until I was sixteen, I always carried a fear of being lost. At times I wondered if God was real and, if so, how could He allow people to spend eternity in hell. I thought about the awesomeness of God. The one thing that would really blow my mind was a passage in the Bible that says, "God is from everlasting to everlasting." In the midst of my deep thoughts, a feeling of realness would come over me like a shadow. At that moment, God was real but yet distant and final. It is said that adolescence is the period when teenagers begin to experiment with heterosexual relationships. When I received Christ at sixteen, I could not have picked a better age. Instead of trying to find love from Jim, John, or Jack, I found love in Jesus. I was completely fulfilled and enthralled by this new and wonderful relationship with the Lord.

[Late adolescence] brought new challenges in my life. It was a time of searching for my place in God and in society. I experienced both spiritual and natural struggles. Approximately around the age of thirteen, I felt an attraction for a particular female character on television. This character portrayed certain characteristics that were opposite from what I had seen in my mother. My mother was a strong authoritarian figure. The character on television was weak and emotional. It was not until much later that I came to understand why I was attracted to this character. All of my childhood years I had been exposed to one extreme side of a woman in my mother. I needed to see and integrate the other extreme side to bring a balance within myself. It was through God's help and my psychological background that I came to this conclusion.

Overall, my adolescent years were pleasant. There were those times of friction between my mother and I because I was pulling away and trying to establish my independence. She did not always understand my desire to isolate myself from everyone at times. Fortunately we developed beyond this period in my life successfully.

In my personal life, I established an intimate relationship with Jesus at the age of sixteen. By the time I reached young adulthood, I desired a more intense and meaningful relationship with the Lord. I was twenty-three before I seriously thought about having a close personal relationship with a man. This desire did not surface until my identity crisis had subsided.

The best way that I can describe myself is as a twenty-seven year old female who is single and content. I have learned to live according to Paul's popular passage in Philippians: to be content in whatsoever state I find myself. The intimacy that I would share with a companion is shared with Christ; therefore I am not lacking in this area. I do look forward to getting married one day and starting a family, but this is not my primary purpose in life. At the present time, I am enjoying my autonomy as a single woman.

Over the past year, I have come to realize a deeper aspect to living which has changed my overall attitude toward life. The golden rule in the Bible has taken on a new meaning. When I came to understand my ultimate purpose, which is to worship God and serve my fellowman, it was an ecstatic awakening. I have found fulfillment in serving others, thus my interest in counseling. I believe that giving of oneself constitutes a mature Christian. My goal is to continue to pursue a vertical relationship with God, and a horizontal relationship with man for the rest of my days on earth. I have come to realize that God owes me nothing, but by His grace and mercy I am blessed in abundance. My outlook on the future is positive. I am sure that as I continue to grow and give, I will receive the desires of my heart in return.

EDUCATION: *I Got a Lot of Praise*

I do not remember my mother "preaching" education in the home, but she seemed to have shown interests in various ways; providing story books, school materials and Bible reading. I remember Maya bringing little books home before we started grade school. My sister Felicia learned to read these books before she started the first grade. Maya once enrolled in an adult education program to further her 3rd grade education. She discontinued the program due to financial pressures at home. I do not recall a specific time set aside for study, but we were prompted to do homework with or without her supervision.

I was an average student in elementary school. I enjoyed individual reading at home and I remember requesting assistance with homework from Maya. Once a week we had Bible Study Hour together as a family where we read passages from the Bible. I never felt pressured to make 'A's and 'B's in school although Felicia was a straight 'A' student.

I continued to be an average student throughout middle school. I knew I had the potential to be above average because I made 'A's and 'B's in the 6th grade. During this period, my social life took precedence over academics. I did not like Science and as a result I was placed in a remedial science class the first 9 weeks of the 8th grade. This was humiliating for me so I decided that I would study and prove to the teacher that I did not belong in a remedial class.

It was this one day, the summer before I began high school (this was before I was going into the ninth grade and I was gonna be starting high school and a new school), I gave myself one of the most important prep talks in the world. I just started doing this self talk. I realized that I had to change because I felt that high school was going to determine the rest of my educational and professional career. It's like some kind of maturity just kicked in all of a sudden. That was strange for this maturity to kick in as far as school was concerned because before I wasn't taking my education very seriously. I didn't know the real significance of it and I didn't know why I had [to] do math and all that stuff. I was more interested in getting outside after we came home from school. I was more interested in going out getting with my friends, playing softball, playing cards, or dancing. That was more important to me—socializing, even in school. It was a social thing. It was all about socializing. And we used to sit in science class back on the back row about five or six of us and we did experi[ments]— I didn't know what the heck was going on, it was a chemistry class. I couldn't tell you nothing about chemistry by the time I got outta that class. We sit back there and set the desk on fire trying to do the experiment. For some reason I started seeing my education as something different because I think I was going to high school and somebody had told me that when it starts to count because you have to have high school credits to graduate and that can determine if you're gonna get a scholarship. Felicia had already gotten a scholarship so see her being there, that was an influence; that influenced me. (Felicia is seven years older than me. She was way ahead. By the time I was in middle school she was in college.)

So I gave myself this serious talk and my whole attitude changed. I said I wasn't gon be hanging out with the same people I had been hanging out with cause they weren't about going anywhere. They weren't as bright as I was and I knew I was bright even though it wasn't showing in grades. In middle school and stuff, I knew I was because when I did put forth the effort and tried, I did very well. And even though I didn't study much, I still did pretty decent. Like in math and stuff, I like math so I made some decent grades. They weren't like all 'A's or anything. But that's when my attitude changed.

My grades were average until high school when they became above average particular 9th and 10th grade. This prep talk changed my whole attitude toward my education and my future. I knew high school grades would determine my college career. This was very serious business. I wanted to follow in my sister's footsteps who had won a scholarship to college. My mother was proud of her achievement and disappointed when she lost her scholarship. I became an honor roll and dean's list student for the next two years.

The summer before my senior year, I got saved. This experience consumed my whole interest and unfortunately I lost the zeal for academic excellence. My grades reflected the change in attitude. All I wanted to do was pray and read the Bible. I almost fasted myself down to a "twig."

The talk didn't fade [when I got saved]. I mean it's just that something came into my life that was more significant I felt—even than making good grades in school. The best way I could describe that experience when I got saved. I was going into the eleventh grade; it was my last year. And the only thing I can really compare it to is when you fall in love with a guy and nothing else in the world matters. You lose interest in your friends, you lose interest in the things that you used to do and all that matters is this one person. This one person becomes the center of your world. And that's what that was like for me. So I lost the interest that I had in school and getting a scholarship and all that making good grades. I lost interest in it. I felt like I didn't wanna be there. The other students, I felt they were immature.

After graduating from high school, I moved to Kramer where I worked at a bank for two years. I made an attempt to start college after resigning from the bank, but other things interferred again. I kept tripping over my religious aspirations. Somehow I perceived ministry and education to be a conflict of interest. Eventually, I got on the right track and have been ever since, that is, educational wise.

One of my most challenging courses in college was my first English Composition class. I tripped over verb agreements again and again that semester. I made 'D's on 'A' and 'B' papers because of this problem. I could not understand how I missed verb agreements in grade school. I learned the hard way that semester. This is still an area I have to be careful with— verb agreements.

Overall, in general, teachers made me feel very good; made me feel real good about my education [and] about myself, especially [in] high school. High school is when I really started coming out academically. [In] elementary school, I can only think of one teacher that I think made me feel less than some of the other students in the class. That was my second grade teacher. I guess you remember the best teachers and then you remember the worst teachers in school. She was definitely worse. She was Black; one of them high yellow kind. She had favoritisms, favorite people in the class, and she showed favoritism. She would go to class and she—this is the second grade now—she would have certain girls, certain students—and she do it every time, she pick the same ones—to take names while she was outta the class for the people who were talking. And they'd sit there and they'd talk among themselves and they write up everybody else's name down in the classroom just about. Even when you weren't talking your name get written down. Cause I was quiet in school. But this happened throughout second grade. And then when she come back to class you get licks in your hand for talking because these seven-year-old kids said you were talking and I just thought that was ridiculous. I've held a grudge against that woman all my life.

I think probably within the last few years I've stopped feeling angry about that. But I felt angry about that for years. And I think I saw her one time. I musta been in high school. I was still living at home. But I saw her one time. She lived somewhere over across the tracks. I didn't say anything to her but I really wanted to. I think I would if I saw her now. I think I would say something to her about that. I mean I know it's over and done with and it really doesn't mean an[ything], but it'd probably make me feel a lot better. Leaving a bunch of seven year olds. But it was just her. I liked all the rest of my elementary teachers.

I wasn't too crazy about my fourth grade teacher. She was burnt out. She just didn't seem to care. She'd go outta the room too. It's like they took their breaks after recess. Now my fourth grade teacher, I know that's what she was doing. She went in the teacher's lounge after recess. And we'd sit in the class for like thirty minutes or something, fifteen to thirty minutes. I don't know. I was in the fourth grade so . . . But we'd sit in there and there was this girl named Veronica. She had a frog voice. And we used to get in a argument just about everyday and entertain the whole class and she would usually start it. So we'd argued until the teacher come in the class. I don't think she was a very good teacher to be truthfully honest with you.

The rest of my teachers I think were very good teachers for the most part. Of course I had a lot of 'em in high school, so there was some that were prejudice. I went to all Black schools until the second half of my sixth grade when we moved out to where we live now, where Maya 'nem live now. That's when I started going to interracial schools. Second half of sixth grade and then from there on I was in interracial schools. Throughout elementary they were all Black. I only had Black teachers all the way through *the sixth grade. Maybe when I went to the interracial school my teacher was Black, it was a Black man. From there, when I started junior high school, that's when I started White teachers.*

I didn't notice any difference [between Black teachers and White teachers] *until I got in high school. Cause even in junior high school it was probably half and half—half Black teachers half* [White teachers]—*because there were a lot of Black teachers teaching at that junior high school and I had quite a few Black teachers there, but I did have some White teachers. And I really didn't see any blatant differences, to be truthfully honest with you, until I got to high school and it was really for the most part just one of my math teachers where there was a blatant difference in the way she treated Black students and the Whi*[te students]*. She was very prejudiced obviously. That wasn't very subtle with her. It was pretty obvious that she treated the White students* [different] *and she helped 'em out more. Like when they came up to her desk to ask questions or if they asked questions while she was standing at the board, she answered their questions and seemed that* [she] *really enjoyed answering. But like if we raised our hand* [or] *didn't understand something, she'd get an attitude and kinda like she made you feel dumb and stupid. And that was in Geometry and I had taken Algebra One and I made straight 'A's in Algebra One. I was halfway teaching the class in Algebra One and that was under a White teacher. But when I took Geometry, by the end of the first school year, that first half of the school year, I had a 'D' in Geometry. I got a 'D' in Geometry for the first half of the school year. And the woman—this was God sent. But she got sick or something happened where she couldn't finish off the rest of the school year so we had to get transferred and I was transferred back to the Algebra teacher that I had and I ended up getting a 'B' in Geometry for that school year. But it's like I didn't even get the foundations. My foundation wasn't really established that well but I still got in there and did well and I know I woulda made straight As in Geometry. I would have liked Geometry a lot better if I'da had a teacher that wasn't like her—that wasn't prejudiced and thought we were all stupid and dumb.*

And I had her for English too. I had her for one of my English classes. And I was an honor roll student. I was on the Dean's list. Took her for English. I think it was my first nine weeks or something, or second, but it may have been the first nine weeks, and I got a 'C' in her class. All the White kids got 'A's and 'B's in the class. Everybody Black got a 'C' and below. I got the highest grade in the class and it was a 'C'. And there was one girl who made staight 'A's. She gave the girl a 'F'. You got straight 'A's and you got a 'F' in English. In English? Excuse me, for crying out loud. I mean English is not that hard. But that's what I mean about it was a blatant difference. It was at Tiberius High before it turned into the Magnet School. I went there for freshman and sophomore and then it became a Magnet school and I just finished my last year cause I graduated as a junior. Back then you could take like seven hours. We were able to go to school an extra hour. We were able to take an extra credit hour and that's how [I was able to graduate high school in three years]. *So when I did that, I forget how many credits I picked up, but I did that for two years straight and I had seven hours. We had to have twenty-one credits or something like that. So seven and seven is fourteen plus six is what? Twenty? So, I don't how that added up to twenty-one unlessen it was twenty hours. But I know in my last year, maybe I took twenty, I took seven hours too. I had to in order to come up with twenty-one. Yeah I guess I did.* [I had intended to graduate early.] *That was my intent. So I just finished my last year there, my eleventh grade. I didn't want to change to go to another school for my last year, so I just finished it off there. It was a whole different student body, a lotta different teachers. It was a whole different school, totally different school.*

I didn't see [differences between how Black males were treated and how Black females were treated]. *That's not something that I saw then. I wasn't aware of that being* [a problem]. *I think I was treated somewhat different, especially in high school, because academically I was doing well. I was excelling academically and I was involved in stuff and I got a lotta praise for that. I got a lotta praise, especially when I started taking my education serious, and that was when I started the ninth grade. I got a lot of encouragement. I got a lot of praise. It really helped my self-esteem. But I attributed that more to the fact that I was a bright student, I was a serious student, and not so much because I was a woman or because I was Black.*

When I look back now I say obviously it was something wrong, but at the time I didn't necessarily pay attention then. Because, for example, [look at] *Marcus and Johnny. Johnny dropped out about in tenth grade. He musta been about sixteen or something like that when he stopped going, when he dropped out. Marcus was going but his reading and spelling was very limited. And I guess I wasn't aware of it at first but later on I started* [to think]. *There was an obvious difference in the way I was excelling in school and the way they were* [and] *we were going to the same schools. I don't think Johnny ever went to Tiberius High, but Marcus sure was going. Seems like Johnny was there at one time when Maya tried to get him back in school. At one point he was going. Johnny's five years older than me so he couldn't ta been. It was Marcus; couldn't ta been Johnny. Felicia and Johnny went to the same schools all the way pretty much. They went to the same schools. Felicia and I did well but the boys did not. The boys did not do the same. And I figure they was intelligent as well. I mean, my goodness, they were raised in the same house. I don't know if there were some things happening differently in the house, but I think the sys- tem had a lot to do with it. I realize now that the system has had a lot to do with it. There're real subtle things that were happening to Black men, with Black children, male children, in school obviously.* [The women had a better opportunity than the men did in school.]

I saw that [my gender and race had an effect] *more when I got in col- lege. That was more obvious. I'm 'on say it's my gender and my race but I guess too it's also the person, the kinda person I am. But I kinda attribute it to gender and race, even now in my work place—especially White males. I have yet to have been around a White male, like as far as profes- sors and even where I work, the Administrators, that didn't like me; that didn't think the world of me. And it was like that in college. They were al- ways encouraging. They would encourage me to go farther, to advance and stuff. They think I'm very intelligent. They value me as a person. I've noticed that especially since I've been from college on to this point. It's almost like, "Wow, what is it?"*

But at Simon Peter University for my graduate work, oh goodness, they couldn't sing enough of my praises. They like just fell in love with me. I know in one class—I was just another student in class right?—we had to stand up and do a project, a presentation, kind of a project of one of the theories in psychology and we did it in groups. And I was the presenter for my group. I got up and I was just presenting the material for my idea. But, my goodness, when I got finished, the professor, he was just like really flabbergasted about how well I did this. And oh, from that day on, it wasn't anything wrong I could do.

There were [other Black women there]. *There were, not many. When I started it wasn't many. It was only maybe, in that particular program that I was in, I think it may have been three. It wasn't that many. It was one Black woman there before I came and then I may have been the second one in that particular program. Now there were other Black women in the seminary. But in that particular program—and especially as far as being in one of his classes—I was one of the few Black women. But now when the other, this other professor I got, he came my second year and we had more Black women in the program then (we probably had maybe five or six or something like that; it increased), but he was pretty much the same way. And, as a matter of fact, he's the one who the part-time work I was telling you about (I'm gonna be starting a part-time job doing groups of substance abuse adolescents next year). He's the one who hooked me up. As a matter of fact, both of them after I graduated, when something came up—like a position came up, whatever—[for] both of them I was like one of the first persons they thought about they wanted. And like with this deal right here, with them starting this new substance abuse program? Well, I've been gone for four years. I see 'em like during a hooding ceremony or something like that, but I've been gone for four years and when this came up I was the person that he really wanted to contact. And he's come in contact with a lot of women—Black women even—by this time. So, I mean it's impressive; it's flattering. I'm not gonna lie about that.*

For the most part [I think the schools that I went to were good schools for learning and that they prepared me for my road to college]. *I mean even Roosevelt, the all Black school. I went to two different elementary schools. The first school I went to, I forget the name of it, but it was over there by where Anne 'nem live. I started Roosevelt in the third grade. So I was there until sixth grade, until half of sixth grade. But I thought they were good schools. And you know, I'm glad I went to all-Black schools to be truthfully honest with you. I'm glad I did because I didn't have to deal with any racial issues per se cause all my teachers were Black; all the students were Black. As far as racism and stuff like that, even though there was like favoritisms shown, like with that one particular teacher, that second grade teacher? And I mean I saw how that made me feel as a person. Because I mean that made me feel less than the ones she favored so I guess that was probably the closest I came to being discriminated against or being made to feel inferior. Because that's how that experience made me feel in the second grade. It made me feel inferior.*

I think schools should prepare students to function adequate in a society that's advanced and is civilized; a society that's developing rapidly in all this modern technology. You have to know how to function. I mean you run into things everyday, like balancing checkbooks. If you gonna have a checking account, you need to know how to balance [your checkbook]. *You need to know how to do that. I mean, my goodness, you need to know how to read. If somebody give you directions to go across town and give you street names, you need to know how to read the street names. It's basic stuff like that. It's the society that we're living in.*

A hundred years ago maybe people didn't [need to know how to read]. *Even though I think reading's always been important, but the world was nothing like it is now. Maybe there wasn't as much of a need for it to function smoothly because of the way it was then. It was a lotta farming and stuff like that and people had gravel roads, they didn't have any cars—cars had just started coming out. But it's* [important] *especially now because of the world we live in. I mean you need to know how to read and write. You need to know how to add and subtract and stuff like that. And I think it does help your self-esteem.*

I figure [school is] *for the people who wanta go to college and who don't want to go to college. I mean even if you don't go, you have* [to] *function in the world with relative ease. Like college is a part of it. That's just one part of it. I don't really see it as being the basic part though. It's something higher that what a person wants to go further, wants to go higher. It certainly prepares you for that. I mean a lotta things are kinda geared toward that. But I guess I'm looking at one basic level; what it does for us.*

[I think the schools] *did it* [for me]. *I think they did it. I mean I can't contribute it to too many other things. I mean of course that's daily living and all that Maya prepared me for a lot of daily living stuff. But school played a big part. School played a big part in helping with the socializing process, conforming to society, what's expected of me, how I should behave, to be able to sit down and listen and then becoming a more civilized, productive individual. They prepared me in that aspect too.*

I guess the only thing I would change [about my education], *I probably should've been more proud of the achievements that I had in high school. At the time, I just didn't make a big deal out of it. Like when I was on the honor roll. I was the only Black student on the honor roll in I think it was the ninth grade. Or was it the tenth grade? One of those grades. But I was the only Black student outta the whole school for the ninth grade or whatever grade I was in (I think I was in the ninth grade) who was on the honor roll. And Maya should've been there but I didn't make no real big deal out of it. It was like, "Well, she's gotta work. Well if she could be there she could be there. It ain't no big thing." And I remember my art teacher telling me. She said, "That is really important." She helped me to see the significance and the seriousness of it. And she said, "Your mom should've been there." But I just didn't make a real big thing out of it cause they had a program and stuff. But then too I guess that falls back on Maya as well. I mean that was an honor and I'm sure there was a letter or something that came up where she was invited or what have you. But it's like because I didn't pressure her to come, because I didn't really strongly encourage her to come, I guess she figure, "Well, it doesn't seem to be all that big deal to her."*

LANGUAGE: *It's What I Feel Comfortable With*

Maya used to always, because she knew she was limited in correct grammar and stuff like that, encourage me to use correct grammar. And she would always say, "Now you in school. You done went further along in school than me and you should know better. You know better than I. You know better than to say things." She would always stop me; she would always correct me or say, "Now that's not right," like verb agreements and stuff. She was real conscious of it. Like she felt that she didn't know any better but I should; that I knew better and yet I still didn't do the right thing. Even up into college she would tell me this when I was at home going to Tiberius State University. She say, "Now you know that's not the right way to say that," and, "You in college. You need to say it right." And I'd say, "Well, I know what's right. I know the right thing to say. This just the way I talk when I get around my family, what have you. It's like this is what I feel comfortable with and this is the way I talk." If I say 'he don't' and 'she don't' or whatever, and she say, "Well, you know that's not [right]," and "You know it's supposed to be . . . So her thing was, "Now you need to practice saying it right all the time so when you really get in a place where you really needed to say it right—because see, if you do that you gon embarrass yourself. You gon find yourself somewhere where you gonna say it wrong where you really shouldn't be saying it wrong." She was right about that. I mean it's like, "Practice saying it the right way. When you say something wrong, go back and correct it right then." That's what she used to say. "Go back and correct this right after you say it. And say it right so that'll just become a part of you."

[Maya]'s right. I know that's right. If I need to stand up in front of an audience and give a speech and it's an audience full of educated people from all walks of life, then I would feel embarrassed about not using correct grammar. I wouldn't want to stand in front and say, "She don't . . ." or "He don't. . . ." I wouldn't want to say that. But the thing is that I say it so much that it's like I know I would say it at a time that I probably shouldn't say it. But the thing is that what I try to do is when I say that in certain circles, I try to correct myself and I find myself thinking in the

*middle of my sentences, "Which word do I say next? Which verb agree-
ment am I supposed to use? Was my subject plural? Was it a plural subject
or was it a singular?" And it's just that certain way you say a sentence
sometimes it's hard to think back of what you said. So I found myself in
the middle of a sentence saying, "Was that a singular?"*

*Good English is proper grammar. Using the proper sujects, verbs and
sentence structure.* [Speaking standard English] *is* [important] *for me but
sometimes I do not use proper English. It's important because it shows
other people that I'm an educated and proper woman.*

*I don't see Black English being any different from regular English. There
are black people who lack the education to speak proper English.* [I do not
think speaking Black English is important because] *Black people understand English period. I don't make a distinction* [between standard English
and Black English]. *I just don't see a difference* [between Black people's
speech and White people's speech]. *I think this has a lot to do with what
Maya used to always say. She came up in the 20s and it's like White
people were some species from another planet. She always made clear
cut differences in White people and Black people. And it's like they were
superior in the way they talk, in the way they behaved and in the way
they handle their family life. It's like they were superior because she was
always making these comparisons about, "White people don't do that."
For example, "Black people always gotta have a house fulla people and
they always coming over uninvited." I'm just using that for example.
"White people don't do that. You don't see White people doing that." It's
always this distinction made between White and Black people and I guess
my perception of them being different definitely came from that. But I'm at
the point where now, to me, there is no difference. I only see a difference in
people living in certain parts of the country as far as accent, a certain vernacular, slangs.*

*I think there's a difference in the tone of voice and resonance and atti-
tudes, but as far as the language itself, no. I think of the difference being
more a culture difference with Blacks—our own li'l culture thing, what
have you. Our voices are richer and deeper—something like that. I guess
we would consider Blacks who haven't gone as far in education, maybe like
Maya 'nem who had second and third grade educations, certain things
she doesn't know any better to say. I guess it's just that part. But then
there are White people who don't use proper English or correct grammar
either. I hear that all the time too. So it's just that at this point I'm able to
invalidate a lot of stuff that she said when I was growing up. I've gotten*

out there and I've lived myself and I've been around all these people and I probably been more exposed to White people than Maya has with being in integrated schools and I've read a lot more.

I don't know what Black English is other than that we say, "Oh Black people talk bad. They talk bad." I don't [believe Black English is bad English] *because White people talk bad too. There are a lotta White people who talk bad too—if we wanna call it bad. But in general, it goes back to slavery and stuff, the way Black people talked back then. That was the difference. There was an obvious difference. And then it probably had a lot to do with them not* [being] *taught. They weren't taught any differ-ent. They brought Blacks over here from Africa. They were speaking a totally different language. They were speaking their own language over in Africa. They bring 'em over here into America and they only supposed to learn this by picking up from White people. They had their own accent. And I guess when they did learn English words, they weren't able to say them, a lot of 'em, the exact way White people pronounced them. Because this is a foreign language to them. It's a different language and they're having to pick this up without really being taught. So when they have chil-dren, well those children are gonna talk the same way their parents were talking cause that's what they're hearing all the time and they gonna talk the way other slaves talk.*

I don't think it was necessarily bad; I don't look at it as being bad as I look at it as being these people were from another country. They spoke their language perfectly I'm sure, whatever language they were speaking when they came over here. I'm sure it was perfect. It was good language. They spoke it the correct way. But you know, if somebody take me and put me in Nigeria and everybody's speaking in that language, a native lan-guage, hey. If I have to pick it up, it could be Spanish. When I say "dinero" (that means money), I probably say it funny to them when they hear me say it. I may not be saying it correct, but that's what I thought I heard them say when they said it. I'm saying like I hear it.

[I talk the way I do] *because it's what I feel comfortable with and the people who I feel most comfortable with are the people who talk that way too. And it's sort of like relating to them. I tend to be more cautious about using correct grammar when I'm around White people in general. It's not all White people. But it's more, I noticed, with White people who I perceive to be more highly* [educated] *than myself—White people who I know they've been to college and stuff and they've even been to graduate school what have you. I'm not as cautious with people that I consider to be my* peers as I am with people in administrative positions, people who have Ph.D.s, like professors—people who are considered to be somebody that I guess in a way I look up to or what have you. I tend to talk differently with them. I'm real aware of how I talk.

But when it's peers or people like friends, even if they're White, it doesn't matter. I'm at a point now where I have White friends at work where I talk the same way around them that I would Black friends. I'm probably more likely to be more aware of using correct grammar around these White people who I perceive to be more educated as opposed to Black people on the same educational level or whatever as these White people that I'm talking about. For example, if it was Maya Angelou who I perceive to be a great [writer] (she's wonderful), I would feel more comfortable interacting with her and I wouldn't be under the pressure that, "Oh, I really need to say this; I need to use this correct grammar and say this right." So in a way, it is a White thing. I would be more comfortable [talking with a Black professor]. I would be more cautious of what I'm saying. I'd be more cautious of using correct grammar with the White person [than with the Black person] regardless of education.

I probably [don't interact with Black people on a higher educational level than me]—or not as much. Even in school [when] I was in the seminary, there was one Black professor and he wasn't African American. He was from Jamaica or somewhere. And he spoke perfect English. He spoke better English than the White people. He had this British kind of a accent even. But, you right. I have not interacted with [Black people on a higher educational level than me]. I went to Tiberius State University. I had one— that I can remember—I had one Black professor at Tiberius State University. Out of my whole career, out of my whole college career. And the Jamaican guy, I didn't even take a class from him. So outta my whole college career, I only had one Black professor. That's six years a college. [I believe this to be true even though I haven't interacted with a lot of Black people at a higher educational level than me].

I'll put it like [this]. I had this friend. She had a Ph.D. She had just gotten a Ph.D., but I felt relatively comfortable. But let me tell you this. With Jackie, one of my best friends, I do because—and I wouldn't've never been aware of this—but like when she calls up to the office, June, the lady who I work with, the social worker, she's a friend of mine too, but she would know the difference. She said, "Were you talking to Jackie? You must've been talking to Jackie." She would know the difference between if I was talking to Jackie or talking to Merla for example. And I say, "Yeah." I say,

"How could you tell?" She say, "Because," she say, "You a lot more formal when you talk to Jackie than when you're talking to Merla." [It's not just a phone thing]. *I think I do it in person too. I think I am more formal with Jackie. And it's because of the way she is. I perceive her to be tremendously knowledgeable. It's like it's almost kinda like it's this perception of she know everything. It's like she's perfect in a way as far as education and stuff like that and she's always correcting me. And it's always been that way. But it's just my perception. And I guess I'll have to say if that's the way I perceive a Black person, then I think I am more aware and more cautious. And I am more cautious with her when I'm talking. I just don't talk any old kinda way with* [her]. *But then she's not talking any kinda* o[ld way]. *It's because it's the way she's talking.* [She normally talks the way that I have this perception of what I should be talking like.] *She's talking like that so it makes me* [talk like that] *even though it's not as conscious as I think it is. But when I'm interacting with her, I tend to try to talk more like she's talking.*

In our society, right now in this country, a lot of us see ourselves having to fit into not only are we a part of a Black culture, but we have to fit into the White culture as well. And so to appear intelligent, I would say that if I went into an interview speaking Black English, then, yeah, it would seem unintelligent, it [would] *seem that I'm unintelligent. I have a tendency to perceive that way too. I've done it. There's a kind of a conforming thing. You have to conform. Speaking standard English to me it's just more of an impressive thing. It's a way of impressing people more and it's not a basic necessity. It's not a necessity, but being literate is.*

L I T E R A C Y :   *I Feel Better about Myself*

Literacy is the way people write and read as well as how they speak a language. Being literate [is important because it] *gives others the impression of one being intelligent and educated. Also being literate improves a person's quality of living. For one thing,* [being literate improves a person's] *self-esteem. If I'm having difficult*[y] *reading a book to my child, that's affecting my quality of life. To be able to sit down and feel good about myself, to be able to sit down and read to my child and feel good about it and enjoy that experience and knowing that the child is learning from that experience—that increases the quality of life with that child. Where if I don't know how to read, then that's something we can't experience together. We can go out and throw some balls. We can experience some* other things together. But it expands a person's perspective on things. And just, like I say, basic simple things: Somebody give directions to go to a neighborhood I've never been in before. If I don't know how to read, I'm 'on have to try to compensate some other kinda way. And I think people that don't know how to read do that. They find some other ways of compensating to get them around and to help them to function. But it makes my life a lot easier and I feel better about myself. I think the quality of life is improved.

I read and write on a daily basis. My reading is almost exclusively for enlightenment and educational purposes. I read a lot of self-help books on communication and relationships. I do periodically read for recreation and entertainment. My job requires extensive writing (i.e. treatment assessment notes, session notes, reports). I also write for personal reason. I keep a journal on hand for emotional purposes. My entries range between daily entries to weekly entries. My writing style at work is concise and clinical, more of a technical style. In my journal I free-style. I sort of flow with my thoughts and feelings. Correct grammar is not my primary concern when journaling.

I think my literacy practices are very good. I enjoy reading and writing although I do not enjoy technical writing as much as my personal writing. Writing is something I've had to acquire a taste for over the past ten years. I'm beginning to feel more comfortable and confident with my writing the more I write. I have to push myself to write but at the same time I view it as a challenge. It's definitely challenging for me. I feel writing is becoming more apart of me. Reading takes time and patience as well as concentration. Reading is one of life's most pleasurable experiences. Reading is like a companion for me. I will always make time in my life to read. I love reading.

[Being able to read is] most definitely [important to me and my life]. Reading has expanded my frame-of-reference and exposed me to other cultures, perspectives and economic/social affairs. [Some of my favorite books are:]

1. "The Road Less Travelled"
2. "Catcher in the Rye"
3. "The Mis-education of the Negro".

The 1st book has become like a bible for me. It lifts me to a higher level psychologically and spiritually. The 3rd book is an ex[tra]ordinary piece of

*work attampting to educate any reader. There's something very real about
the 2nd book. I can identify with the mood swings of the character in
the book.*

*Reading has been an activity I've always enjoyed even during elemen-
tary school. Reading is like a companion to me at times. I do a tremendous
amount of reading on my own, even now. It comes natural for me to read.
I'm currently reading a book now.* [My] *reading level/ability is relatively
high due to* [my] *advanced/higher educational level. "Men Are From Mars,
Women Are From Venus." I do find this book helpful. I first heard about
this book on the "Oprah Winfrey Show."*

I think [the difference between a person who is a good reader and a person who is a poor reader] *is probably a combination. I don't believe it's
genetic. If an individual is not diagnosed to be borderline or intellectual
functioning, I don't think it should effect the way they read. Genetics I
don't believe play any part in this, unlessen there's some kind of a mental
deficiency. And even if it's that, I think it's a combination of parents and
school teachers—the methods that they use. Everybody's different, everybody's unique, everybody's different and it takes different things to help
some people* [or] *to make people catch on or click and you just have to find
out what it is. And I think that has a lot to do with the teaching, with the
method of teaching and even parents—that's important too. To say somebody's a bad reader to me is to say that they weren't properly taught. The
time and the patience weren't* [there]. *They didn't receive the time and
patience that they required because they're different. They might not
catch on to reading or what as quick as I did. Like Marcus and Johnny.
They needed another method. They needed another way of helping them
to catch on to some of those things. But you know, a lot of us was thrown
in class together and you either sink or swim. I think that's ridiculous. I just
think that's terrible.*

[Being able to write is] *most definitely* [important to me and my life].
*50% of what I do on my job requires writing. Writing has become a signifi-
cant tool for me in my emotional healing process. I do a lot of clinical writing at work and I keep a journal on a consistent basis. The purpose for the
journal is to help me explore feelings that have been repressed/suppressed
for years as well as current feelings.*

*Writing has been an activity that I have not always enjoyed because
it requires focus, thinking and energy. I have come to appreciate writing
more because it helps me to express myself more concisely, clear and objectively. I usually write different than I speak but I'm beginning to express*

myself verbally the way I write. I still do not enjoy writing reports. I don't really enjoy writing the answers to [some of your] *questions. I'd much rather just talk about* [them].

My writing is different from my speaking. There's a big difference. My writing is a lot more concise, to the point, than my speaking. For example, spending four years in college made a significant difference than if I wouldn't have gone to college. If I woulda just stopped at high school, it's a world of difference in the way that I'm able to express myself verbally. My vocabulary has increased because I've been exposed to college-level writing. I was exposed to that for six years—four years undergrad, two years graduate. And it's much easier for me to express myself verbally. Certain words that I wanta use even though like today talkin' I would've liked to have used another word. But sometimes I have to just stop and really think what I'm writing. Those words seems to come to me quicker. When I'm writing in my reports at work and my review notes for my treatment plan, for example, I don't say, "He shows more interest in his treatment issues." I'll say, "He displays more interest in his treatment issues." It's just certain words what I consider I'll take 'em a peg or two up. I don't use certain things like, "He tends to get bored in group." I'll change that where it's not, "He tends to get bored . . ." I'll just do it with 'get' all together and just change the whole structure where I may say, for example, "He has a tendency toward indifference at . . ." Things like that because my vocabulary, it's expanded. I use bigger words, stuff like that. And the more I write, especially with what I'm doing at work, I am finding that it is easier for me to express myself verbally and I don't have to struggle so much to find the words that I wanta use. It's like I have easier access to words that I wanta use tha[n] *like six, seven years ago. Because I used to get frustrated before I started college. When I was talking, it was frustrating because it's like I know I wanted to use another word, I wanted to use a bigger* [word] *than what I was using, but I couldn't cause I didn't know the word to use. But I just knew there's another word I wanta use here. I wanta say this in a different way. But I couldn't because I just didn't have the vocabulary to do that with.*

I think that [the difference between a good writer and a poor writer is] *probably the same thing* [as the difference between a good reader and a bad reader]. *Again it has to do with method. I think it has to do with the time that's taken up and given to them. I think it probably takes more time to write. I mean because even now, for me, it's a lot more difficult to write than it is to read. Reading is more of a passive kind of a thing. But in elev-*

enth [and] *twelfth grade, no I wasn't critical at all. I accepted what I read. I mean you're actively reading, but you don't have to put out the energy and the effort in reading that you have to put in writing. It's a lot more difficult because for one thing when you writing you're having to formulate your own thoughts. You composing your own things. You're relying on your own thinking abilities and your own perception.* [With writing, you have to create the product; with reading the product is already there.]

Reading is a more passive activity that requires concentration but little energy. I use the word passive for a lack of a better term. Reading is a behavior; it's something that you actively do. But it's kinda like watching television. Ok, it requires thinking, but I guess what I was saying writing is much more difficult than it is to read. You have to put more effort in writing than you do reading. You're creating something when you write. When you reading, you not. You're using your thinking ability or what have you and your concentration. You're trying to comprehend what you're reading and it requires energy. But it's just that it's already there. It's something that's already created. Whereas when I sit and I have a blank piece of paper, I have to create that. So, that's the difference that I see.

Writing and reading goes together. I mean if you inadequate at one you gonna be [inadequate in the other] *although I realize it seems easier to catch on to reading and for a person to read than to write. I noticed that with the boys I work with, with the residents I work with, some of 'em are good readers. I mean they can read quite well. But when it comes down to putting that pen on paper—oh no. I mean poor skills and just really underdeveloped skills in writing. But you know they read well. I think it has to do with method.*

Knowing how to read and write helps us to function everyday in this world and it's one of those basic things that we need. It's not as significant as needing food and water, but if I had to rate it on a scale of one to ten, I'm gonna rate it up to like around seven or eight because it improves the quality of life that we have here and it feeds into our self-esteem.

GOALS AND POSSIBLE SELVES:
I'm Just Kinda Trying to Take Life as It Comes

I used to wanta be a teacher. When I was in elementary school, I wanted to be a teacher—which is usually what most kids wanna do. But I wanted to be a teacher. I like writing on the board. They write on the board. I used to come home and I'ah have to get these li'l color charks, different color chalks. I don't know where I got 'em from, I guess Maya bought 'em or something. When we went to the store I may have asked for 'em. But I take the little chalk and I'd go outside. We had this white house we lived [in] on Berry Street. I used to go on the side of the house and write on the side of the house like it was a board. I liked doing that stuff then. I wanted to be a teacher—till I got in fifth grade.

When I got in the fifth grade I had a Cuban teacher and she was very short. She was like my height when I was ten years old. But she was the cutest little something. And this was a all-Black school and some of these kids were pretty wild. I'm not saying they wild, cause I wasn't wild. But they had some real discipline problem. I guess it coulda been in a White school just the same. But they tested her and they gave her a rough time. I know one time she ran outta the class in tears. She used to try to discipline some of the kids like she get the ruler and give 'em those licks on their hands. And they'd throw the ruler outside. We were on the second floor and they'd throw the ruler outside the window. Then one girl told her mom about this. I guess at the time we probably figured she was different. She wasn't Black; she was different. I guess we probably thought she was White. But somehow I knew she was Cuban. I knew she wasn't White. She didn't quite look White, but she was different. So I remember this girl. She paddled this girl on the hand and she went home and told her mother. And supposedly her mother came up there and really cussed out the teacher.

[But nobody complained about the second-grade teacher even though she was doing the same thing], probably because she was Black. Nobody complained about that at all. But in the fifth grade, she was different. If she had been Black, I don't think it woulda been this little girl run home and say, "Oh Mama, this White lady, she did this and did that to me," and then her mother comes charging up there to jump on the woman or cuss her out. But no, there is no comparison between my fifth grade teacher and my second grade teacher. None whatsoever. Because those kids deserved that. Those kids were bad. And she wouldn't leave the class. She was a good teacher. She stayed in the class, but she had some real discipline problems with the students there. They just didn't respect her. She didn't establish that with 'em. She was too nice. She was probably just outta college. She was young and she just didn't really know how to handle that kinda stuff. So she didn't have control of her class a lot a times. But she was one of my favorite teachers.

After that class, after I saw what they did to her, that's when I changed [my mind about becoming a teacher]. *I said I don't ever wanta be a teacher. Forget that one. From that point until probably until high school I didn't really have any* [plans] *as far as career, what I want to do as a career. I didn't really think about it like that. It wasn't anything particularly that I dreamed of being, that I wanted to be. At least I don't remember, even in middle school. I don't remember wanting to be* [anything]. *I hadn't really thought about what I wanted to do, what I wanted to be. Felicia was a role model. I figured I was gonna go to college. By the time I was in middle school she was in college. So I figured yeah I'm gonna go to college, but I didn't know what I wanted to do, wanted to be, in college.*

As I look back over my academic career, I am proud of myself. Throughout high school and college, I've received recognition and honor for my academic achievements. I was the first person in my family to have completed a Master's Degree. Education is one of the most valuable things anyone can do for themselves and I strongly encourage my clients and family to go-for-it. I would like to write a few books in the field of behavior and social science. I want to one day build a foundation that will be a solution to the declining black community. This foundation would offer alternatives to delinquency and teen pregnancy. We could build recreation centers for the youth, teach parenting skills. I want to prevent the problem and not wait until a crisis occur to do something. My ultimate goal is to worship God the Creator and serve my fellowman.

DEIDRA
A Mother's Love Is the Greatest Love of All

Language is the only homeland.

—Paule Marshall, *Reena*

• • •

I Remember when I was five my mother and Sister would come to see me in Tiberius, I never really knew my mother, but she would always pick me up and kiss me for [a] long period of time and take me with her wherever she went. But she would always bring me back to my Grandparents house afterwards. My mother would then leave again and I would'nt see her for a while. My Grandparents had five children of their own. As I got older around six years old, Then I began to realize who my mother was. I was always angry with her because she would always leave me and take my sister, but I didn't know why. When I got older, I began riding the bus to Picard for the Summer to see my mother and Sister. I would be so happy to see them and they would be happy to see me to.

My Sister would always treat me unfairly. And I would always fight her because I was already angry that she was living with our mom and I wasn't. When Chistmas time would come my mother would always call and ask me what I wanted, And She would buy exactly what I wanted because she wanted to see me happy. And thats why I would always tell people I'm Raising my own children no matter what the situation is because I k[n]ow that a mother's love is the greatest love of all.

When I was 8 years old in Elementary School, I started Running track for the Track Team that we Formed. I continued running track throughtout my Junior high School year and my Sr. high school year. During the time I was Running track in Jr. High School I was one of the fastest Runners there, Yet I was always upset because I wasn't maintaining the proper grades. Therefore I would[n't] recieve an award for my accomplishments. I would always be hurt each year I ran.

Furthermore when I was coming up no one took time out to teach me to Read, Write, or Spell so I went throughtout my whole education not comprehending half of my School work. As I go[t] older I learned more on my own yet it was not enough for me. I was quiet in school because I was scared that someone wou'ld know that I couldn't read. Also, I fright in school.

In junior high school the 9th grade was very hard For me; so hard that I Fell it and had to go to summer classes. At the time [I failed,] *it was like* [I] *wasn't interested because I didn't know. I didn't know anything. I couldn't even tell you about junior high that much. And I guess that's the reason why I fail because it was history and I just couldn't understand that for nothing. And when I failed, I mean, it was like nobody really, I mean, it wasn't like, "Oh well you gonna be punished and get a whipping," or, I mean, anything. It was like, "Well, I guess you'ah have to go to summer school and make up for it so you can go to high school." Because the school that I went to in junior high it went to the ninth grade so therefore I wasn't in high school at the time. I was still in junior high. And I guess they didn't want me to be embarrass or nothing so they sent me to the summer program and I passed. I went through the math part because I knew math a little more than I knew history because history was a lot of reading and I knew I couldn't comprehend on that part that well. So I took the math course because I fail math and history. So I took the math and I passed it and I moved on to high school, but still not knowing everything that I supposed to had been knowing in math either. Cause throughout high school the teacher that we had—I had and a lotta other kids had— she was a alcoholic. She didn't really teach us that well for math. There were another teacher there but it was like, "I'm staying in this class because I don't know that much and I figure I can pass." So I'n't switch out of the class. I was hiding. I didn't know. I was scared.*

I don't blame [the teachers or the schools]. *I think I blame more of my family because my grandmother and my grandfather, they didn't know. And even if they did know they didn't try to get any help. And it was very difficult because, I mean, if you bringing home 'F's and 'D's and 'C's you should notice that a child has a problem. I wouldn't say anything cause they wouldn't confront me with my grades.* [My parents] *would just say, "Well, do better next time." But next time wasn't really as good as it was 'pose to had been though.*

Althroughout high school I had a hard time writing papers for class and Reading books that i could have enjoy but i was scared to Read because I knew that I had a problem. Althrough High School i did whatever it was in class just to get buy. I would only pick up my books when the teacher will give home[work]. even in college i will che[a]t somethimes to get a good grade on my test. But deep down inside I wanted to be like the another student.

In college [is] when I started really noticing that I had a problem. I didn't feel comfortable at all with the teachers. I didn't feel relaxed. It was like one teacher said, "Well you need to get some more help or something or maybe you could get a tutor or something because you not passing the class."

"Are you having a problem?" You know, they use to ask me, "Are you having a problem? Are you aware that you don't know how to write and read and stuff like that?" At that point in time I knew that I couldn't. When I was in the twelfth grade (I would go back to high school right now), I never want to get up and talk. I always wanted to just sit down and listen because I know that I didn't know the work and I didn't know what I was really doing. So I didn't want to talk about it. I didn't want the teacher to ask me any questions because I was scared that someone in the class or the kids in the class would laugh and they'ah notice that I couldn't read and stuff like that. So I didn't wanna ever stand up and read even in college. I didn't want to but at one point in time I had to. No one laugh but it was like one guy said, "Why—what's wrong? You—why you can't read that well?" And it was like trying to explain but really not knowing how to explain it because I was just beginning to learn what my problem was. So, I felt very uncomfortable at the classrooms.

At the age of twenty one I moved to Picard with my mother and Step-father. My sister was off in college. I resided in Picard for about seven years. After moving to Picard I realized how much my mom and I are alike to say we never really lived together before. Moving to picard made me understand life more as well as responsibilty. living with my Grand-parents was like living in a make believe world because I wasn't growing up at all. Moving to picard with my mother was the best decision I could have made.

During that time I got to know myself more, what I felt and what I wanted out of life. Also during that time my mother and I became Good friends. To have a Friendship type of relationship with my mother meant happiness to me. I moved out of my mother house and moved back to Tiberius w[h]ere I was raised and move on with my life, and I feel so good about myself right now. I Love my mother and sister and brother's and I love my Dad know matter what he Does.

EDUCATION: *I Didn't Get that Part*

[When I was going through school, my teachers] *were like even—fifty fifty—White and Black. I notice that the Whites will fail you quicker than the Blacks will but other than that no extensions* [i.e., distinctions]. *They sure will. You'ah be done failed and everything.* [But I do] *not really* [think race or gender had any effect on my education. I don't feel I was treated differently because of my race or gender.] *I just feel like that part was up to me. Because I mean in the class you either get it or you don't. The White kids, they knew more and the teachers respond to them more and call on them more, but I guess it was up to us to really get off into it and make them notice us as well as the White kids. So I don't blame anybody. I mean if I would have known, believe me I pro'bly been jumping out of my chair too wanting to answer questions and go to the board. But since I didn't know I didn't really care about it. It didn't really come to me or nothing like that.*

In college, I just felt like it was—well it was a all Black college so it wasn't really like it was, "Oh well, this person here is White and we got to do this and that." But I mean even the Black kids who were very smart they responded to them more and paid attention to them more than what they did to the kids who wasn't really at the college level that they suppose to had been at. So I mean I can't feel bad. I don't think I can because it shoulda been something I gotten through elementary and junior and on up. It just something that wasn't there.

[Schools should be] *preparing* [students] *for the outside world. Preparing them to be at a point in life where the education that they have gotten is something where they can get a job—a decent job—and basically have a family. Because without a good job and without something that you can depend on and provide for, you can't have any kids. It's hard to have children and you don't have any money and anything that is, I would say, over twenty-five thousand dollars a year. I mean with one child you can make it with that but basically, education-wise, if you don't have it you not gonna make that type of money unless you been on a job for years. And I just feel like education is something that we all need because it prepares for life and it prepares for whatever the life that we wanna lead and whatever we want to become and how we wanna live our life. No* [the schools didn't do that for me]. *No. I knew I didn't get that part.*

I'm in a lower middle class. I'm not in a middle, I mean a lower class, but it's in between. I just feel like at thirty I can be more in a higher middle class than what I am but because of education wise I'm not. So, [my level of education] *has a lot to do with my economic status, yes it does.*

I look at some kids as I was teaching. I had little four year olds. [This] *was before I started getting into nursing, really getting off into nursing. They would pick up books and they would read them and they knew what they were reading and they really understood what they was reading. And I think* [becoming a good reader] *comes from that. I think it's good teaching and good learning style. I think it comes from the child at a age where they would want to do it. I don't know who's pushing them or if the parents are pushing them, because I'm pretty sure parents have to be buying books and stuff like that to get them interested in reading. So therefore I think it's kinda up to the child to pick up the book and read. I don't know that much about that part, but I never picked up a book. I mean even in high school, I didn't even pick up a book really. I just got outta high school.*

[For example, your language and literacy compared to my language and literacy are] *totally totally different. Totally different. I couldn't even compare myself to your language and writing and stuff because I'm not on the level that you're on. I guess I can say you were interested in your writing and your language and how you felt and I wasn't because no one taught me anything. You had someone in school to really push you. I didn't have anybody to push me. One time I ask, you told me it was a lady who use to make y'all get the dictionary when you was in what, elementary school or something? It's some teachers help you when you at that level and I didn't get that part. So you and I are just, when it comes to that literacy or anything, we are totally the opposite. In that way you know more than me. I could know more than you in some other ways but in that way we're just totally different.*

I can't say that [the schools I went to were not good schools]. *I mean to me they wasn't because I felt uncomfortable in school. But they were good schools because there're other kids who graduated and went to school with me who are practically on the level that they need to be on. It just were me. So I just felt like I just didn't get the education that I needed. But they were pretty good schools. I guess I could say they were pretty good schools.*

I'm not happy with [my education and educational experiences]. *I always felt like I could have gotten some help or something when I was growing up. I realize that i had a problem but know one side* [i.e., said] *eventhing* [i.e., anything] *about it are try to get me some help. But I guess nobody noticed that I had a literacy problem. And I never got that help. If only someone would had, maybe my life would have been different. Know I haven't been happy with my literacy but it's there and i have to deal with it. I have a literacy problem and I'm getting help.*

[If I had it to do all over again] *I don't know* [what I would change about my education or my educational experience]. *I don't like to think about if when I was coming up would I have changed or what I woulda did. But I can say now I'm in a program to help me more with that and as of this point in my life I want to change it. But I can't speak for back then because I didn't know and what you don't know you can't really say I wanna change it. But if that was possible, I wish that I could have been more open and said that I had a problem, but I didn't so it's something that I have to deal with now and get the help that I have to get.* [The thing I like about myself now] *is that I'm getting help with my literacy.*

L A N G U A G E : *People Just Speak the Way They Know*

[My grandparents did not contribute to my language and literacy development] *cause they didn't know. They talk bad language. They talk bad English. So I mean they didn't know. They didn't even get outta eight years. They didn't know how to teach me how to better myself.*

[Bad English and Black English are] *two different things. Because a lot of Black people doesn't speak the way they* [i.e., Deidra's paternal grandparents] *speak. I mean I guess by them being older they just say whatever they wanna say and it doesn't matter to them how they saying it. To a younger person it matters the way they speak, but to them it just doesn't really matter to them.*

[Speaking Black English is] *knowing what your Black culture is about. And how the*[y] *uses their English. What type of words the*[y] *uses. and understand the Black world. I'm not sure* [if speaking Black English is important]. *Unless your speaking to a Black Brother or Sister. I guess understanding t*[he] *Black language.* [I value Black English more than I value standard English] *because I can understand Black English better than I can understand standard English and not that I feel as if I'm Black and I suppose to.* [But I also value Black English more than standard English because most of the people I associate with] *is Black.*

[Standard English is important to some extent for me if I see a connection with reading and writing. For me it's not to speak it, it's] *just to understand it better. But if I were Black and can speak standard English, and*

*there are Black people who speak good English, then I wouldn't see a prob-
lem with that. I'm not saying that I don't understand the standard English.
I do understand it because when someone is talking to me now, I understand* [them] *perfectly. I mean back then I prob'ly wouldn't have understand anything. But now I understand when people are talking to me
because half of the people here in Tiberius don't speak good English
at all.*

I feel like Black[s] *know their English and they know what they can comprehend and understand what each other is talking about compared to
someone who speak proper English or good English.* [Sometimes people
who speak standard English] *do* [have a problem understanding people
who speak Black English]. *They have a problem understanding, far as if
you wanna look at the Blacks. They might not understand what they are
saying but in some ways they do understand because, I mean, I heard
people say something like, "Well, explain to me what you're talking about,
you know, from a Black point of view. Tell me what you mean by what
you're saying?" Even though they speak correct English they also learn
that there are different cultures and they learn their languages somewhat
because everybody doesn't talk the same. It wouldn't be a problem then* [if
we take slang out of this. Then] *we all understand each other. The way you
use the words and the way you present the words in the sentence is totally
different. I mean everybody use slang words but some people presenting
sentences and trying to make a statement might be totally different and a
person who speak proper English might not understand what they're trying to say.*

*The way you talk effect the way you basically read and write because if
you don't understand the way you're talking, what you're saying and talking about, then how are you gonna relate to the reading and writing part
cause you wouldn't understand what you writing or reading. I can say that
I have improved a good 15% on that part and now I understand a little
more on that. I don't think half of the people that speak good English, half
of 'em can't probably read and write. I have heard that some people can
just sit down and read and from that reading and stuff from the knowledge that they hear other people talking. Some people can talk the way
other people talk and it can be proper. For instance, like a young child can
hear their parents talking correct English because that's the way they talk
and they grow up talking like that. That doesn't mean that they know how
to read and write. So therefore, it's not like it's a big deal to me because I
might be a person that can read and write and might can't talk that well.*

No [I don't make fun of the way some people speak] *because I can't speak that well myself. So I don't make fun of anybody language because I learned that people just speak the way they know. I mean at one point in time I use to speak terribly. I talk better now. I don't like to use "ain't" and "I did dat" and stuff like that a lot. I can't really say that it's bad language. It depends on who's talking. Everybody talk different. Everybody have a way of speaking.*

[Speaking standard English is important] *only if you believe it is. Sometimes for a job it's good. People talk the way they wanna talk long as you understand. It's not that important to me. I mean standard English is a English that who prefer, want to better themself in talking that way. When I say that someone speaks well are talks good, it's because the*[y] *have study hard in life. I don't care for talking proper or talking good English because long as I know what I'm saying and someone's understanding me, it's not that important. I don't think so.*

I talk the way that I talk because I'm trying to better myself. Sometime I might just say something and it might be like, "Now you know you wasn't supposed to say it. And look at the way you said it. You know that wasn't right. You 'pose to had said it this way."

There are distinctions that I do [make]. *Sometime, when you around your color and they not talking properly, you tend to kinda say anything really.*

I probably will talk different to a man than I will a woman because women are different from men so you have a tendency to say certain things that you wouldn't say to a man. [For example,] *with a friend girl, I might say, "Girl, shit." I might say anything. But with a man I might have to . . .*

With you I talk totally different. Conversation wise it's totally different because it's certain things that I would talk to you about and then it's certain things that I would talk to them about. I mean it depends on the person that I'm talking to. Cause you're not really interested in half of the things that I want to say. So basically I don't talk to you like I would talk to Geneva or Darrell or somebody like that because I just feel like I can talk to them about any anything and they would be listening, but I mean with my sister I can't talk like that cause she's not really interested in half of the things that I have to say. I mean you might listen but I mean it's not like you really would be a person who would just really say, "Well Sis I think such and such." She not interested in some of the things that I'm interested in so therefore talking to you would be inrelevant because you prob-

ably wouldn't even know how to answer me the way I would like for you to answer me so I wouldn't want to get into a conversation on that part.

But I try to talk better regardless to who I'm with. I always try to say correct words. I don't care who it is. I always try to talk correctly because I don't wanna be embarrassed when I'm talking and someone say, "Oh that's doesn't—that's not what you suppose to say. You suppose to had said this." But I'm glad. I like people to correct me if I'm saying something wrong and if I'm not using the proper English when I'm saying it because it helps me when I say it again. I think I'ma think about it before I say it. So I try to think before I say something now. I don't care who it is. And far as other people talking, I mean I can't control their talking, but I can try to better myself on my language and everything.

L I T E R A C Y :   *I Have a Literacy Problem and I'm Getting Help*

[Literacy is] *a person who can read and write but can not explain it. It's when a person is having* [a] *problem with reading and writing. Can read and write but scared. Some people can read and write but don't understand what they're writing, and some people can read and write and don't understand anything.* [Illiteracy is] *a person who has a deficiency problem of reading and writing. I don't know* [the difference between literacy and illiteracy] *I guess,* [but] *like I say a person who has a deficiency problem, a reading* [problem], *a comprehending problem.*

I'm not satisfied with [the type of writing and reading that I do]. *It's not up to the level that I need to be on as a out-of-college student. I have a reading problem. I'm not comfortable reading out loud. I have a problem with mostly spelling words and the meaning of the word and that is the most important thing of my reading and understanding what I'm reading. I hadn't graduated, but in college I wasn't on the level that I need to be on far as my reading and writing and stuff like that. So it's like I'm on a seventh, a twelve-year-old reading level when I need to be on a eighteen, seventeen far as getting it to the point I need to be at. But it's not . . .*

Now that [I] *am older I'm reading better and writing more.* [Reading is important to me and my life] *because one day I would like to have children and knowing that I could help them is very important to me. I'm reading a book now. the name of the* [book] *is, "Are You the One For Me?" I'm enjoying it. Felicia told me about it. and I wanted to know if something in this book relation to me. and I do read stories. But basically I don't have that much time to read* [so] *I don't read that much. Not that much. Maybe*

once are twice out of a week. You know, the sales paper. But I enjoy read-
ing love stories and books that I feel pertain to my life story. [Being literate
is important] *because it's important to me to know how to read and write*
without having to ask someone to read it and make sure what I'm writing
is good to turn in and get a 'A' or 'B' on it.

I'm also starting an adult progree [called the] *Adult Learning Program*
that could help me with my literacy so that I could somewhat get on the
level that I need to be on for college because that's the only way that I
could go back and get an Education. I go like three days out of a week if
I can. Sometime I go two days out of a week and I go for like two three
hours. It's like a formal classroom setting. You go in, you read stories and
you do a test after each story that you do. Right now I'm on the comput-
ers and you read a little short paragraph of a story and you go back and
they have words listed where you pick out the word that would pertain
to that story, that would fit that story. And believe me, you would think
you have everything right and you have maybe five or six right out of the
whole fifteen. But you continue doing it until you get it right. You continue
reading the same thing until you get it right. Basically, it's one-on-one even
though it's people, maybe a lot of people, in there. But the instructors are
only one-on-one with you when you go there. It's a one-on-one thing. But
sometime they don't know half of the stuff. [Still] *it can help me in some*
ways and then I would probably have to move on to something else. It is
design for [moving you to a twelfth-grade reading level or higher]. *It's*
definitely design for that but I guess it depends on the type of help that I
can get from someone in there who can just [work with me one-on-one].
I think I need a one-on-one; I mean just no one there but me and the
instructor. And when I don't understand something if she's there, I can
ask her and we can refer to the dictionary, show me how to go back and
say read and look up the word and see if that word pertain to what I'm
reading. But now it's difficult because it's more kids in there because [even
though] *it's really adult learning, it's other kids in there and it's other*
adults in there and it's like they can't just stay one-on-one with you the
whole while you in there. But it can be something beneficial.

I wouldn't go back to college right now. I'm not gonna go to any school
knowing I have a problem because it's not gonna help the situation. And I
definitely wouldn't want to go to nursing school and get into clinical and
not know what I'm really doing because it's not gonna work. It's a very
difficult course and you have to know how to somewhat read. I mean
everybody in nursing, I can't say they know how to read everything but

I need to know what I'm doing before I can get to that point and I will not go back to college.

My attitude about education is that i hope that one day I could get a degree in college. i couldn't go back to college knowing how i Feel about my literacy without getting help with my problem. So right now it's like one day at a time trying to read and stuff like that and comprehend everything that I'm supposed to be reading. It's very difficult when you have that type of problem. But it's not bad as it used to be when I was in high school and college because I read a little more than I did then and I understand a little more. So when I'm reading it's a li'l more better but it's just not on what I want it to be on, what I think it should be. So I'm not happy with that at all. And my writing is not where it need to be either because I get scared when I'm writing because I'm scared I'm gonna make a mistake and everything is not gonna coordinate together, not gonna correspond together, it's not gonna sound right. So I don't like to write. I know I need to, but I don't.

A good writer comes from reading really and reading has a lot to do with writing because when you reading, you see the format of things that you reading and when you writing, a good writer would know that the format that I need to write in is when I'm reading a book or something. I'm not sure how to do that part. But if I was reading a book, I would like to form my words like that if I'm gonna write a paper because that's the way I want to do it. But if I didn't have the book to read and go back and write a paper about it, I wouldn't know how to write it that well because I'm not a good writer and a good writer wouldn't have to pick up a book. He would just write. They would just start writing any thoughts or whatever. I'm not good at putting my thoughts down because I'm not sure that they would be in the same order that they suppose to be even though I'm thinking and writing at the same time. I don't think they would. They don't come out that way and I would have to just go back and continue reading and reading and reading until I get it to the point that I need it to be at. So, I'm not sure. I don't know how a good writer would start out writing.

[Writing is important to me] *because to become a RN are psychology I need to know how to write a paper and take good notes. also when writing friends.* [I do] *not* [write] *much. I can write but not that good. My writing is somewhat poor. I write at work, write papers and notes and stuff for patients. When I was in High School I use*[d] *to write down things that I felt and what is going on in my life at that time. When I was dating this guy in the army I would write to him and we would write back and forth and that kinda help me with my writing. When writing letters are papers sometime I need help with knowing if I'm useing the right pattern. Are if what I'm writing sound good. Once I started really writing, like just all the time at one set, I learn to write more and put things in order so you can understand what I'm trying to say.*

I don't write as good as I talk. Totally different from the way I talk and write because I can talk and say the things that I wanna say. But if I put it on paper it's not the way that I'm talking,. It's totally different because I cannot spell half of the words that I'm talking unless I just look in the dictionary. If I'm talking [and] I'm writing at the same time, it's not gon come out right. I have to go back, get the dictionary to fill in everything that I'm saying to make sure that everything is spelled correctly, everything is said correctly and everything. I would say that if I'm writing, I can write what I'm saying in some ways but when I go back to read it I have to put the correct word because I'm writing and I'm not putting the correct words that I'm thinking.

GOALS AND POSSIBLE SELVES:
I Wanna Have It Together

When I was in college (I'm still a junior in college), I met this professor and she just had everything together. Like she had everything together and sometime you notice that and you say, "Well I wanna be just like that. I wanna have it together. I wanna be able to do the things that she can do." She get up in front of the class and it's like she just had it together and that kinda made me want to strive more. And then listening to talk shows and stuff like that of Blacks [and] going to see shows that pertain to Black and telling us how we need a education and stuff like that, some kinda way it kinda made me give a little more into my studies (because I didn't like to study at all cause I couldn't comprehend what I was reading that well so I didn't wanna study and I ain't wanna pick up a book). But once I got off into them and kinda seeing them as I got older, it kinda made me want to do better.

Now I work up in the hospital. I just love this lady there, the way she do with the patients and treat 'em and stuff like that. And I started off in nursing. As I been into this hospital and working, I say to myself, "One day I'm going back to nursing," cause I wanna be just like her and I don't want to be the type of nurse that some of those people are. They don't wanna help or do anything. They like, "Oh I have my RN license and I'm not doing anything. That's not for me to do." But she's like a total care person on a patient and I admire her. And I like when she does that because it makes me do my work better also and it helps me with my thinking and stuff like that. And all of 'em tell me I need to get in school and try to become a RN cause I'ah make a good nurse.

The language, only the language. The language must be careful and must appear effortless. It must not sweat. It must suggest and be provocative at the same time. It is the thing that black people love so much—the saying of words, holding them on the tongue, experimenting with them, playing with them. It's a love, a passion. Its function is like a preacher's: to make you stand up out of your seat, make you lose yourself and hear yourself. The worst of all possible things that could happen would be to lose that language. There are certain things I cannot say without recourse to my language. It's terrible to think that a child with five different present tenses comes to school to be faced with those books that are less than his own language. And then to be told things about his language, which is him, that are sometimes permanently damaging.

—Toni Morrison, in an interview with Thomas LeClair

• • •

I was in the fifth grade. It was my second year in a magnet school where I was being bused from my home in a working-class neighborhood. The school was in the middle of a white, middle-class neighborhood that didn't resemble mine at all. All of the teachers there were white as I recall. The students of color that attended the school were all bused in from my part of town. We took long bus rides in the morning and afternoon to get there. It was a big change for me, but I liked the school. I got along wonderfully with my teachers. My fifth-grade teacher was Mr. Thames. I thought he was wonderful. He liked me too. Sometimes I would sit next to him at lunch and we would talk about all kinds of stuff. Once he had me guess his age during lunch and I guessed it correctly. To this day I'm not sure that was a good thing to do. One day in class we were doing an activity. Students were all over the room. Curtis, one of the kids being bused to the school like me, was fiddling with something and Mr. Thames yelled to him, "Get your black hands off of that." He had never told anyone to get their "white" hands off of anything. Why did he have to say "black"? Why did he have to say it so loud and so hurtful? I don't know how I changed at that time, but I must have because we all do. I still had white friends at school and special friendships, but I always remember that day and it always hurts me deeply.

I am a Black woman and I am proud of it. . . . I don't wonder what it's like to be white. I wonder what it's like to be Black and respected or to be Black and equal in the eyes of society.

—Excerpt from my 1992 paper for a graduate class in gender and literacy

When I was an undergraduate student, I don't remember doing much writing except for exams. I didn't have a lot of papers to write even though I was an English major. Actually, I really committed to being an English major late in my college career. When I did do so (I was accepted by the Honors English program which allowed me special honors in English for graduation because I had to complete an undergraduate thesis as one of the requirements), I think that is when the bulk of my writing in college (undergraduate, that is) was done.

Before that commitment, I was a business major with the idea of going into corporate law, but I dropped that idea before I even attended a class at college. I had gotten a lot of pressure from my parents and others to not go into teaching, which is what I had always dreamed of doing. A neighbor and family friend who works in education tried to discourage my teaching interests because she felt I could do more. To her, teaching was something African Americans who wanted a college education were historically limited to. She felt that I should and could use my intelligence and opportunities to do more than that. Ironically, I found more African Americans in the business school or preparing for the business school than almost any other place. I guess a lot of African American kids were getting a similar message to the one I got. There was also the money issue as well. Besides, to them, there wasn't enough prestige in teaching. I could certainly do better than that.

At some point and with some strength, I decided that I had to do what I wanted to do and not what my parents or others wanted me to do because I would be the one who would have to live with my career choice, so I dropped the business and corporate law idea and I began to explore other majors like speech pathology (when I was still a prescriptivist) and math. I also seriously considered teacher certification for secondary or elementary, but I didn't do that either. At one point, I was seeking a dual degree in math and English, but I never really took any math classes beyond calculus to demonstrate that interest and I eventually decided to only seek a B. A. in English. I regret that sometimes. I think the challenge would have been good for me, but I think the problem was that I am a split between an intrinsically goal oriented person and an extrinsically goal oriented person.

I think that has been represented throughout my academic career. I didn't take some "hard" classes in high school because I was conscious of my academic standing and the competition with other students in my honor's track classes. However, I remember being very hurt when I was not put into a special honors class in high school because my counselor didn't think I was up to the same level as the others chosen for the class. I eventually got over it (kind of) given the amount of work they had to do. What also made me feel better (in a way) was that some of the people chosen for that class eventually didn't do as well as I did in school—both high school and college.

Two students from my high school who also went to college with me but as National Merit Fellows, flunked out and lost their scholarships. I'm not glad they lost their fellowships or anything like that, but their experiences in their last year in high school and their brief years in college showed me that I won't always get the opportunities and privileges that I think I deserve or can handle. They did well on standardized tests and I didn't. They didn't work very hard—especially in their senior year at high school—but I worked hard enough to rank ahead of both of them in my class standing and to a prestigious graduate school. Unfortunately, both of them were the only other African Americans who ranked as high as I did. Essentially, they let me down as an African American, but they also let themselves down. I wonder where they are now and what they are doing. I hope they got their acts together.

Anyway, when I think back to that class, I still feel a little hurt now. I think that class would have been beneficial to me, but maybe the counselor was right given my split. I believe my desire to learn and my desire to be competitive made me compromise my academic career. I was interested in mastery, challenge, and learning (intrinsic goal orientation), but I was also interested in grades, rewards, and approval from others (extrinsic goal orientation). I feel the educational system I have been involved in up to now has emphasized the latter more than the former—so I did as well. Now, however, I am much more concerned about showing how competent

I am. I want my work to be good—no, excellent—and anything less is a big disappointment and embarrassing to me. After being in predominantly White college institutions, I have learned that as an African American I have to do better than my White counterparts, both in appearance and in actuality. If I don't, I can easily be labeled as an incompetent, mediocre, or poor scholar who got the breaks she did because of her gender and ethnicity. I don't intend on being anyone's token in that sense. If I am going to be a token, I will be one who strives for excellence and achieves it as an African American, a woman, and a human being. I don't think I can or should settle for less.

E D U C AT I O N : *I've Been Going to School All My Life*

I kinda tended to be a teacher's pet kinda person at least as I can remember through elementary school. They pretty much made me feel like I was a smart student and as a person, I don't think my teachers did anything to make me feel that I wasn't smart or that I wasn't a worthy person or anything like that. So I don't think that they interfered with my self-esteem in a negative way.

From kindergarten through third grade, I think I went to predominantly Black schools because you went to schools that were in your neighborhood and I lived in a predominantly Black neighborhood. I had one Hispanic teacher I remember and one White teacher and I assume the other teachers that I had were Black. That particular area is now considered a really bad part of town, but like I said I thought my second grade teacher was a really good teacher for me at least.

For fourth, fifth and sixth grade I went to a magnet school in music which was in a predominantly White area. And I was bussed in there—it took forever to get to that school from where I lived. I guess it was a pretty good school. It introduced me to music and I was interested in the piano, and my parents eventually bought me a piano and I sort of practice on that for a while. My crowning moment was when I got to play a revised version of the theme for "The Young and the Restless". And I was in the choir there so I got to do that. I just had lots of opportunities when I was at Longfellow and that was probably the most positive time in my education that I think back on and remember despite the incident with the fifth grade teacher. I had positive experiences there and I was just exposed to so much and it was just fun it seemed being in that school.

My junior high school I guess was pretty typical, it was pretty average. I *don't know if it stood out in any particular way. I don't think the high school that I went to was that great of a high school. The way that the lines were drawn for what school you went to had it so that the high school I went to was a predominantly minority school, probably predominantly Black, but it was really well mixed with other ethnic groups, but there weren't many Whites there. And the other two schools were in rich suburban White areas. So for the most part, the Whites went to the other two schools and the Blacks went to my high school. And I certainly feel that those students who went to the other two schools got a better education and I think they had better opportunities than I did. Take tennis for example. Our tennis coach was pretty pitiful as a tennis coach. He was just doing it to get the extra money I think even though he did play tennis and he liked the game. It was always a struggle for us to get t-shirts or tennis balls or equipment or stuff like that. Whereas at the other two schools they have this wonderful program and their tennis courts were kept up really nice and they had neat uniforms and stuff like that. And it wasn't that same type a struggle. And they had like real tennis coaches who were interested in doing that as a tennis coaching job whereas our coach was trying to move up into being a football coach as well. So I think I missed out on some opportunities there. It was certainly better than average and I sort of pulled it together after my first year there and I was able to graduate like number six in my class out of four hundred and ten students which got me a five-year scholarship to college. But I can't really say that there was any school that I went to with the exception of Thoreau that sort of stood out and maybe gave me that start in terms of language and literacy development. I think I went to a pretty good college. I think I've developed a lot since being in graduate school but I don't think there's anything special I could say about most of the schooling that I had.*

I certainly think race had an effect on my education because Blacks lived in particular areas of town and certainly for elementary schools, you went to schools in your neighborhood except when I got the opportunity for bussing, so all the schools were Black. I had exposure to White people even though I lived in an essentially Black area of town until I was twelve years old, but I had the opportunity to go to a school where I was no longer surrounded mostly by Blacks and I don't know if you want to say that's positive or negative. It was positive for me in the extent that I had certain opportunities that I most assuredly wouldn't have had had I just went through elementary school in my neighborhood. And that was probably a good move on my mom's part.

The incident in fifth grade certainly brought the issue of race into that particular class. At that time I was in a school that was in a White neighborhood and I was being bussed from a predominantly Black area to that school. So there were very few Black students in the school to begin with. And I don't know if before that I was conscious of it or I can't even say at the time if I was very conscious of racial issues being at that school but I mean for me and looking back at it, it has an effect. I can feel sort of this effect because I really liked that teacher and we would sit together at lunch sometimes and we'd talk and it was just kinda fun. But on that particular day, I can still see the expression on his face and I'm sure he was probably embarrassed for having said it, but it was said by then. I'm not sure how our relationship changed after that or anything like that but I mean I can even still see the face of the kid he said that to. And I can't imagine him actually saying something like that to me, partly because of our relationship but also partly because I was never a student to get into trouble and I think Troy was a pretty average student and did things I guess that boys do in school sometimes. But for him to say it like that. There were other students in that class that were Black—other male students in that class that were Black—and I don't know if he woulda said that to them or not. But when I look back at that I think sometimes you just don't know what a person is sort of thinking or feeling about you as an African American or even as a female. At the time I don't know if I was conscious of it, but now when I look back at that, I really think you can't tell. You don't know what people are thinking or feeling.

Although I certainly don't think my grades were suffering in any type of way because I was Black because, like I said, I was always one of the top students in the class (although it could've had an indirect effect for me if I look back at the incident with the fifth grade teacher and if that's a particular feeling that he had). So for me the way that I see race affecting me is when I was blocked or locked into predominantly Black schools that didn't get the same type of opportunities that White schools in even the same district got. I think there was definitely an imbalance there, this inequity that existed there because we played tennis matches against 'em and when we went to the newer school and walked through there, boy what a beautiful school that was. And the tennis courts were great. We'd come back to our school where the wind screens were falling down and no one was gonna put them up and we didn't have really uniforms or something like that and we had all these dead balls—our tennis coach didn't want us to use up all the good balls cause we only got so many and stuff like that— we had no real training program, no real coaching because he wouldn't be there half the time and it was just stuff like that I guess that I noticed. I don't think that was going on at the other two schools—the two White schools—in our district. I know I focused on extra-curricular stuff but in terms of educational stuff, I'm not sure. The concept was that we always thought that the teachers at our school didn't want to be there and they wanted to really go to one of the other two schools 'cause the students were better, right, because they were all White. And that just the whole system over there was a lot better than it was at our schools. You knew that other people in the district were saying, "Oh you go to the Black school," and "It's not as good a school."

Up until when I was going through high school, I didn't realize that I was actually gonna go to college. I never really thought about that. And so I guess I wasn't thinking about "Oh gee, if I'm going to this Black school and I want to go to college, I might not have as good a chance to go to a particular college because of the way that the colleges choose students for schools is different based upon how your school ranks." And I knew our school couldn'ta ranked too high, so you really had to do well in order to even be considered for a scholarship. On the other hand, being there could've worked to my advantage because if a college that is predominantly White wanted Black students, well certainly our school would have been the place to go if they wanted to say, take the top ten students out of that particular school. So in some ways I guess it had a positive effect and other ways I think it had a negative effect. I don't know if I would've had the same opportunity or been in the same situation if I'd been at one of the White schools because I don't know if I would've chosen to compete with the students that were there. Not to say that I wasn't as smart but to say that at that time in my life, I was only putting forth enough effort to stay in the honors' level classes. And I was making good grades because I think I have some sort of intelligence. It may have been an inferior school, but I did what I could to stand out in some particular way.

And as far as gender, I don't know if I would've had as positive relationships with as many teachers as I had, had I been a male. For certain I don't recall any Black males being like in the top of our class for except maybe one. And they would fluctuate between being in the level one class and the level two classes. I think they were like split. I can't think of a Black male right now who went through all level one classes with all of us, and most of them in those classes were women anyway. So, I don't know what that says about the Black men that I went to school with, but what that says about gender and how that sort of worked with Blacks in the school. I don't know; that's sort of curious for me to think about. Would I have had the same type of relationship with the teachers in the schools that I went to had I been a male. So maybe gender in that respect worked as a positive thing for me. Especially in like college where you have sort of the quota thing going and you want the double minority and by me being Black and female, maybe that helped in some way.

I think my high school experience that stands out for me is my relationship with Mrs. Gee. She was a woman who replaced, when I was in junior high, my Social Studies teacher who I also had a crush on. And I was really angry with her when she replaced him. I was really mean to her at first but then I grew to have a really nice relationship with her, and I really respected her. And I appreciated the way that she pushed us in my senior English class. And I even wrote to her a couple of times after I left there. And when I would go back home, I'd go and visit her. I think that was the first time I read a book—a complete book—that I really liked and still think about, think of as one of my favorite books of all time, which was Jane Eyre.

Mom says I've been going to school all my life cause I started going to like daycare when I was two months old. I remember having books at home. I remember like having a children's Bible. But I don't remember my parents reading bedtime stories to me at night and stuff like that. A lot of the stuff that I recall learning that children learn, I recall learning it when I was in daycare. All of the songs that I learned, all of the stories that I knew. I don't remember my parents reading stories to me or teaching me songs, or teaching me about reading and writing or helping me with my homework really. Because it seemed at some point in my schooling, I had actually outdone them in a way. I mean I would be the one that would go around correcting them in their language or something like that. By the time I reached high school, I was the one that they would ask questions of. I didn't go to my parents and say, "Would you help me with my homework," or "Can you help me figure this out." That wasn't the sort of situation that my parents were in because neither one of them I don't think felt particularly confident in their language and literacy capabilities. So it was sort of a reverse situation for me. I would be the one helping them and I think the help that I got came from whatever initiative that I had and just from being in school all that time. I mean I can't remember not being in school. That's the only place I can think of that I learned about being a kid. Because that's where we played our games, and that's how I learned *about being a student and sort of the whole game of being a student. I sort of learned how to interact with adults that were teachers in a particular way because those were the people that I was around for a lot of the time of the day since both of my parents worked and didn't pick me up until late in the afternoon. Because even if I was in elementary school, I'd have to go to a school after that because my mom wasn't gonna be home until a certain time and I couldn't stay at home by myself until I got a little older. So for me honestly I'd have to say, I really don't think they played a direct role in my language and literacy development. Maybe my Mom played an indirect role in the fact that she was the one putting me into these schools.*

Education should expose students to lots of things to get to show them all of the opportunities that they could have. I think they should give all students a chance to actually sort of pursue those opportunities, even if they seem really slim. I don't think right now that there's any indication that schools sort of take into effect that people actually change. And so that you—you're not always gonna be the same way that you are. And that's why it's important for you to be exposed to lots of things because you might be able to remember these other opportunities that you can actually have based upon how you're continually changing. So I think the purpose of education should be equal to opportunity and just sort of doors opening, doors of your mind sort of opening, that is.

In terms of the purpose of education and reading and writing, I went through this period where I thought students shouldn't be forced to learn a language or even in reading and writing something that I didn't think was part of their culture. But I think reading—reading about something like this, reading about literacy and reading about language—has had a tremendous influence on me so I think at this point I would have to say that I think at least literacy is very important. That every student, every person, should be given the opportunity—a good opportunity—to learn to read, to write, to critically think, to become literate. I think that's very important because that allows them to be in a position to make particular choices for themselves that if they're not, they're sort of limited. They don't realize particular opportunities that they may have; that they're restricted from opportunities that they could've had. So I think literacy is important and I think schools need to do a better job of helping students along this road to literacy. For me I think it's a lifelong process.

As far as language, that's another issue. Students know how to speak, students know language before they go to school. Because language is a socialization thing that you have to be exposed to, you're gonna learn language. If you haven't learned language by a particular point, then you're not gonna learn it all. So the fact that students can speak when they go to school, they're in a constant process of learning language by the time they get there and they know pretty much most of what they need to know about language by the time they get to school. The problem comes when schools don't want certain languages there. And I have a problem with that. I think a school is there to teach you. I think the part about literacy development is the number one priority out of the two things because you know the language once you go there.

Would I change something about my education? I don't know. One thing I'd like to change about my education was to have been able to finish Thoreau so I wouldn't feel like I had been cheated. And I don't mind the moving, I understand why my parents moved. They wanted to move to a better neighborhood and to some extent they wanted to get me out of an environment that I was having some problems in and so they wanted to move me and hopefully that would make a change, and it did have a great effect upon me. I think I made this drastic leap, so I guess I don't mind the moving as much as the timing of the move for me. I can't think of anything about my education right now I would change, other than things about myself.

LANGUAGE: *I Sometimes Feel Uncomfortable*

"Standard" English is an idealistic normative variety of a language. It is the variety that the power structure promotes and expects. It is arbitrary as to what is the standard in that it's essentially chance. "Standard" English is a myth because there really is not consensus on what the norm is.

Speaking "standard" English is important in situations where the power structure thinks it should be used, but not so in that it doesn't exist. There are some things that are more acceptable than others and one may want to be careful since how you talk affects how people view you. But given the definition of "standard" English, this question becomes problematic because the part of the country you're in affects what the standard is.

African American English is a variety of English spoken primarily by African Americans if you buy the dialectology view. Otherwise, African American English is a creole—derived from African and English languages—if you buy the creolist position. I'm not sure which I buy. I think a combo of *both may be in order. In any event, it is a language spoken primarily by African Americans.*

I think speaking African American English is important. I think it's important for people to value their culture and heritage. Language is a major part of one's culture. Not valuing it jeopardizes the people that speak it. I think it is essential for those who speak it and value it and realize it for what it is.

I see there are linguistic differences between standard English and Black English, but I don't see the differences, just like I don't see the differences between standard English and New York English or what have you, as being a difference that connotates good versus bad or proper versus bad or incorrect versus correct. I see them as just being differences devoid of quality.

I guess I value Black English more than standard English because I'm sort of going to an extreme and saying I'm going to appreciate Black English more than standard English when I hear it because so many other people don't. I don't know if I would call it BEV [Black English Vernacular] *envy as much as an admiration and sort of a respect for it that I don't see.*

I think I'm kind of in a love/hate relationship with standard English because so many people are pushing this valuing of standard English and a not valuing of Black English that I'm sort of going to the opposite and saying I'm gonna highly value Black English and not value standard English as much because it's a cultural issue for me. It's a issue of identity and I have a strong reaction to that. I've also begun to feel uncomfortable when I've chosen specifically, consciously chosen to say I wanta speak standard English in this particular case for whatever reason because to me that's like buying into the whole system of it. To some extent I still try to be practical in some of the cases and say look there are these people who don't share your beliefs and they're sitting here saying this person sounds like a Black person and I don't want to have as much to do with her or I might not want to hire her for this job or whatever. I mean I'm gonna have enough problems dealing with hair, do I want to add the language thing to it also? It becomes a practical issue to me. A practical issue but also sort of an intellectual dilemma as well.

Lots of times I have felt insecure about my language and literacy. I didn't feel comfortable with writing until I got in graduate school and sort of realized how important writing can be and how important it can at least be for me and it can have a purpose for me. Because before it was all, you wrote for somebody else, you didn't really write for yourself. You were writing to fulfill some requirement. But when I was in this one professor's classes, I just really felt like I was writing for me. I was given that opportunity to do something for me. And I started making a connection that writing and reading were important for me. It could actually serve me in some particular way instead of serving someone else who wanted you to complete some requirement on a test or something like that and was judging you on the way that you wrote out your answer, based upon your language.

I feel insecure about my use of Black English Vernacular since I don't have all of the salient features of that in my use. I feel uncomfortable in certain situations. I can give you a good example of that. I saw Brianna [an African American graduate student in my husband's department] *yesterday. She had the poodle hair going. She was talking and she definitely speaks Black English Vernacular, but she also I think can speak standard English from what I've heard. I felt uncomfortable because even though she was a person who chose to speak Black English and I knew she chose to speak it, but because of my uncomfortableness with it and not knowing her that well, I can't respond to her in that way. I sound awkward when I speak Black English and I tried to speak Black English. I sound awkward and I know it and that's uncomfortable and I get the feeling sometimes when I'm with people who speak Black English, like my sister or even my Mom sometimes that they think I'm trying to show them up or something or that I'm trying to make some kind of impression that I'm better than them or something. I can't think of the word. But that makes me uncomfortable because that's not what I'm doing. It's just that I don't know any other way really to do it. My linguistic repertoire overlaps with theirs, but it's not a complete overlap. I don't talk the same way that they do, and that makes me feel uncomfortable in certain situations.*

I sometimes feel uncomfortable with standard English because there's some things I don't buy into for standard English and therefore I don't practice it. Like I always have a problem with 'lay'; 'lie' versus 'lay' versus 'laid' versus 'lain' and when do you use all of those things. I have problems with that and I feel uncomfortable in using some of those things and I know that people are gonna look at you. But then again I think most people don't know the difference so to that extent that gives me some comfort in that. But I mean in terms of my literacy I feel more secure with it I guess. I think I went through understanding more about literacy and maybe feeling less secure but now feeling a little more secure because I'm more aware of it. Now that I'm aware of it I think I can sort of understand it better and I can feel a little more secure about it. But I still have times where I'm sort of insecure about the language thing and about the literacy thing. But at least I'm aware of it and I can sort of adjust and get through that.

Yes, I guess I do talk differently to White people in general than I do to Black people in general. Depending upon who the people are, I'll talk more of what's thought of as standard English to Whites. But it could also depend upon who the Black people are too. For example, I think education level and how the particular person presents themselves have something to do with it. I probably approximate more of the concept of standard English with say a Black professor that I don't know who comes across to me as speaking standard English and that's a big issue with them. And the same thing with a White person than I would if it was the hair stylist talking about a soap opera and not approximating standard English. That's how I would differentiate in that.

I think that what I said just before still has a bearing on how I would talk to someone I don't know—Black or White. But once I get to know that person more and if that person also is sort of relinquishing this grip on standard English, then so will I. For example, I was much more apt to approximate more of this concept of standard English when I first met the people I play softball with more so than I do now. However, I am still conscious of it and I realize how I am talking when I talk with them. Because of some comments that have been by the manager of my Monday team, I realize or think that maybe I should keep up the formal talk since how you talk, at least to some extent, seems to be tied to intelligence. That link also appears to be seen even more so when the person doing the talking is African American.

I would talk different to Black people that I know based upon how they choose to speak. So if I'm talking to a Black person that I know who typically uses Black English Vernacular, say like my sister, I can try to accommodate 'em to an extent, but I don't have a full blown Black English Vernacular.

I've tried to make a connection between the way I talk and the way I write. I've tried to write more like I would talk. Not necessarily the way I would talk in like a casual conversation, but try sometimes not to make my writing as stilted, depending upon what I'm writing. Sometimes I write and I try to be sort of this professional scholar writing and using the jargon and stuff like that, but there are always going to be places I think in my writing where I'm gonna try to sound as natural as I want to be even within the context of a scholarly piece.

Given my beliefs about language and knowing what I know about the way people speak, and the way some people think about how others speak, I talk the way I naturally do because the more that I read and the more that I think about it, the more that I get angry. I feel the injustice of judging people on the way that they speak and just trying to judge their intelligence, their abilities. It bothers me and I think that's why I make a conscious effort to not use standard English a lot more now than I did say four years ago. I don't think that I consistently talk the same now than I did four years ago. I read some stuff where there are people who are talking about Black kids having to speak standard English. I have a problem with that; why do Blacks have to speak standard English? They're not gonna learn it for one if they don't want to know it and I think that points to a problem that I mentioned earlier with education.

I make a conscious effort to talk however I choose to talk. For this interview I'm probably talking more standard than I maybe would over the course of the day. I know that during the course of the summer when I was doing those DS1 set of tapes, that I was choosing to try to use as much Black English Vernacular as was possible for me. When I listened to those tapes I don't like the quality of my voice. But when I listen to those tapes, I heard that I'm doing that and it almost sounds phony to me because I know I don't really talk that way on a regular basis. I talk much more like I'm talking now than I did on those tapes. I know that I was making conscious efforts in particular cases to do that. Like when I went to my mom's job and would talk to people there, that I was making a conscious effort to talk. . . . My mom didn't say anything about it so I guess for her it was normal because my Mom makes comments about my speech and so do some other people I think in my family make comments about my speech being this proper speech, "Oh she's all proper on us," or something like that. I guess I can't deny that I talk differently to my parents or people in my family than I do to other people outside of my family because they certainly notice a difference when I'm talking one way than when I'm talking another. Because I remember there was an instance where this was maybe a couple of years ago, or maybe last year when I may have been talking to them and you may have come into the room, and then they'll say, "Oh look at her talking all proper now," or something like that. So I know my parents or people in my family have made comments about my language. So they must notice a distinction between the two, but they don't say *something like that. They wouldn't have said something like that like after graduation when I was talking to my professors; they wouldn't have said anything like that. Because one, they're also trying to approximate this concept of standard English that they had while they're talking to them. So they would have known what was the situation what was going on and that I wasn't making a switch, that that's just pretty much the way that I talk and they know that that's how I probably talk when I'm not with them.*

LITERACY: *A Purpose of My Own*

Literacy is multidimensional, it is a social construction, and it's more than just reading and writing. Critical thinking is important. I think it can be transforming. It is an individual's way of expression, comprehension, valuing, understanding, contributing, and being. Being literate is important. I can say that because I don't see it as merely reading and writing. If I can use my definition I say it is very important, regardless of culture. If you say literacy is reading and writing then I say no. You also exclude a lot when you use such a narrow, prescriptive/biased definition.

Being able to read is important to me and my life. Since I've been in graduate school, I've learned to appreciate reading more even though I am still confused/shaky about literacy—that is the development, teaching, etc. I guess it's important for me because I read for a purpose of my own. I don't do much reading that I don't want to do. That seems important. So, I have a desire to read and to learn. I would venture to say that not a day goes by that I don't read something.

I'm a slow reader. It's as if I have to read and soak in every word. I'm getting better at skimming, not reading every word, probably because I realize more and more how short time is. Sometimes I read for reading without getting any of what I read. That's when I'm not critically reading and my eyes are just moving across the page. I've gotten better at critically reading, but I do sometimes still read for reading. When I read for myself and it's interesting, I understand what I'm reading. I enjoy reading what I choose and sometimes what I don't. I have learned to appreciate reading and what it can do for me—and others.

I think being able to read means you are able to actually say and understand the words that you come across on a page or whatever, some sort of written text. That you're able to read it, comprehend it and critically think about it. My mom can read the words on a page, my dad can read the words on a page, they can pretty much read the words on a page, but I don't know if that's reading if you have a problem with understanding. So I think reading has to entail, not only being able to read the text, but also being able to understand the text.

A good reader is a reader who can read the words, who understands the words and then who can take that a step further and sort of try to integrate what's been read with the experiences that they've had, with what they've seen, with what they do, who they are—sort of incorporate that into their entire being, and that becomes a part of them. I think that's what good readers do. I think a good reader is the one who actually gets something out of the reading or can take something from that and move on and try to take that a step further. A poor reader is one who can't do that. A poor reader is one who either can't read the words on the page, who doesn't understand what they've read or who isn't able to move beyond just what's written on the page, or sort of think about what's written on the page, or whatever the text is.

I think some of the reasons for the difference between a good reader and a poor reader can be approaches that people take towards their concept of reading, that their teachers may take towards their concept of what reading is. I don't think it's necessarily a genetic thing unless you have some problem with your brain. But I think certainly the culture you come from has a lot to do with it because how that culture values it is important. Because if the culture, the environment that you come from doesn't value it, then you're gonna run into a problem when you go into the school situations, that's gonna be a conflict with the school and the teacher.

Put that aside, the teacher has a lot to do with it because teachers have different views about reading, what good reading is. You might have one teacher who deals with someone and says she's a good reader she just doesn't understand. Well for me that means she's not a good reader. The individual obviously has a lot to say about that because regardless of the culture that you come from and the teachers, it's gonna come down to your individual responsibility. What do you take responsibility for, what is it that you want. And I know that's a lot to say to someone who's four, five, six, seven, eight, nine, ten years old, but at some point the responsibility is gonna fall upon them. Through those years they need a lot of support from the environment, the parents, the culture and the school and somehow they need to sort of get some sort of consensus on what they want.

Being able to write is important to me and my life. I've learned to value *writing. I see the possibilities I have with writing. I didn't realize this until graduate school. I wrote a conversation (paper) about it in a class. I can express my thoughts and feelings—which I found is therapeutic in some ways; I can make a difference when writing a paper for class or an article for a conference; and it provides me with voice. I don't have to be silenced or silent as long as I can read and write.*

I think I have the potential to be a good writer. I think about creative writing sometimes. Writing is difficult to start—and finish sometimes—when it's an article or essay. I find I like to quote other people more than I should but I am usually genuinely interested in their words. I don't think I have a monopoly on ideas or expressing myself. Maybe it points to something about me—that is that I like to quote—but I do sometimes get enamored almost by some of the quotes I use. I enjoy personal writing and I enjoy my finished products, but the process is excruciating.

Being able to write means physically being able to put pen to paper and do that or fingers to keyboard or whatever. Being able to construct I guess, that's what being able to write is. Your ability to create a text.

A good writer is the one who's actually constructing and creating and not like copying or rehashing. A poor writer would be the one who a teacher asks a question and they give them this sort of typical response, it's almost a reflex response. It doesn't require much thought at all. I think a good writer is someone who definitely shows some thought in their writing. I mean something creative, some thought that reflects who they are because I think if you're a good writer, someone picks up your work and is able to actually make certain judgments or whatever about you based upon your writing. A good writer, in the writing, gives clues about who they are because that becomes inseparable I think from their writing to some extent. I think a poor writer is one who the creativity is not there, they're just going through the motions of writing because someone asked them to do it. There's just really nothing reflective about the writing at all. There's nothing really that they have to construct—creatively construct. It's just something that's just being put down on a page because someone said I want you to put this down on the page. They may as well've dictated it to them.

I think what you have to say sort of beats how you say it. It is important that people understand what you have to say, but it first starts off with you being able to understand it. I just think it's important what you write, what you have to say and with some help, some people can work

*through getting it written in a particular way to communicate that with
other [people]. I think if you don't have the ideas then you don't have anything really to write down.*

*The process you go through to get the stuff down on paper is more
important than what ends up on the paper though I think the process is
linked to the product. I think the process that you go through is important.
That goes back to what I said about what a good writer is. And a good
writer, one thing I mentioned is that's the person who creates and con-
structs and if you're creating and constructing, you're going through
a process. There's something that you're thinking about because that's
what you're building on, you're building stuff in your mind. If you've gone
through this whole process, the product in some way is gonna reflect that
obviously. I remember those days in school where the product was my trying to sort of reword what I got from Encyclopedia Britannica or something
like that. The only process really involved in that was getting the encyclopedia and then how can I figure out whether this is plagiarized, but it's
pretty much what the teacher would want to hear. I certainly wouldn't say
that's good writing. It might be creative writing to some extent, but I don't
think it's certainly good writing because it wasn't a creating and constructing process that was going on. It wasn't me going to something, reading
it, and reading other things along with that and trying to construct in my
mind what this actually was and how does this actually relate to me and
what can I do with that and sort of expand on that.*

*Your ideas are important and that supercedes what it looks like on the
paper. What you went through to write it on the paper is primary. If I say
process is most important, that doesn't mean that the product isn't important that just says that I'm putting one above the other in rankings. The
product obviously is important because that's the actual communicative
part. That's the part that someone picks up and reads and that's all
they're gonna see. They may not necessarily know the process that
you've gone through to write that. So they're basing their judgment
on you on that particular product. The process that you went through is
important. Though someone who picks up your paper to read doesn't
know what process you went through, that process is very important
nonetheless if you intend to continue to write. They may only see that
one product but you may have many more products and whether they
see what you went through or go through to get there, you DO need a
way to get there.*

GOALS AND POSSIBLE SELVES: *I Want to Be a Teacher*

*I dreamed of becoming a teacher when I was young. I was always gonna
be a teacher. I mean there was nothing else in my mind except being a
teacher. I would have play school in my garage or something like that. I'd
bring out my little workbooks and stuff and make up lessons and stuff like
that. I even remember when I was in junior high school in my biology
class. The teacher allowed me to make up an exam for the class and that
was my crowning achievement. And I was like, "Oh wow, I can make up
this test for the class," and it was a really bad test that I made up. Cause I
was trying to make it be this really hard test and I'd have these fill-in-the-
blanks that would take a word from the book and I'd write out the sentence and take out one word from the book that they should've had or
something like that. So it was a really bad test and I don't think she used
it but that was kind of typical of the relationship that I would have with
teachers in school and I'm not quite sure why.*

*But I always wanted to be a teacher. I don't know. I'm not sure. I cer-
tainly wasn't thinking of money and I certainly wasn't thinking of vaca-
tions off, I don't believe. It was just I wanted to teach. And I guess my concept of that was you had a classroom and you had students and you went
in and you told them about some particular subject that whatever it is
that you taught, and you gave tests and you know just what I saw as a
elementary student whatever. That's what I saw for teaching—you had
this interaction in class. Maybe because I loved elementary school. At least
I loved Longfellow. When I was at Longfellow, those were probably the best
years of my educational life through elementary and secondary school. But
that's the only thing that I can ever remember saying that's what I wanta
be. I want to be a teacher.*

*Unfortunately, by the time I was actually going to college, I was really
being discouraged from doing that by my parents or by other people. I
was struggling with this doing what other people are telling you to do and
doing what I really wanted to do. And I said I'm gonna go into Speech
Pathology, which sort of fell in with my language thing and I went through
all of these different phases, still struggling with this concept of teaching,
but I mean in the end I still said, that's what I wanna be. That's what I
always wanted to be and I couldn't really think of anything else and
despite my mother continually telling me throughout the course of my
life that I wouldn't be a good teacher for various reasons.*

THE ANALYSES
Surreality[1]

*You educated and I'm not. I'm not up to the stan-
dard that you are. I know I'm way beneath you.
But it doesn't worry me. Things like that doesn't
worry me, see. I'm just knowing you more educated than me. I got more wisdom than you now.
When it comes down to wisdom, I got that old wisdom. I can think deep and look deep at a person.
You know what I'm saying? You don't have as
much wisdom. I'm pretty sure. You have wisdom,
but not like me.* —Maya's interview

Part Two

*I think your language and literacy and writing, you
know, all that stuff, I think it's great compared to
mines. It's no comparison. There is no comparison.*
—Grace's interview

*I think you are understanding English language
more than I do. I think your grammar is more correct. I kinda put you in the same boat in many
ways that I do Jackie. Even though with you it's
easier for me to talk. I don't feel as pressured with
you. You don't correct me as much—but you don't
have to correct me as much. I'll say wrong stuff
around you and you don't think anything of it
really. I'll say something that's really, you know,
grossly incorrect and I just don't think about it.
Reading and writing. Oh you write—oh my goodness. To me when you were what thirteen, you
were writing like somebody in college as far as I
was concerned. You were thirteen your writing was
tremendously advanced from my perception. I've
read your writing. I've perceived your writing to be
more advanced than mine. It's more like a book;
like a textbook or something. I don't consider my
writing to be textbook writing.* —Reia's interview

*Oh, totally totally different. Totally different. I
mean I couldn't even compare myself to your language and writing and stuff because I'm not on
the level that you're on. I guess I can say you were
interested in your writing and your language and
how you felt and I wasn't because no one taught
me anything. You had someone in school to really
push you. I didn't have anybody to push me. I
didn't get that part. So you and I are just—when
it comes to that literacy or anything—we are
totally the opposite. In that way, you know more
than me. I mean I could know more than you in
some other ways, but in that way we're just totally
different.* —Deidra's interview

*In considering Maya's actual writing abilities,
there's no comparison. Grace and Deidra are
ahead of her in that respect simply because Maya
has a hard time writing. However, in terms of
speech I would put Maya ahead of Deidra though
maybe not ahead of Grace. In reference to language I would put it as me, Reia, Grace, Maya,
and Deidra. In the whole scheme of language and
uses of literacy I would put it as me, Reia, Grace,
Deidra, and then Maya.* —Sonja's interview

The narratives . . . that kept me company, along
with the living, breathing people in my life,
were those that talked honestly about growing
up black in America. They burst into my silence,
and in my head, they shouted and chattered
and whispered and sang together. I am writing
. . . to become part of that unruly conversation,
and to bring my experience back to the community of minds that made it possible.
—Lorene Cary, in Johnson, *Proud Sisters*

MAYA
I'm Comfortable Like I Am

I make my own decisions and couldn't imagine anyone else doing
that, because I'm in control of my own destiny. And if anything
happens, or if a mistake is ever made, it's because it's something I
chose to do.   Janet Jackson, in Johnson, *Proud Sisters*

● ● ●

Doing What I Got To Do

Maya really does appear to be quite comfortable with her life, both past
and present. Although she would like some things about her life to have
been different, she does not mourn lost possible selves or what might
have been. She is quite practical about her life and what was and is still
possible for her. In response to various questions about her goals,[1] she is
brief but consistent. She says she expects or desires to (be/have):

doing my housework, doing what I got to do
[in good] *health*
stronger mind
going to church
going to nursing home to pray for others
take a vacation with John

She is certainly modest in her goals, which can be characterized as Personal Well-Being (i.e., *doing my housework, doing what I got to do,* [in
good] *health, stronger mind*), Social Helping (i.e., *going to nursing home to
pray for others*), and Travel and Adventure (i.e., *take a vacation with John*)
goals. Although these goals are not rank-ordered by Maya, I would venture to say that her religious goal (i.e., *going to church*) is of great importance to her since religious goals consistently occurred as goals and because she is a fundamentalist Christian.

Her statement *"I'm comfortable like I am"* and her age may indicate
why her list of goals is so short. When talking about possible selves, she

was quite willing to engage the likelihood of being or realizing various language and literacy possible selves, but she did not expect to actualize the possible selves that did not already describe her. Where she is now is where she thinks she will be in the future with respect to her language and literacy possible selves.[2]

Her responses to the questions on the Possible Selves Inventory[3] about reading, writing, and literacy accurately reflect her narrative. She describes her present reading and writing abilities as poor, but she sees reading as more important to her present and future life than is writing. As long as she is able to read the Bible, participate in her religious activities with her present abilities, and use the telephone, she does not see a need for writing. However, she does view both reading and literacy as desirable but unlikely possible selves. It appears she sees little possibility of improving her reading, writing, and literacy, but she can at least maintain them in the future, and she wants to. Still, her third-grade education has gotten her far and she is able to read at a level she is comfortable with.

Maya's view of her language possible selves also corresponded with her narrative and the other information I collected from her (such as her interview). She was quite candid about her language abilities and possibilities. She wants to speak "standard" English but she does not see very much likelihood that she will ever speak it. She believes she speaks both African American English and "bad" English and that she will continue to do so. Since she thinks she speaks both and she is often unclear when responding to questions about definitions for African American English and "standard" English, it may not be a stretch to say that she believes the two are the same (as do many people) even though they are not, but it is still likely that she does not equate the two. She believes she speaks African American English, but she does not find that to be particularly problematic as a possible self. In considering her African American English and "standard" English possible selves together, Maya indicates more of an affiliation with African American English than with "standard" English even though she would like to be able to speak "standard" English. Nevertheless, she chooses to maintain her identity with African American English, or at least accepts that as what she speaks and what she will continue to speak because she is not going to make any changes now.

She does not hold her speech in high regard compared to her perception of "standard" English as the benchmark for American English, but she is quite unflappable in her resolve that over the course of her life she has done all she can under the circumstances and that that is all she can do or expect unless someone or something intervenes to make those hoped-for possible selves probable. In any event, she is able to do what needs to be done in her life through her own knowledge and with a little help from her family.

Maya does not mourn what might have been, nor does she dream about it. Her language and literacy possible selves are things she values in the overall scheme of interpersonal communication and insight, but they are not goals she is committed to achieving. Her narrative and data reflect where possible selves and goals "are different and separable from the current or now selves, yet are intimately connected." Her reason for not having them as goals appears to be quite practical in her mind: *"But now since I got this old and everything, I don't worry about that. I wouldn't worry about that at all."* But is this really true?

SPEAK TO ME

Since Maya was unable to adequately comprehend the instruments that required a lot of reading and writing, I have ample speech data from the tape recordings of her responses for those instruments. However, she had the least amount of speech data used for analysis because of her formal speech data (i.e., the interview talk speech sample). Her interview took the least amount of time to complete (approximately 82 minutes on a 90-minute audio tape). The first 45-minute segment for Maya went up to the beginning of the second handout (i.e., the reading passages) for the interview. That portion of the interview for everyone consisted of less speech because they were simply stating their level of agreement or disagreement with the ideology statements using a 7-point scale. In other words, there was little extended discourse by any participant during that time in the interview.

Of the 33 pages of her Interview Talk (INT) speech sample transcript,[4] only 16 (less than half) consisted of her talk alone (i.e., not including my speech as the interviewer). Of the 11,798 words total for the INT speech sample, only 5,467 were Maya's alone (again, less than half). Still, that produced approximately 39 minutes of speech for Maya's INT speech sample out of 82 minutes for the entire interview—a quantity adequate for analysis.

For the first 30 pages of her informal speech data transcript, the Kitchen Talk (KT) speech sample, only 14 pages (again less than half), for a total of 3,802 words, consisted of her talk alone (i.e., not including transcriptions of anyone else's speech from the audio tape). As such, I included additional KT speech for Maya and, subsequently, everyone else beyond my initial goal of using only one side of a 90-minute audio tape for analysis. Combined, Maya has 35 pages (16 for INT and 19 for KT) of speech consisting of 10,203 words (5,467 for INT and 4,736 for KT) used for analysis. Hence, her speech comprised less than half of the transcript for both her INT and KT speech samples but she does have at least 30 minutes of speech for her KT speech sample (as do all the participants). Nevertheless, her speech data overall is fairly comparable to that of the other participants.

Because I had more opportunities to record Maya, my triangulation of her data is largely based on what she said rather than what she wrote. As such, there were times when I had to ask her similar questions to which I would get similar responses. At various times throughout the recordings, almost to the point of being a refrain, she comments, "*I don't let it worry me.*" That statement typifies her attitude concerning the issues addressed in the study, but is it an accurate perception given her practices? Does context really matter so little to her at this point in her life?

In a comparison of her KT with her INT, we see that the informality of the one compared to the formality of the other does influence how she chooses to speak with respect to the phonological and syntactic features analyzed. Of the 18 African American English features I charted, Maya's speech contained 17 of the 18 in the KT sample and all 18 in the INT sample. So, the African American English linguistic features follow an expected pattern: there are more African American English features present in the KT sample compared to the INT sample.

Maya's use of African American English phonological, morphological, and syntactic features in her INT speech sample context is significantly different from that in her KT speech sample context.[5] So, it would appear that Maya is concerned about and conscious of her speech, even when she is familiar with the interlocutors and they are African American.

Maya is able to speak more like her notion of "standard" English than she believes, and she is more likely to exhibit that "unexpected" behavior in more formal situations for the African American English features charted. Overall, she used African American English linguistic features 32% of the time (329/1,028) during her INT speech sample and 57% of the time (647/1,139) during her KT speech sample.[6] That is the second-highest combined increase in usage (i.e., 25%) of all the participants. I guess she still does care—at least a little.

Though Maya produced very little writing (only 127 words)—the least amount of any participant—she provided enough for a brief analysis. Her letter was her only written data. Based upon Mina Shaughnessy's five levels of punctuation, with 1 being the lowest level and 5 being the highest level, her punctuation is definitely at level 1.[7] Although her punctuation was problematic, I could understand what she wrote. She did have at least one indentation for a paragraph. She mostly used periods and capitalization inappropriately. There were a couple of instances where I did not know what the punctuation mark was though I was fairly sure it was a mark of punctuation. In one case, it appears she might have even used a dash, which would be interesting.

Her writing included two African American English linguistic features—for example, *"bone"* instead of "born" and *"I stop going . . ."* (i.e., no past tense marker)—along with several misspellings (e.g., *"maried"* instead of "married" and *"rocing"* instead of "raising"). However, her short composition was remarkably well organized given her educational background.

She seemed to write with difficulty, as evidenced by the jagged appearance of her characters. The act of writing, both physically and mentally, might have been a little difficult for her. When she did not know how to spell a word (e.g., *"favoret"* instead of "favorite"), she usually seemed to rely on how she said the word.

Maya's lack of writing samples was a good example of her writing practices, or at least the lack thereof. She had no writing samples aside from the letter I requested of everyone. It is true that on most occasions she has had other people write out her checks and other items of importance, such as letters, when needed. She has written checks at the grocery store (though she often has had the cashier do it) and brief notes when at church or when studying the Bible.

Maya is able to read and write. She demonstrated she could write with her letter. She also demonstrated she could read during the interview section that requested her to do so. I found it interesting and worth noting that she understood the passage from linguist John Baugh's article

"Language and Race" the best, possibly because it was depicted partly in African American English:

J: O. K., so what happened?

DJ: Oh, yeah, now, check it out. I'm riding down the street, all right? I got me a blue Monza, and my lady by my side. We pull up to a stop sign, you know, and I stop. Y'know? I look both ways and then I starts to go. Well, midway up the next block, up slides this policeman who tells me, "Pull over!" Y'know, like, he pulls up along side me and then parks his bike in front of my car.

J: Uh huh.

DJ: So, he gets off the ol' bike and starts walkin' back to my car, and I'm sayin' to myself, "Why me?" So, he tell me, "You ran the stop sign back there and your brake light's out." I said, "I ain't run the stop sign," and he said, "You ran it!" So he take my license and proceeds to start writin' up this ticket when it dawns on me what's happenin'. I said, "Well, wait a minute man; if I didn't stop at the stop sign and you came from 'round the corner, then you've never seen the back of my car; you pulled in front of me. So how can you tell me my brake light is out 'less I stepped on the brake for the stop sign?" (Imitating the officer's voice) "Well, you just a smart [@#$!] ain't ya kid?"

Below is Maya's reading of the passage (brackets, [ ], indicate overlapping speech, usually me pronouncing a word Maya is having trouble reading; <x> indicates unintelligible speech):

Maya: *Ok. So what happened. Oh, oh, oh yes now check it out. I am reading down the—I am driving down—no riding down the street, alright. I got me a blue* [Monza] *Monza—that's a car?* [yeah] *and my lady by my side. Ok we pull up to a stop sign, you know and I stop. Now that—that 'y'* [that's like an abbreviation for you know, it's like saying y'know] *Ok and I stopped you know. I looked both ways and then I started to go. Well uh, midway up the next block, up slides this uh, policeman who tells me "pullover" . . . Now you say what this word is again?* [y'know] *y'know, like the like he pulls up alongside me and then parks his bike in front of me—in front of my car. Ok.* [That's just "uh huh"] *That's just "uh huh."*

Sonja: That—that—that word—those two words I mean are "uh huh."

Maya: *Uh huh. So he gets uh—he gets off the o—*[ole, you know like you say] *ole bike and starts walking back to my car and I'm saying to myself why me? So he tells me—he tell me you can—you are the—you are the stop sign back* [no you ran the stop sign] *ok he say you ran—ok, you ran the stop sign back there and your brakes lights up, I said I'm—I—I'm running, a-i-n-t—I ain't running the stop sign. And he said you ran it. So he take my license—so he take my license plate uh proceeds—that he take my license and proceeds to start writing up this ticket when it dawns on me what's happening. I said well wait a minute, man. If I done—if I didn't stop at the stop sign and you came from round the corner, then you—then you never seen the back—the back of my car. You pulled in front of me so how can you tell me my brakes light is out unless I stopped on the—stepped on the brake s-t-e-p-p-e-d—stepped on the brake. So he pulled in front of him @ so <x> <x> alright now. If you out in front of me now ok, how can you tell—wait a minute there—how can I stepped on the brakes ok for the stop sign, that's the last one.*

Sonja: Umm hmm. So what do you think he's saying.

Maya: *I'm—that I am imitating the officer's voice, ok. Well you just a smart* [that was a curse word that you <x>] *or ain't related anyway so I ain't gon say that.*

She did, however, have difficulty understanding the reading passages that were not in African American English, such as the one below by Ruth Finnegan:

Some would interpret this literacy myth not just as a misleading and incomplete picture but a smoke screen masking past and present inequalities. The myth can be seen as playing an essential ideological function for the governing social, political or educational order, whether the earlier imperial expansion or current national or international inequalities: so when people might want, say, houses or jobs or economic reform they are instead given literacy programs, even blamed for their own poverty which the dominant myth can present as the result not of social inequalities but of their illiteracy. This may be an extreme view, more applicable in some cases than in others—but it may indeed have some grain of truth.

Here is Maya's reading of the Finnegan passage:

That is—that's a question to ask 'im, if he on the side of 'im, how @ how he could knew that, he didn't step on his brake. Ok. Well this uh starting now, I don't need—I just say. [some] *Some would interpreted this* [literacy] *litershry moth—that's moth?* [myth] *myth not just as a—just not just as a misleading and incomplete picture, but a smoke screen mistaken* [masking] *masking* [like hiding] *yeah masking, p-a-s-t paste* [past] *past* [it would be paste if there was an 'e'] *ok but a smoking screen mask past and a person* [present] *and a present in* [inequalities, unequal] *inqualities unequal. The moth, is that moth?* [myth] *The myth can be seen as plainly—that's p-l-a-y-i-n-g, playning* [playing] *playing an essential* [mmm hmm . . .] *oh that's right we talked about that one—*[ideological] *inealogical* [ideological] *ideol* [ideo] *ideo* [logical] *logical, ok, function for the—for the governing society* [social] *for the governing social, political or—or educational order* [umm hmm]. *Whether the earlier* [imperial] *imperial extinct—exponsion or something?* [expansion] *expansion* [like getting bigger] *expansion or current national or international* [umm hmm] *and equalizing?* [inequalities] *inequalities so when people might want—when people might want say houses or jobs or economics reform, they are in—instant given* [instead] *instead given literatures* [literacy] *literashry* [lit-er-a-cy] *liter-acy programs. Even blamed for their own poverty* [umm hmm] *which the d-o-m-i-n-a-n-t d- dom . . .* [dominant] *dominick dominick moth* [myth] *myth can present as the result. Not all society* [social] *social in- uh inqualities* [oh yeah you got it that time] *ok, social inqualities but of their liter—literature* [illiteracy] *literace* [no this one is ILLiteracy, you got a 'il' there] *@ illiterastry—I can't say that too good. @ I mean uh, illiter—I can't say that period. This may be an @—this may be an uh e-x-t-r-e extreme view more uh, more I know what that is, applicator?* [applicable] *applicalel* [appli-ca-ble] *app-pli-ca-ble* [mmm hmm] *in some cases than in others. But it may indeed have some grain of truth.*

She has much more trouble reading the latter passage than the former one. She likened the Baugh passage to her own speech while at the same time she commented that the speech in the passage was *"not too good."* (Hmmm, maybe those dialect readers of the 1970s were not such a bad idea after all, as suggested by linguist John Rickford and educator Angela

Rickford.) Though I do not think the reading passages I selected could necessarily determine one's state of literacy, Maya did not understand most of them after having read them herself and after I reread them to her.

WHAT TO BELIEVE

During the interview, I asked each participant to respond to 30 statements based on the three ideologies I had delineated for language (namely "standard" English) and literacy: 8 statements for the Ideology of Opportunity, 15 for the Ideology of Progress, and 7 for the Ideology of Emancipation (see note 2 of the introduction for a list of the statements). On a scale of 1 (strongly disagree) to 7 (strongly agree), Maya's average score for each ideology was 6.3 or higher. Maya not only strongly believes in each ideology but also in each individual statement used for the ideologies with very little divergence (her lowest score for any particular statement was 6).

It is no surprise that Maya strongly believed in these ideologies at the time of the study based upon her narrative and her sociocultural and historical contexts. Maya came of age during a time when most Americans espoused the Protestant work ethic. As seen in Maya's narrative, effort and hard work were how one achieved success or at least was able to have a decent life. Maya believed in hard work because she believed that was how she could earn money and take care of herself. You may recall I mentioned that Maya was mistreated by her brother's wife, with whom she lived after her parents died. Although Maya did not discuss her background in very much detail, that was not the only mistreatment or abuse she saw in her life. Maya still will not discuss the things that happened to her as an adolescent and young adult. I can only imagine what happened to a child who had no real home and moved from one relative to another searching for a place to call home and someone like parents to love her. I will not speculate about her circumstances or situation or share what she chose not to share. Suffice it to say that, as was common during her youth, most people did not finish high school, much less go to college, Black or White. A high school diploma in those days was equivalent to a college degree in many ways. So it is no surprise that Maya and most of the people in her life did not finish grammar school. The economy of the South was still more agricultural and service oriented. As Reia indicates in her narrative,

A hundred years ago maybe people didn't [need to know how to read]. *Even though I think reading's always been important, but the world was nothing like it is now. Maybe there wasn't as much of a need for it to function smoothly because of the way it was then. It was a lotta farming and stuff like that and people had gravel roads, they didn't have any cars—cars had just started coming out. But it's* [important] *especially now because of the world we live in. I mean you need to know how to read and write. You need to know how to add and sub-tract and stuff like that. And I think it does help your self-esteem.*

In order to be able to account for why Maya strongly identified with the Ideology of Opportunity, I had to recognize not only the environment of her life but also the context of the times she lived through. Maya was born in 1920. She grew up between World Wars I and II. She lived through the Great Depression and the Great Migration early in her life. Her adulthood was in full bloom during the 1950s. However, she also lived through the 1960s and Civil Rights (I still remember my mom telling me stories of how they boycotted riding the bus) and the 1970s era of "peace" and "equality." She lived through the Reagan and Bush years. She has lived through multiple times and generations, and she could not be the same person now who she was then, because she has seen too much.

I would venture to say that fifty or even forty years ago, Maya did not believe in the Ideology of Opportunity or even the Ideology of Progress with respect to language, education, or literacy, but did do so with respect to hard work. But the ideologies for America have changed over the decades, and so has Maya. Nowadays we are told that life chances for success greatly diminish without a college degree, and in some cases a graduate degree. The times, they are a-changing.

The changes in Maya are made evident by the differing narratives of Grace and Reia with respect to their views about their mom. As Grace said, *"See, school was not important to Maya. That was just a state law to her, so we had to go. Maya felt if you could cook and clean that was your B.A. and B.S. degree. She felt when you got married that was your Master's degree"*—because that was Maya's Ideology of Opportunity and Ideology of Progress and possibly her Ideology of Emancipation. That was in the 1950s and 1960s. For the 1970s, Reia writes, *"I do not remember my mother "preaching" education in the home, but she seemed to have shown interests in various ways; providing story books, school materials and Bible readings."* During the 1970s Maya accepted Jesus Christ as her personal

Lord and Savior. The Bible became her textbook, and she shared that with her remaining four children at home. *"Once a week we had Bible Study Hour together as a family where we read passages from the Bible . . . Maya once enrolled in an adult education program to further her 3rd-grade education. She discontinued the program due to financial pressures at home."* But Reia goes on to end her education narrative by saying:

> *I guess the only thing I would change* [about my education], *I probably should've been more proud of the achievements that I had in high school. At the time, I just didn't make a big deal out of it. Like when I was on the honor roll. I was the only Black student on the honor roll in I think it was the ninth grade. Or was it the tenth grade? One of those grades. But I was the only Black student outta the whole school for the ninth grade or whatever grade I was in (I think I was in the ninth grade) who was on the honor roll. And Maya should've been there but I didn't make no real big deal out of it. It was like, "Well, she's gotta work. Well if she could be there she could be there. It ain't no big thing." And I remember my art teacher telling me. She said, "That is really important." She helped me to see the significance and the seriousness of it. And she said, "Your mom should've been there." But I just didn't make a real big thing out of it cause they had a program and stuff. But then too I guess that falls back on Maya as well. I mean that was an honor and I'm sure there was a letter or something that came up where she was invited or what have you. But it's like because I didn't pressure her to come, because I didn't really strongly encourage her to come, I guess she figure, "Well, it doesn't seem to be all that big deal to her."*

Reia assumes that Maya could read the note if one did come home about the program, but she also assumes that education did or at least should have meant more to Maya than it appeared to at that time. I believe that it was not until Maya saw what education did for Felicia that she realized the possible value of education. I do not think anyone realized the significance of that event in Maya's life. Maya, for the first time, had a child who not only was going to finish high school on time with a high school diploma but also, because of good grades, was going to go to college, and with a full scholarship. Felicia got her bachelor's degree—the first in our family. Maya saw the difference an education could make and she finally, as indicated in her narrative, realized the importance of education: *"I think everybody should* [go to college], *but I know everybody don't want to. I think they should get an education, everybody, if they can. Just like I say, I wish I had got a education—good education. But I don't have it and I don't let it just worry me so."*

Despite her strong belief in each ideology, it would seem, at least from her point of view, that the three ideologies are not mutually exclusive. Apparently she can believe in all three but not necessarily without contradiction. In the Possible Selves Inventory, her responses to "In order to succeed in this country, I (like everyone else) must speak standard, or 'good,' English" and "In order to succeed in this country, I (like everyone else) must be literate" were "slightly disagree" and "strongly agree," respectively. This points either to a contradiction or to her distinction between literacy and language ideologies. In either case, there might be something different for her about the power of language and the power of literacy. If so, they might have different effects on her. She responded with "neither agree nor disagree" and "strongly disagree" to "I feel I do not have much to be proud of because of my language and literacy" and "I sometimes don't like myself that much because of my language and literacy," respectively. The different responses support her position that she might not be at the level of language and uses of literacy she would like. Although language and literacy are important to her and have meaning, they are not end-alls. Goals and possible selves cannot be overlooked in this case.

Maya has a positive self-image overall, as demonstrated by an average well above 6 (strongly agree) for the positive statements in the last section of the Possible Selves Inventory (e.g., "I like most things about myself" and "I am happy the way I am") and averages above 5 for the positive possible selves (e.g., "self-confident" and "motivated"). In other words, she was positive at the time and planned to continue to be positive about herself despite the negative outlook for her language and literacy. She defined herself by more than her language and literacy abilities. She might not be proud of her language and literacy inabilities, but she believed she had much to offer and much to do for others. As she said in her narrative, *"I'm important to somebody. A lot of people I'm important to. Now I might not be important* [to everybody, but] *I don't think any of us is important to everybody."* From all other accounts, Maya was looking forward, not back, to all the goodness that awaited her for all the people who cared about her and for the many she cared for. I'd say that's pretty important.

A surprising aspect of Maya's narrative is that she believes more in the effects of the ideologies and education than in the effects of race and gender on her life. Despite the time in which she grew up, the environment of her childhood and young adulthood, she can see how education might have been a way to success despite the entrenched institutional racism of her time—*"I coulda had a better job and I'da been a educated person. I really and truly in the past just wished I went on through and got an education. Cause I could get better jobs"*—a way to make your dreams come true—*"I dreamed a lot of things when I was young. But the education is the one that kinda hemmed up some of my dreams"*—(that *is* the Ideology of Opportunity). "[I don't think that because I was Black or because I was a woman that that affected my education.] *Like I say, I just stop going to school. It's just the individual."* I believe there may have been some revisionist history going on or some unreflective thinking (or remembering) since Maya also says:

> I guess it was something about my parents dying. See I probably would have been more educated and everything else if they woulda lived. I was staying from here to yonder. I would stay with one a while and the other'n a while. And well my mind just got off a school and I just went on to work. Course they didn't make me go to work, but the other girls was working, my brother's wife nieces . . . and they didn't put any pressure on me to go to school, get your education. But I wasn't nothing but a kid and so it didn't make me no difference. That's the way I was thinking. See I didn't know the value then. And so that's how that was.

She didn't know the value then, and neither did anyone else in her world.

This might also mean that Maya defined success in a way different from what I might have, and it points to something Grace has said about Maya on more than one occasion: No matter how difficult the situation, how hard the times, Maya always held her head high. So, even though racism and sexism were prominent in her day, they did not control her destiny—she did. She alone was ultimately responsible for any and all decisions she made and she would live with those decisions for good or ill because what else was there to do—blame someone else? No. Accept what you cannot change, and move on.

A belief in the importance of education did not become part of Maya's psyche until she was in her fifties, with her second group of children. But her lack of education affected the quality of her tutoring and made an early end to the help she could offer her children: *"I remember helping them when they was in the lower grades. But now when they got up to like fifth grade or something, like that, I couldn't help 'em. I help them as far as I knew."* Maya did the best she could with what she had. Her situation is a good example of the problem with relying on parents to tutor their children. Not all parents can do the school's job. If a child has a problem learning at school, schools expect parents to pay for tutoring or to provide extra help at home. But what happens when the parents do not have the money to pay for tutoring or the education themselves necessary to help their children? Even if the majority of parents can afford the extra help or provide it themselves, what about the minority?

Maya did the best she could and the best she knew how to do given her sociocultural and historical contexts. The result was having only three of eight children earn a high school diploma (not counting a GED) and higher. The others dropped out of school or earned a GED later. In "Applying Linguistic Knowledge of African American English to Help Students Learn and Teachers Teach," linguistic educator John Baugh indicates that collaborative cooperation among adult educational advocates (e.g., parents or guardians), professional educators (e.g., administrators, teachers, and staff members), and students is needed in any successful educational enterprise. However, in Maya's case, she could not bear her role for financial and educational reasons which, in the end, had differing effects on her children. According to current standards, the system did not work for Maya, but given the environment of her times and her steadfast belief in the power of one, it is not surprising to see she surpassed her third-grade education and accepted her life and her choices for what they were and not for what they could have been: *"You gotta work at anything for to get anything good. You gotta put some effort forth if you want whatever it is. That's right. . . . It's in a person mind what they really wants in life and they go for it . . . this is up to the individual."*

GRACE
If I Could've Gotten into a Trade School

*I always thought when I turned 50 years old I would have achieved
everything I wanted. When you are young you feel you have a lifetime
to do all the things you want to do—everything. I always put off today
until tomorrow and that didn't work. I am approaching 50 years old
and I feel I should have done more in life and accomplished more than I
have. I thought I would be financially secure and that my home would
be furnished like I want it to be. I have never had a house where it was
furnished like I wanted it to be.* —Grace in her 1993 interview

• • •

I'm Getting Older Now

Unlike her mother, Maya, Grace has many regrets about education as
well as unresolved anger about her experiences. She can remember few
good times about her schooling. From her experiences and her reflections on them, she has formed some interesting opinions about what
education should and should not be, what the role of teachers really is,
and how children should be treated and cared for in schools and out. She
has also thought a lot about language, literacy, and possible selves. I cannot help wondering if she will view her experiences as Maya does in another twenty-five years or so. She seems to be headed in that direction:
*"But I've done it for so long. And you keep thinking you getting older and I
say, 'Oh well, I'm getting older now. I'm not going to worry about it.'"* I do
not know if she really won't *"worry about it"* in the years to come, but at
the time of her interviews, language, literacy, goals, and possible selves
were at the forefront of her thoughts.

Grace had much to say about her goals and possible selves. She made
an extensive list of goals and she carefully considered her possible selves.
Even though she has many goals and she can envision a number of possible selves, she is not actively pursuing any of them. This may in part be
due to her sense of lost time, as is the case with Maya. Even though she
says she is *"not going to worry about it"* since she is *"getting older,"* she

has not let go of her goals or possible selves. In any event, I would not discount Grace's faith in possibilities. She listed too many goals (more than twenty in every goal domain except Friendship) and still dreams too much not to make some attempt at achieving her potential. Grace's goals are:

Educational Goals:
> *A degree—So I can better myself*
> *Education—Go to school, get a degree in nursing.*

Family Goals:
> *Financial Success—So I can help my children and family because most black people do not think of their children welfare; they only look out for themselves spending all their money on clothes and cars.*

Occupational Goals:
> *Retiring from my job getting a degree in nursing don't do anything for a year and go back to Farpoint and work part time as a nurse giving immunization shots to children. I would really like that.*

Personal Well-Being Goals:
> *Get a tutorial to help me read better, write better, and comprehend better to achieve understanding*
> *Read better*
> *Write better*
> *Comprehend better/achieve understanding*
> *Knowledge—Have that key to success and power*
> *Wisdom—to achieve understanding*
> *Success—Mental, Physical and Spiritual*
> *Control—Take (control) of my own life and stop living for other people*
> *Happeness. Love—For someone to love me for me, and be for me, do for me, take care of me, and I will do the same for them*

Physical Comfort Goals:
> *A (Mercedes Bend); a nice one payed for*
> *My own (home) payed for*
> *Own a long (mink coat)*

Power and Wealth Goals:
> *Financial Success*

Religious Goals:

> *Peace—With myself and God I would like to find out who I am, my purpose on this earth, and work toward that purpose*
>
> *Salvation—With my Lord and Savior Jesus Christ. Success—Mental, Physical and Spiritual.*

Social Helping Goals:

> *My own (business) in helping others to succeed in life*
>
> *I want to give back to others by getting out working in the church and in the community*

Travel and Adventure Goals:

> *Traveling—Seeing the country and places I have read about and seen on TV eating different kind of foods and injoying myself in "Paris" and other places in this world*

Her two most important hoped-for possible selves are Education and Occupation goals: getting a degree and retiring. That looks odd to me because I envision getting a degree as a beginning, not an end. Yet she couples this beginning with an ending: retiring. Although she says she would come out of retirement after getting a degree in nursing to pursue a new career as a nurse who gives immunization shots to children, I am not sure how reconciled those two goals are. She only intends to do the latter part-time and she does not indicate what else she plans to do despite the goals she lists that would require financing. Still, she has many other goals she could pursue.

Her two most feared possible selves are not related to her two most hoped-for possible selves, but they indicate what it is important to her to avoid: being the victim of a crime and getting cancer, both of which she has limited control over. Both are Personal Well-Being goals (the goal domain containing more goals than any other for her). Still, one's feared possible selves are just as important as one's hoped-for possible selves and should not be excluded from consideration since what we do not want to become is as important as what we do want to become.

It is interesting to note that she has control over fulfilling her hoped-for possible selves but very limited control over her feared possible selves. This reflects another implied aspect of Grace's narrative: she feels as though she has had little control over her life because of circumstances, and that has been frustrating for her. Although she accepts personal responsibility for the decisions she has made during her life and the too often not-so-welcome consequences, she feels she was limited in her ability to make better decisions because of environmental factors; hence, the opening to her narrative, *"I always wondered if my life would have been different if . . ."* Though she talks about her mother, her teachers, her stepfather, and so forth, she essentially is saying she needed help to do a better job with her life than what she did. This is very different from the position Maya takes.

Maya may not have liked some of the decisions she made, such as not getting an education, but she does not look outside herself (e.g., parents, racism, gender) to explain why she did not do something or how things might have gone differently. She specifically talks about her decisions as being her own and no one else's. She made the choices she did because they were what she wanted to do or felt she needed to do at the time. Grace, on the other hand, looks outside herself because she is not comfortable with herself or the choices she made.

> [I didn't make that dream come true] *because I had no guidance in growing up or anyone to talk to me, to help me to get through school and to tell me the importance of going to college and to try to make something outta myself and get some type of degree. But if I would've had someone to just help me and to make me feel that I was important and I was better than just somebody to cook and clean up and take care of children all the time, see that's what I felt I was cut out for. Because I guess you look at your parents and you see what they do and you feel, "Well, I guess this is the life* [for me]. [This is] *what I'ah be doing." I just felt I would be cleaning up people house like my mom was cleaning up people house and coming home cooking, having a house full of children. That's what I thought at that time. Because I couldn't see. I couldn't see any further than that. I couldn't see past that. Because there was no one to help me see past that. Cause I thought that was life and I looked at all of my sisters and stuff and look what they were doing. So I just thought . . .*

She constantly reviews the past and her mistakes and contemplates how she might have done something differently, without seeming to accept that those choices have been made and are over with. There is nothing she can do to change the past, although she can change her present and her future based on where and who she is now. Grace can list twenty-five or fifty possible selves, but she will not achieve them until she can accept who she is and the life she has lived and start from where she is and with what she's got. She has to take control of the here and now. I think Maya might offer this prayer for and to Grace to help her along:

God,
Grant me the
Serenity to accept the things I cannot change,
Courage to change the things I can, and the
Wisdom to know the difference.

She has the tools, but does she have the conviction? According to her goals, she at least has some realization of the issues involved, given her desire for peace and control.

I Guess This Is What I'll Be Doing

Grace's dilemma is that she has many goals and possible selves, but does not believe in herself enough to achieve her goals. Even though she knows she wants to read, write, and talk better, she is almost paralyzed with self-doubt. She has no confidence. Though she indicates that she will achieve her possible selves, it appears that some are more important to her than others.

Grace indicates she is interested in improving her reading and writing. Like Maya, Grace does not see reading and writing as the only components to literacy. Comprehension is apparently also a large factor, as we hear in her narrative. She sees writing as a skill, but she sees reading as more than a skill. Just as literacy is more than components to be separated, reading is more than saying the words on a page as indicated in her response to the fifth reading passage in the interview (i.e., the one I wrote):

He's saying that just because you can read and you can write doesn't necessarily mean that you are literate. Because if you are not understanding what you are reading and writing, it has no meaning to it. I do agree with it. Because that's what I be saying, if you read, you don't know what you're reading. Just because you can read and write, I see this saying it doesn't make you literate. Because if you're not understanding what you're reading and writing, you could put this paper down and you have read it but you don't know what you read. Just like up here, when I was reading and

I say, "Well, I don't get that one." See I would have to read over and over before I could get it. I'ah eventually get it, but I have to continue to read it over and over. But see that's the thing. You have to know what you are reading and you have to comprehend what you're reading and writing.

Even before reading and responding to the passage in the interview, Grace indicates the importance of comprehension for both reading and literacy. Her lack of comprehension is what she sees as her basic problem. *"I will read something and I don't understand what it means sometimes. I have to read it over and over."* It may also be that she believes reading is more complex because reading presents others' thoughts whereas writing is something she produces. Even though she has difficulty producing texts, at least they are under her control, unlike reading. She is in charge of the level of complexity of her writing, but she often has little control over the complexity of her reading, especially at her job.

Another relevant issue is her sense of conflict, which may in part stem from the language and literacy ideologies she has as well as from her lack of confidence. This sense of conflict is present in most of her data, but especially in her possible selves. When comparing her African American English possible selves (i.e., "speak African American English" and "value African American English") to her "standard" English possible selves (i.e., "speak 'standard' English" and "value 'standard' English"), Grace does not identify very much with either African American English or "standard" English. She does not want to continue to speak African American English (though she indicates she only speaks it "somewhat" right now), but neither does she strongly choose to want to speak "standard" English. The general pattern of her possible selves increases with the more prestigious "standard" English and decreases with the less prestigious but more comfortable African American English. Still, if she speaks African American English only somewhat and "standard" English even less so, what does she actually speak? She does not think she speaks "bad" English. Does she therefore speak a mixture of the two (or three) or something in between?

According to sociolinguist William Labov, African American Vernacular English (AAVE) is a language system that coexists with other American dialects (OAD). AAVE consists of two distinct components: General English (GE), which is similar to the grammar of OAD, and African American (AA). As such, AAVE has access to the same linguistic features as OAD for much the same purposes as OAD through its GE component.

The AA component is not a complete grammar but a subset of linguistic features used in combination with much of the grammatical inventory of GE. AA is therefore complementary to OAD and GE is the default component of AAVE. In other words, when no AA element is supplied, the GE component is used. As such, AAVE and OAD are coexistent systems with each accounting for different parts of Grace's language. So, if Labov is correct, Grace speaks AAVE and accesses the GE component when she chooses not to use an AA component or none is available. This would be the same for Maya as well. It is just that some AAVE speakers access their GE component less than other AAVE speakers or less at some times and in some contexts than at other times or in other contexts. This notion is intriguing because I think it further complicates the nature of bidialectalism (and, as a result, is relevant to bilingualism), the state of the participants' language use (i.e., their access to and use of two distinct language varieties).

Grace's narrative indicates she does not like the way she talks, but that is only when she feels there are others around her who speak "standard" English and expect to engage in conversation using "standard" English. She seems perfectly fine talking with others who talk like her, but she wants to be able to use various modes of discourse to adapt to her current circumstances and to the speakers she wants to identify with or recognize at any given time. The problem is that she is not currently able to do so.

I find it hard to believe that she does not want to continue to speak African American English, given her ties to a community that uses African American English, but I do not find it hard to believe that she is struggling with this issue. Unlike Maya, Grace has not reconciled herself to the issues of language and literacy. She has not reconciled her goals and possible selves to her identity. She is still learning and thinking and, consequently, struggling with her ideologies and the reality she lives everyday.

I know a lotta educated people who know how to speak better and they don't. Let me tell you something. There are people that I speak with a lot and they feel comfortable talking with me and they talk worse than me. But if they have to write something on a piece of paper, write a letter or write something or had to make a speech, they would do so much better than me because then they know how to do it. But just in the everyday, they talk just like me and I would like to do that—know how to read and write, even though I may not use it all the time, but I would love to know how.

Despite her statements about African American English, Grace clearly possesses some salient characteristics of African American English, as shown, for example, by her use of the African American English syntactic features I charted. She used African American English syntactic features 73% of the time possible during the KT sample. In the INT sample, she used only the African American English syntactic features 20% of the time when possible. That is an increase of 53%, the second largest for any participant for any category in either speech context. However, for all categories combined, 14% of her INT sample consisted of African American English features charted while 32% of her KT sample did, an 18% increase. Syntax is clearly her African American English stronghold (see Appendix 2 for a more detailed representation of Grace's, as well as the other participants', use of the African American English linguistic features charted between the two speech contexts).

Grace did show increases from the INT to KT speech samples across all three categories, though not as drastically for phonological (i.e., having to do with pronunciation) and morphological (i.e., having to do with structure at the word level) African American English features. Neither was as dominant in her speech as were African American English syntactic (i.e., having to do with structure at the sentence level) features, but there is a significant difference between Grace's INT and KT samples with respect to phonology and syntax. She seems to know more "good" English than she believes she does.

Interestingly enough, the very linguistic anxiety Grace discussed in her narrative (i.e., subject-verb agreement, or SVA) is evidenced in the morphology category and the syntax category. Since a couple of SVA features are salient African American English linguistic features, I charted all subsets of SVA because of Grace's anxiety about it and analyzed one of them (i.e., generalization of *is* and *was*). She has more SVAs (75 total) than any other participant. However, what is so interesting is that she has a much greater amount in the INT sample (71) than in the KT sample (4). This may be because of both her increased anxiety about her speech during the interview and the greater length of the INT sample. She was so preoccupied with speaking "good" English that she possibly hypercorrected. This would be analogous to the excessive use of "whom" because it sounds right or educated even when "who" is the prescribed form.

Of the 18 African American English linguistic features I analyzed, Grace used all but 2 of them in her speech samples: lowering of /ɪ/ > /æ/ before /ŋ/ and labialization of voiceless interdental fricative (i.e., /θ/ > /f/).

All the African American English linguistic features she did use occurred in both her INT and KT speech samples.

In contextualizing Grace's speech data, one should keep in mind its construction. Grace's INT data contained 18,668 of her own words out of 27,868 words overall (two-thirds). Of the 73 double-spaced pages of transcription for her INT speech sample, 48 of those (almost two-thirds) consisted wholly of her own speech. Such a total indicates that in her INT sample she did most of the talking; in fact, she did a lot of talking. Her interview was longer by far than any other interview—180 minutes. She talked approximately 120 of those 180 minutes (again, two-thirds of the time).

Grace's KT speech sample consisted of 19 pages and 5,300 words of her own speech. Over the course of the first 45 minutes of her KT sample, she spoke almost half of the time (15 of 33 double-spaced pages consisted only of her speech). That is a high percentage since there were as many as four people involved in the conversation during the speech sample used. Overall, she produced the most speech for the two contexts: 67 pages (10 more pages than the next closest participant) and 23,968 words (1,260 words more than the next closest participant).

HOW DO YOU GET TO CARNEGIE HALL?

Practice. Practice. Practice. That's what you can do to improve your reading and writing. You can become a better reader by reading. You can become a better writer by reading and writing.

But I could write for a year. I could write for ten years and never know how to break it down into sentences and stuff, where my periods and stuff go. It wouldn't help.

It wouldn't hurt either.

But I need guidance in the beginning.

You need to practice.

That wouldn't bother me if I'm just writing for myself and I'm just writing something happened in my life. It wouldn't bother me. But to write something to give to somebody? I wouldn't want to just write anything

*and give to someone to read. But if I'm writing for myself and just writ-
ing, I still don't know how to punctuate that. I still don't know if my
sentence is right. So if I'm getting ready to write something for somebody else, I still don't know.*

Start writing for yourself then. The rest will come later.

Of all the responses I received to my first letter to the participants,
Grace's was the most intriguing. She wrote in a very conversational tone,
and she used it as an opportunity to make some interesting points about
her life and her education. In reading the drafts and the final draft of her
letter response, I found them to be very moving. Nevertheless, if she
were to go to college, she would most likely be classified as a Basic Writer
because she has problems with punctuation (she is at Level 1) and mechanics, as she openly admits. Still, Grace is not a bad writer. Her writing is coherent and understandable, and she has interesting things to
say. If she used a computer to write, her writing would "look better" because she would do away with many of her spelling mistakes and possibly some grammatical problems (I know a few people whose computer
makes them appear more grammatically and lexically proficient than
they actually are). She comes across as a woman with ideas and thoughts
to express but with an insecurity in her ability to express them. She
could use a lot of encouragement and guidance.

Several features of African American English appeared in her writing:
"mine" instead of "mind" (i.e., final consonant cluster reduction); *"doing"* instead of "during" (i.e., /r/ deletion); *"first, second, & third grade"*
(i.e., no plural marker); *"my best friend name was . . . "* (i.e., no possessive marker); *"but now he see . . . "* (i.e., no third person singular -s
marker); *"it was suppose to be . . . "* (i.e., no past tense marker); *"to us we
was having fun"* (i.e., generalization of *was*); *" . . . that over with"* (i.e.,
zero copula; and *"she was not going to stay with no man that fights"* (i.e.,
negative concord); and one that did not appear in her speech, *"thank-
ing"* instead of "thinking" (i.e., lowering of /ɪ/ > /æ/ before /ŋ/). The occurrence in her writing could just be a misspelling, but its presence at all
is of interest. She also made some misspellings (e.g., *"injoying"* instead of
"enjoying" and *"payed"* instead of "paid"). One curious feature was that
she consistently wrote *"durning"* instead of "doing" while once she wrote
"doing" instead of "during," which clearly reflects a typical African American English pronunciation of the latter (/r/ deletion).

Grace had no writing samples per se, but she did include a draft of the letter she wrote in response to my first letter as well as two cover letters, her information questionnaire, and two additional responses in writing that totaled 5,156 words. Again, I think the lack of writing samples is indicative of her writing practices. In her narrative, she says she occasionally writes messages, notes, and memos for her job. She also writes checks and sends birthday cards. However, she does not write extended prose, at least none she shared with me. So, if she took more time to read and write she would become a better writer. *"If I would take time to read more I would be a better reader."* There is a fear-of-embarrassment factor that must be taken into account as to why Grace does neither as often as she realizes she should if she wants to become her hoped-for possible selves of a good writer and a good reader.

There is little question that Grace can read. During the reading phase of the interview, she was able to say the words. That was not a real problem for her. But as Grace has indicated, there is more to it than that.

> *I don't comprehend well at all, I will read something and I don't understand what it means sometimes, I have to read it over and over. Then I get frustrated and stop. If I'm around somebody, I don't know what I'm reading. I'm just reading. I'm just saying words.*

Even though she read the passages by herself while I was out of the room until she was ready to discuss them, she still had a problem understanding them.

Grace: *When I'm pressured to do something like that I don't understand.*

Sonja: I gave you time. I tried to give you time.

Grace: *Well, I still had to say it. But see afterwards then I was doing it on my own. Then I could think better. When you're under pressure you can't think straight.*

Sonja: Why were you under pressure?

Grace: *Because you was going to ask me those questions and that was enough right there to make me forget.*

After completing the interview, Grace read each of the reading passages over to try to understand them better (that is when the above conversation took place). She says she understood them better after doing that, but she had a hard time understanding them for the interview because she was anxious about the discussion that was to take place after she completed her reading.

Like Maya, Grace understood the passage in African American English better than most of the other passages. When asked if she thought it was an example of African American English, she responded, *"It's worse. Yeah."* When asked if she thought the African American English speaker showed logical, analytic, critical thinking she responded, *"Yes. That doesn't make you not think well or have common sense. Common sense will outsmart a person who speaks well. I've always told you that. If you don't have any common sense, you'll sit right there and let him give you a ticket and you never would've thought of that."* So, even though she says that the way the African American English speaker in the passage talked did not hinder communication or indicate a lack of intelligence, she believes that it is bad English, or at least something worse than African American English, but that its use is not indicative of intelligence level.

This attitude is not exactly reflected in Grace's responses to the ideologies explored in the interview (see Appendix 3 for more detail about Grace's responses to the ideologies). The Ideology of Opportunity and the Ideology of Emancipation have high averages and low standard deviations (i.e., she believes in each aspect of the ideologies in a consistently high manner). The Ideology of Progress ranks third among the three. The standard deviation for the Ideology of Progress is highest among the three because she disagrees that literacy and/or "standard" English lead(s) to a society with political democracy, a society with urbanization, and people who are less likely to commit a crime. Hence, she does not believe in the various aspects of the Ideology of Progress as consistently as she does those of the other two ideologies. However, she strongly agrees that literacy and/or "standard" English lead(s) to people who have a skeptical and questioning attitude; people who are more capable of general and abstract uses of language; and people who are more capable of logical, analytic, and rational thinking. Yet, in the very next section of the interview (the reading passages), she rejects what she had just strongly believed in.

If we look at Grace's Possible Selves Inventory responses again, we find some similarly intriguing things going on. Although she is ambivalent about identifying with the six positive possible selves (e.g., "Successful" and "Motivated"), she does want and expect to identify with them in the future. Also, she is consistently ambivalent in her responses to the positive statements in the last section of the inventory (e.g., "I think I have good ideas" and "I am happy with the way I am") with an average slightly above 5 (i.e., "slightly agree" on a scale from 1 to 7) for the five items. However, her average of 5 for the two negative language and literacy statements about her in the last section of the inventory (i.e., "I feel I do not have much to be proud of because of my language and literacy" and "I sometimes don't like myself that much because of my language and literacy") in conjunction with her average of 5 for the two ideological statements about language and literacy (i.e., "In order to succeed in this country, I must speak standard, or 'good,' English" and "In order to succeed or function in this country, I must be literate") indicate not only that her identity is related to her language and literacy ideologies but also that there is a conflict between her reality and her self-image.

Grace believes she is not stupid or incompetent, that when she does something she does it well, and that her common sense can more than adequately compensate for her perceived lack of linguistic and literacy dexterity, but she also gives credence to the Ideologies of Opportunity and Progress. Grace is at a point where she is questioning the validity of these ideological categories she says she identifies with when she is confronted with reality. When she applies these ideologies to her life and experiences, they do not always ring true. She does the same with the Ideology of Opportunity, though to a lesser extent, when she talks about Byron in her narrative.

So if you can understand what you're reading and what you're writing, sure it helps you. And you understand and you comprehend what is going on. It helps. But then there are people like Byron [a relative], for instance. Somebody like him who is not educated and you look at him and you talk with him, look at the kinda sense he have. He can go on a job interview and clean hisself up and put some false teeth in his mouth and stuff. He'ah get him a job. Some people can't read and write, but they got a lotta common sense and that's what help. That takes the place of it. They can figure they way out. They can get a good job. You'll be surprised of people that is illiterate. But they have a lotta common sense and that's how they get over.

Grace, like many of us, holds contradictory beliefs right now. Some of those contradictions may be resolved as she continues to ponder her life and experiences. These issues are very real and very meaningful to her at this time. They may continue to be so as long as there are proclamations like the following:

> A t-shirt at a bookstore with the word "Literacy" printed on it. A light bulb next to it was illuminated indicating that the light, or an idea, comes on when you are literate.
> A billboard which said: "America's Leaders Are America's Readers."
> A radio commercial that says: "Everything begins with reading and reading begins with Hooked on Phonics."

Why Is This Child Not Showing Any Interest in School?

I am not sure of the answer to the above question, but somebody needs to care. *"It all comes back to help. Somebody helping somebody."* Of all the narratives, Grace's is the most contemplative when it comes to education, and is also the one that has influenced my thinking the most. She has thought about many issues in relationship to her own education as well as others. That is not surprising since, unlike Maya, Grace tends to keep revisiting her past introspectively in part to help others when her advice is sought, but also to contemplate what might have been and what might still be possible, if . . .

> *When I turned about 13 or 14 years old I was the oldest at home. That's when my life turned around. I was a child responsible for 4 children. That wasn't easy. Maya was single and going out all the time. I was the babysitter. I couldn't have a life of my own. Going to school, cooking and cleaning for 4 children, getting them dressed in the morning, and fixing them breakfast—that was too much for a 14 year old child who was trying to go to school and learn. I didn't have a lot of time for homework.*

What should teachers or schools do in situations like this? I think it depends, in part, on the goals of education and schooling. If one of the goals is to teach all children what they need to know in order to be lifelong, self-regulated learners, then schooling failed both Grace and Maya (as well as Deidra). I do not think Grace's situation was or is an anomaly. *"Maybe sometimes if they see that a child is having a problem they should try and help by taking up more time with the slower kids instead of leaving them behind. That makes children drop out of school."* No one should be left behind or matriculated without being literate, but this happens all too often. In Grace's case, she matriculated with inadequate literacy skills, at least in her opinion, and no confidence.

In thinking about this aspect of Grace's narrative, I have to wonder if hers is the generation in which the seeds of disillusionment with education and schooling were sown for African Americans with the unfulfilled promises of *Brown vs. Board of Education* (1954). Grace would have been nearing middle school at that time. Though the schools were still segregated throughout her schooling despite the court decision, surely there was a sense of hope that Blacks would finally get the same education as Whites. Yet, we have Grace still asking how White children are educated differently than Black children fifty years later.

I don't know what goes on in those schools [White, middle-class/affluent] *or how they're* [children in those White, middle-class/affluent schools] *taught. . . . I always felt that the other races got a better education than we got for some reason. And I don't know what manner it was, how they were taught or what. But we were always left behind. And I'm sure it's because of race. They will not let you catch up with them. And that's why they didn't want integration I'm sure.*

Though race was not a factor in Maya's narrative, it is prominent in Grace's. Grace came into adulthood during the 1960s, a time of civil unrest and a quest for liberation by the oppressed. A key impetus for this season of discontent was racism. So, though Maya grew up during a time when racism was so entrenched and so seemingly omnipresent, Grace grew up in a time when racism was no longer being accepted as "the way it is" but being challenged. She believes that her education and her opportunities were limited, in part, because of race. In her opinion, White, middle-class/affluent children receive a different and better education than Black children—regardless of socioeconomic status. She does not know how the schools are different, but she believes they are. I cannot provide evidence to the contrary since there is little if anything to support the notion that Black children, poor children, the "other" children receive the same education as White, middle-class/affluent children or even just a good education.

Another issue relevant to the above is the rise of racialization in schools after *Brown vs. Board of Education* as well as the current topic of the potential benefits of educational resegregation for Black students in K–12. In his latest book, *Beyond Ebonics,* sociolinguist John Baugh relates a statement made by Professor Richard Wright of Howard University during a guest appearance on the Gordon Elliot television show in January 1997:

> I wanted to make a statement that the whole problem of black children going to school and not learning standard English is a relatively recent phenomenon. It is not the case that black people used to go to school came out the way they went in, okay? I went to school during the 1940s and 50s. We didn't go to school as speakers of black English. We went to school understanding that the purpose of school was to clean up whatever you took in. . . . Since desegregation you've had to deal with the weight of color. When we went to school, we just went to school. You didn't go to school as a black child, you just went to school as a child. . . . The weight of race is something black people have to carry today. When I went to school I did not carry the weight of race. [109] . . . During the period of segregation there was not such a thing in your mind as you were going to a black school. . . . You were simply going to school and the assumption was that you were going to school to learn because you had something to do there you couldn't do away from school, and that's learn something. [110]

This excerpt reinforces a recurring message in *Beyond Ebonics:* this nation will not heal and cannot move forward educationally, socially, or politically until it redresses not only the linguistic consequences of slavery in America, but all consequences. In other words, as long as there is racism and its ill effects, Grace will be asking her question and relating her comments for the rest of her life. The slogan of an NPR (National Public Radio) program emphasizes this idea that we fail or succeed together, not individually: "If it's important to Latinos [and we could add American slave descendants, descendants of Chinese railroad builders, survivors and descendants of Japanese internment camps, etc.], it's important to America."

There is another prominent feature in Grace's narrative. Research shows that children develop resilience when they have a supportive adult in their lives who helps and enables them to believe in themselves and their abilities. According to psychologist Albert Bandura, the development of a stable social bond with a competent, caring adult is a crucial factor in the management of adversity. Parents can (and should) be enablers of resilience, but supportive teachers can often be important enabling influences in the lives of children, particularly children faced with (severe) adversity. Grace was certainly one of those children faced with adversity:

When I turned about 13 or 14 years old I was the oldest at home. That's when my life turned around. I was a child responsible for 4 children. That wasn't easy. Maya was single and going out all the time. I was the babysitter. I couldn't have a life of my own. Going to school, cooking and cleaning for 4 children, getting them dressed in the morning, and fixing them breakfast—that was too much for a 14 year old child who was trying to go to school and learn. I didn't have a lot of time for homework. [In] Elementary *[I made]* 'A's and 'B's, *[in]* High School 'C's and 'D's. *I eventually lost interest in school. . . . Maya fussed so much. Growing up I didn't feel loved at all. I was insecure and I had no self-esteem. She was very abusive to us mentally and physically. When she would get up in the mornings she wanted you up. Maybe that is why I stay in bed so long in the mornings now. I was always a nervous child from the fussing. And sometimes she and Mr. John would fight. That was too much for me. I would go outside and sit on the porch and cry. She tells everybody I was her smartest child in the house. That's because I went on and did what was needed to be done so she wouldn't fuss. I couldn't take that all the time. I didn't have a good teen life at all, not at all. Maya did teach us values of life and morals; thank God for that.*

In Grace's narrative, we can see that she did not have that enabling, supporting caregiver or teacher in her life:

You know, I always wondered if my life would have been different if Maya would have motivated me as far as getting an education and being independent and if I would have learned how to read real good and comprehend good and if she would have taught me how to choose a husband. Mr. John was there most of the time so we did have food and clothing, but he didn't pay any attention to us. It was like we weren't there. I feel I could have gotten a better education if I would have had the time to apply myself and someone to help me understand the importance of education. . . . I blame myself and the school teachers. see I feel teachers should try to find out why children are not doing well in class and counsel you on you[r]* grades.*

As she states simply, *"I didn't have anybody."* It is not difficult to see why Grace is not as resilient as she might have been.

Given her experiences in and out of school, Grace has a few ideas about how schools can be better for Black children or any children not receiving the education all children deserve regardless of race, ethnicity, income, or ability.

1. *You should be allowed to do you work at school and somebody there to help you . . . because* [some children] cant do it when [they] go home because it's nobody to help [them] or to support [them].

2. *There are students there that need more attention than other students. . . . But I feel since you are there and they are the teacher, they should recognize when a child is not doing what they should do. It's something wrong. Only thing I would say if you would just make one phone call and ask the parent. Try to find what kind of household this person came from. What is going on there; this child can't do they homework or whatever. Yeah they do what they suppose to do. To teach you. And if you can't catch on and you can't get it, well they just leave you behind. But I don't think they should do that.*

3. *I think there should be tutors at school too, not to be paid, but to help the slower students so they can keep up in class. Because there are people who can't afford a tutor. And I think it's wrong because you're going to school to get an education to better yourself and I think all that should be there at certain hours, even if it's after class or before or during. You should have a study period for to go to a tutor to help you keep up. They will be surprised at how many children learn how to read, write, catch on and everything. But no, you have to pay for this services, although you going to school and the teachers are there to teach you. And if you a slow child and you can't catch on, you got to pay somebody twenty dollars an hour to tutor you. And I think that's wrong when that's what you going to school for.*

4. *And I think they should give you aptitude tests and all kinda stuff. And when your score is low, below a certain level, you think they try to come and try to find out why? They just continue to teach and leave you right behind, and I think it's wrong. . . . Because I think they should have other people, professional people, come in and those children who had low scores and stuff like that, give them some other kind of test to try to find out if these children have some type of Dyslexy or*

what they have and try to help them in some kinda way. Because
everybody pay tax and I know they have enough money.

I agree with much of what Grace has to say. Some of it echoes Maya's comments about education and the purpose of education, and relates to points in journalist Dale Mezzacappa's report on an education summit addressed by President Clinton:

> At the third national education summit held in Palisades, New York, October 1999, President Clinton said that American policymakers are asking the wrong question. The question is not whether all kids can learn, Clinton said: "You can take a brain scan to show that." The right question is "can we teach them all?" The 114 summit participants—governors from 24 states, corporate CEO's and educators, including the heads of both major teachers unions, agreed that it's not enough to set high academic standards for all students, which most states have now done. The next step is to provide a teaching corps that is competent to teach them. And while many states are also moving to raise standards for new teachers, keeping and retaining the best remains a challenge for all schools, but especially for those with the poorest students and most difficult conditions.

A lawsuit filed recently by the ACLU on behalf of students at several schools in California claimed that the state has failed to educate certain children because of poor school building conditions, high numbers of uncertified teachers, overcrowded classrooms and schools, and insufficient resources (some schools do not have enough textbooks to distribute to their students). Under such conditions, is the problem really that the students cannot learn? Of course, these were schools that predominantly served "other" children—the poor, the disadvantaged, the non-White. In California in particular, *"everybody pay tax and I know they have enough money."* When small, resale homes are selling for well over $500,000 in Silicon Valley and prices for many services and goods are triple the price elsewhere in the United States, surely there is enough money to at least pretend you care about all children equally.

Imagine thinking that black people write only about being black and not about being people.

—Alice Walker, *You Can't Keep a Good Woman Down*

• • •

I Probably Should've Been More Proud

Reia may not have been proud of her accomplishments at the time she made them, but she certainly is now. She exudes self-confidence, and she still has much more to do. Unlike Maya and Grace, Reia desires many things that she believes she can attain as long as they are things she is in control of, and that is quite a bit. She is not completely comfortable with certain aspects of her life, but she is not going to let them get in the way of her reaching her goals. She has several goals, some of them grand and some of them typical. Still, she appears guaranteed to make the most of what she has and can accomplish.

Reia listed fourteen goals across all goal domains except Friendship. Reia's goals and hoped for possible selves include the following:

Educational Goals:
> *Enroll in a Ph.D. program to further my studies and do the research that will lead to my future books.*

Family Goals:
> *Wife/married*
> *Mother*

Occupational Goals:
> *Television Director*
> *Psychologist, Ph.D.*

Personal Well-Being Goals:
> *Fully Self-Actualized Person*
> *Perfect size "6"*
> *Write a few books in the field of behavior and social science*

Physical Comfort Goals:
  Owner of a beautiful home
Power and Wealth Goals:
  Wealthy Individual
Religious Goals:
  Worship God the Creator
Social Helping Goals:
  Build a foundation that will be a solution to the declining black community.
  Serve my fellowman
Travel and Adventure Goals:
  World Traveller

As was the case with Maya, Reia did list hoped-for possible selves and feared possible selves as well as her two most hoped for—*"Mother"* and *"Fully Self-Actualized Person"*—and two most feared goals—*"Widowed"* and *"Motherless"*—something most of the participants did not do. Under the circumstances, I would say she really wants to be a mother. But then, for as long as I can remember she has wanted to have a family. Her responses to questions about her actions with respect to these possible selves are interesting. When asked what she had recently done to make her most hoped-for possible self of "Mother" come true, she said, *"I am putting out more mental energy toward finding a suitable companion. I am changing my attitude toward men and I feel more open for romance."* For her most feared possible selves of *"Widowed"* and *"Motherless,"* she said, *"I have not gotten married,"* and *"I am making more effort to prepare myself to receive the man God has for me,"* for what she had done to not make them come true. The logic seems clear but conflicting. Though it is true that one can have a child without getting married and having a husband, that does not fit what she states among her goals. On the other hand, if your most feared possible self is also that you will be widowed, then not marrying is one way to prevent that from happening. In any event, this is a good example of how one's feared possible selves are as important as one's hoped-for possible selves. It also shows how we can be working for and against a goal at the same time. The goal we attain is the one we are most committed to. When asked what she had done to make her hoped-for possible self less likely to come true, she did go on to say, *"It's more of what I have not done. I'm not making myself more available by seeking out the places I can meet educated, professional men."* So, she was aware of the problem. The next step would be to do something about it.

Another interesting point is that as important as she believes education to be, she does not mention that as one of her two most hoped-for possible selves. I suggest this may have to do with what I mentioned previously about control. She certainly has much more control over her education than she does over having a family in the way she wants. Reia is very specific about the kind of man she wants for a husband. She may want to accomplish the general and familiar goal of having a husband, but she does not desire just any man. That makes the goal more challenging. Research indicates that this can actually be a good thing in terms of accomplishing a goal.

According to educational psychologists Edwin Locke and Gary Latham, goals tend to be the most useful when they are challenging yet realistic. Goals should be set so they are just beyond our reach. When goals are too easy we tend to lose interest; when they are too difficult, they can soon become overwhelming. Also, according to educational psychologist Paul Schutz, goals that are specific and measurable tend to be more useful than goals that are general. Specific and measurable goals are important because during the process of working toward a goal you need feedback to regulate and monitor your progress. If a goal is general, it is hard to tell where you are in relationship to where you want to be. Specificity, then, improves the usefulness of the goal because it provides more information about where you want to be. According to educational psychologists Miriam Erez and Isaac Zidon, the evidence also seems clear that commitment to the goal is important. If there is little or no commitment, little progress toward a goal can be expected. Reia seems to have met these criteria. The next step is to actually learn and have what it takes to accomplish the goal. I remember someone saying that people often want a particular kind of person as a mate, but are they the kind of person the person they are seeking actually would want? I cannot answer that question for Reia, but that is at least part of what makes this goal less controllable than some of the other goals she is more confident of though no less committed to. I do not know if she has a plan for accomplishing the other goals, but at least she has a diverse set of goals that seem to be part of a larger plan.

Reia's confidence can be seen in her view of her reading, writing, and literacy possible selves. She has quite a bit to say in her narrative about reading, writing, and literacy. Although she has no reading goals listed (not counting the inevitable reading necessary to complete a Ph.D.), she does have a writing goal listed. Though she greatly values and enjoys reading and it is important to her life, she is a little more ambivalent about writing, yet it appears as one of her goals. Writing is more challenging for her than reading, but it is obviously no less important to her, or at least that is the way she sees it for the future. Her current valuing of writing is tied to her sense that writing is more difficult than reading and writing is a challenge she intends to conquer over time. Reading does not provide the same challenge—at least not at this point in her life—because she considers it something she has mastered; hence, an average score of 7 on a scale of 1 to 7 (and, therefore, a standard deviation of 0 since each possible self garnered a 7) on her Possible Selves Inventory for all her reading possible selves (i.e., good reader, value reading, enjoy reading, and read on a regular basis) as well as her literacy possible selves when expressing her commitment to achieving or sustaining those possible selves for "describes me now," "would like to describe me in the future," "and will describe me in the future." In other words, those goals have already been accomplished and there is no need to look back. The next challenge is writing, and it is formidable because, according to Reia,

> It's a lot more difficult to write than it is to read . . . because for one thing when you writing you're having to formulate your own thoughts. You composing your own things. You're relying on your own thinking abilities and your own perception. [With writing, you have to create the product; with reading the product is already there.] You have to put more effort in writing than you do reading. You're creating something when you write. When you reading, you not. You're using your thinking ability or what have you and your concentration. You're trying to comprehend what you're reading and it requires energy. But it's just that it's already there. It's something that's already created. Whereas when I sit and I have a blank piece of paper, I have to create that.

I can certainly understand that feeling.

Unlike Maya and Grace, Reia does not talk about literacy as something more than reading and writing. Also unlike Maya and Grace, Reia sees literacy as an integral part of who she is and what it says about her as a person as well as how she values herself as a person. *"Being literate gives others the impression of one being intelligent and educated. Also being literate improves a person's quality of living. For one thing, self-esteem."* Maya and

Grace distance the intrapersonal possibilities of literacy whereas Reia sees it as an intricate and important part of the very person she is. As a result, Reia affords more status and importance to literacy than does either Maya or Grace. That may very well be because Maya and Grace have differing abilities with respect to literacy compared to Reia; she has it and they don't. In other words, if it is something you do not have and have not had and you are making it without it, then its value is less for you. Reia does not quite see it that way. She believes you are not complete and cannot experience life to its fullest if you are not literate. *"It makes my life a lot easier and I feel better about myself. I think the quality of life is improved."*

Interestingly enough, Reia sees a natural connection between literacy and language. *"Literacy is the way people write and read as well as how they speak a language."* Competence is integral for her at every step. It is no surprise then that Reia does not value African American English in the way she does "standard" English. In part, she is uncertain or possibly confused by the whole issue of African American English; hence, her equivocal ratings for "speak African American English" and "value African American English" (all 4s on a scale from 1 to 7). Until she comes to terms with and understands her position on African American English, it is likely she will continue in this uncertainty.

> *I don't see Black English being any different from regular English. There are black people who lack the education to speak proper English. I don't make a distinction* [between standard English and Black English]. *I just don't see a difference. . . . I only see a difference in people living in certain parts of the country as far as accent, a certain vernacular, slangs. . . . I don't know what Black English is other than that we say, "Oh Black people talk bad. They talk bad." I don't* [believe Black English is bad English] *because White people talk bad too. There are a lotta White people who talk bad too—if we wanna call it bad.*

But Reia speaks African American English. She claims there is no difference between African American English and "standard" English, but she then makes a distinction between her African American English and "standard" English possible selves (see Appendix 1 for more detail about Reia's responses to the possible selves).

Reia believes "standard" English is important and that *"it's much easier for me to express myself verbally,"* but speaking is what trips her up the most, according to her narrative. She mentions one person who constantly stays on her case because of her speaking, Maya.

> *"Now you in school. You done went further along in school than me and you should know better. You know better than I. You know better than to say things." She would always stop me; she would always correct me "Now you know that's not the right way to say that," and, "You in college. You need to say it right." And I'd say, "Well, I know what's right. I know the right thing to say. This just the way I talk when I get around my family, what have you. It's like this is what I feel comfortable with and this is the way I talk."*

In spite of Reia's uncertainty about her language use and how she can comfortably distinguish African American English and "standard" English given the way she speaks, her education, and how she feels most comfortable speaking, like Maya and Grace with literacy, she is able to brush it off in the end.

ACTS OF IDENTITY

According to creolist Robert LePage and associates,

> People create their linguistic systems (and we all have more than one) so as to resemble those of the groups with which from time to time they wish to identify. Both the groups, and their linguistic attributes, exist solely in the mind of each individual. When we talk we project the universe as we see it on to others as on to a cinema screen in our own images, expressed in the language we consider appropriate at that moment, and we invite others by these acts to share our universe. This does not necessarily mean that we accommodate our behaviour to resemble that of our audience, though we may do so. Rather, we behave in the way that—unconsciously or consciously—we think appropriate to the group with which at that moment we wish to identify. This may be quite distinct from the group we are talking to.

No truer words have been said, at least in regard to Reia's narrative and speech. There is little doubt in my mind that Reia speaks African American English. The extent of its use may be different from what is seen with the other participants, but she speaks African American English none-theless. Ironically, the range of style shifting Reia displays and the con-fidence she has in her ability to style shift are the very things Grace says she would most like to have and do with her own language. Reia can comfortably perform her acts of identity, but Grace regrettably cannot.

Reia produced the second highest total of speech data analyzed—sec-ond only to Grace—because of the length of her interview. Of the 56 to-tal pages and 24,375 total words transcribed for her INT speech sample, 42 pages and 18,000 words (three-quarters worth) consisted of her speech alone. That translates to a total of approximately 101 minutes of Reia's speech for her INT speech sample out of a total interview time of 135 min-utes (again, three-quarters worth). Reia's numbers are second only to one other participant and show that Reia talked most of the time during the interview, unlike Maya. (In fact, Maya is the only participant who did not talk at least 60% of the time during the interview.) Unlike her INT speech sample, Reia's KT speech sample is the shortest of all the partici-pants. Her KT sample is 15 pages of her speech alone for a total of 4,708 words. With the INT and KT speech samples combined, the total for her speech alone is 57 pages and 22,708 words—both second only to Grace's speech sample totals by 10 pages and almost 1,300 words. However, the next closest participant has a total of 13 pages and over 8,800 words less for her speech sample totals. So, despite the difference in INT and KT speech data for Reia, she provided ample speech data for me to analyze.

Despite Reia's ambivalence about her speech, only one African Amer-ican English linguistic feature I analyzed is not present in her speech samples—labialization of the voiceless interdental fricative (i.e., $/\theta/ >$ $/f/$). All other features occur at least once in one of the two speech con-texts. The one feature that occurs the most with respect to number is zero copula. That would certainly address her anxiety about verb agree-ment since there is no verb to deal with on the surface.

In comparing her INT and KT speech samples, we see that, as would be expected, Reia's use of the African American English linguistic fea-tures I analyzed is different for the two contexts. Numerically, more fea-tures consistently occur in the KT speech sample (224) than in the INT speech sample (87), but she has the second lowest percentage change be-tween the two contexts (17%). Her use of morphological features was not statistically significant between the two contexts, but her use of phonological and syntactic features was. In fact, the difference between her use of African American English syntactic features in Kitchen Talk and Interview Talk is greater than any category for any other participant. It is unquestionable that Reia uses these African American English syntactic features very differently in the two speech contexts. So, even though she may have some anxiety about subject-verb agreement, she knows enough about the differences between African American English and "standard" English to get the "standard" English variant (or GE component, according to Labov's hypothesis) most of the time when she chooses to do so.

Reia exhibits similar abilities in her writing. She included various writing samples for the project, mostly papers from her psychology classes. In all, her writing samples consisted of three responses to the letters I wrote, her information questionnaire, and five writing samples from class papers for a total of 7,847 words. According to Shaughnessy's five levels of punctuation, her punctuation is approximately level 4. Several African American English features I analyzed were in her writing samples —*"pass"* instead of "past" (i.e., final consonant cluster reduction); *stated* instead of "started" (i.e., /r/ deletion); *"9th and 10th grade"* (no plural *-s* marker); *"The clients interaction with males"* (no actual possessive *-s* marker); *"not wait until a crisis occur"* (no third-person singular *-s* marker); *"The 'pink eye' was experience once"* (no past tense marker); and *"Piaget's concepts on child development is applicable"* (i.e., generalization of *is*)—but there were no African American English syntactic features present in her writing samples. She had more occurrences of zero plural *-s* and zero possessive *-s* in her writing samples than she did in her INT and KT speech samples combined. Overall, she is able to control the occurrence of African American English syntactic and phonological features in her speech and writing more than she can her African American English morphological features. Her writing may be different from her speaking, but not necessarily in the way she meant or thought. This pattern with African American English morphological features seems to be consistent with what we have seen so far with Maya and Grace as well. Of course, this is no surprise to me since what most strikes me about Reia's speech as being African American is the way it sounds.

It's the Society That We're Living In

A hundred years ago maybe people didn't [need to know how to read]. *Even though I think reading's always been important, but the world was nothing like it is now. Maybe there wasn't as much of a need for it to function smoothly because of the way it was then. But it's [impor-tant] especially now because of the world we live in. I mean you need to know how to read and write. You need to know how to add and sub-tract and stuff like that. And I think it does help your self-esteem.*

Reia appears to have bought into the Ideologies of Opportunity, Prog-ress, and Emancipation much more so for literacy than for language. The literacy section of her narrative portrays her firm grasp on the ideologies, but she is a bit less convinced about the impact of language in part be-cause that seems to be more variable than literacy. After all, she does say that Whites speak "bad" just like Blacks. So, whereas language is a little more subjective and volatile, literacy is steady as she goes because re-gardless of one's language abilities, one still has to be able *"to read and write . . . add and subtract."* Although in her definition of literacy she does include language, it must not play as big a role in her concept of lit-eracy as might seem from her definition (it is listed last). This distinction might, therefore, explain why her average scores for the three ideologies are not as high as one might first expect from her narrative. What is even more surprising to me is that her average score for the Ideology of Eman-cipation is lower than that for the Ideologies of Opportunity and Prog-ress even though that is one of the aspects of the ideologies she seems most convinced by, especially when she talks about self-esteem. It is lower than the others because she says she neither agrees or disagrees for both "autonomous" and "empowered." The only other ideologies she rates at that level or lower are "less likely to commit a crime," which she strongly agrees with, and "productive," which she neither agrees or disagrees with —both components of the Ideology of Progress, which accounts for the large standard deviation (i.e., a large range in scores) for that ideology compared to the other ideologies.

Of the three participants analyzed so far, Reia seems to have believed in the ideologies in a way different from Maya and Grace. She appears to be the one most indoctrinated by schooling.

Maya prepared me for a lot of daily living stuff. But school played a big part. School played a big part in helping with the socializing process, conforming to society, what's expected of me, how I should behave, to be able to sit down and listen and then becoming a more civilized, pro-ductive individual.

She bought what schooling had to offer hook, line, and sinker—for literacy, socialization, etc. But that was not quite the case for language, as can be seen by her self-conflict about what language really is and what it is for her in particular. She may have gotten the message that you have to speak "standard" English to get along in this world, but she does not articulate that in a way that jibes with her lived experience. She does note that she sees a connection between perception of intelligence and language use, but her confidence is such that she believes she is intelligent and others come to believe that as well despite the African American English linguistic features she uses in both speech and writing. So, in theory, language use may matter; in practice, language use can matter, but there are these mitigating factors that are not always accounted for.

She notes that many people may have been able to get along fine in society in the past because literacy was not as important then as it is now. Society has changed, and it is more damaging to be illiterate today than it was then. However, that does not seem to be the same with language. I think it points to the fact that as long as we do not have a brain injury or mental deficiency that prevents us from learning and using language, we speak in a way that allows others to understand us. It is not that everyone understands us or even chooses to understand us, but there is a community of speakers that does understand us. That may or may not be the community of one's enculturation, but it is a community of speakers we are most comfortable with and with whom we choose to identify ourselves. That strong presence of acts of identity in Reia makes her do wrong when she wants to do right, so to speak, because that is just who she is and all the indoctrination in the world has not changed her experiences or her reality. *"I know the right thing to say. This just the way I talk when I get around my family, what have you. It's like this is what I feel comfortable with and this is the way I talk."*

However, despite her confidence in her own abilities, she is not confident in the abilities of others based on their speech. It may be that Reia (as I will illustrate for Grace also) accepts the legitimacy of some African American English linguistic features more than others. There are, apparently, just some things that are not acceptable.

When I was watching the talk show one day and they had three Black guys on this talk show who were going around I guess pimping women some kinda way because they like, "Well you know, we can get any [woman], we can talk to any woman. We go around and we hit on pro-

*fessional women, professional educated women, that's who we get. We
don't deal with anybody. We deal with professional educated women
and we can just about talk them into doing anything. We get money
out of 'em." They weren't working. They said they were living off these
women, mooching off these women. All three of 'em, they were sittin'
up there talkin' like, you know, saying 'dat' and 'dis' and they just
sound. . . . And a lot of the Black women in the audience said, "I don't
see how because all you have to do is open your mouth when you first
say . . . ," and that's what I was thinking too; that's what I was saying.
He comes up to talk to me, when he opens his mouth I'm gonna . . .
you know the way he talks that's gonna turn me off. I'm a professional
educated woman.*

It may be that labialization (/θ/ > /f/) or stopping (/ð/ > /d/) of the interdental fricatives (orthographically "th") is unacceptable and/or it may
be that she is not aware that she uses some of the very African American
English linguistic features that she has on her blacklist. In any event,
there is clearly a line that is not to be crossed by certain others (consider
the earlier discussion about the "right" man for her). I think her level of
indoctrination and the extent of her belief in the ideologies can best be
seen and understood from her own words.

*Knowing how to read and write helps us to function everyday in this
world and it's one of those basic things that we need. It's not as significant as needing food and water, but if I had to rate it on a scale of one
to ten, I'm gonna rate it up to like around seven or eight because it
improves the quality of life that we have here and it feeds into our self-
esteem. Speaking standard English to me it's just more of an impressive
thing. It's a way of impressing people more and it's not a basic necessity. It's not a necessity, but being literate is.*

It Takes Different Things to Help Some People

Reia, for the most part, fit the mold for schooling. She was good at the
school game, as evidenced by her graduating from both high school and
college early. She had more positive things to say about schooling than
any other participant. She believes in schooling and what it can do. She
exudes confidence in herself and her abilities. At one point in her narrative, she attributes her resilience not only to Maya, but also to the fact

that she was in all-Black schools during her formative, elementary school years: *"I'm glad I went to all-Black schools to be truthfully honest with you. I'm glad I did because I didn't have to deal with any racial issues per se cause all my teachers were Black; all the students were Black."* Unlike Maya and Grace (and Deidra, as I will discuss), Reia had teachers in her life who enabled her self-efficacy (to use Bandura's term) and resilience. She mentions several teachers, from elementary to graduate school, who were encouraging and supportive and enabled her to believe in herself because they could believe in her and help her to see her self-worth and strength as a person: *"They would encourage me to go farther, to advance and stuff. They think I'm very intelligent. They value me as a person."* As a result of such praise and encouragement and guidance, Reia is very bright, motivated, self-efficacious, and resilient. So, unlike Maya and Grace, Reia has received a post-baccalaureate degree because she had good educational experiences for the most part and people who believed in her: *"Overall, in general, teachers made me feel very good; made me feel real good about my education* [and] *about myself. . . . I got a lot of encouragement. I got a lot of praise. It really helped my self-esteem."* She also had a role model at home in her sister Felicia. *"I remember Maya bringing little books home before we started grade school. My sister Felicia learned to read these books before she started the first grade. . . . Felicia was a straight 'A' student."*

Teachers can make a difference in a child's life for good or bad. Fortunately, Reia had more good teachers than bad. However, her point about race and education should not be overlooked. Grace talked about attending all-Black schools as a positive and negative: it was good to be around other Blacks who supported students and cared about their well-being, but it would have been better to have the same resources as the all-White schools of the time. *Brown vs. Board of Education* was supposed to deliver on that promise. By the time Reia was in school, she still attended all-Black schools and they were still supportive. We can infer as well that the resources were at least adequate since Reia seems to have benefited from them and, one might say, flourished with them. The question Reia raises though is whether her experience would have been as positive had she not had that foundation of an all-Black caring and supportive environment during her formative years in the 1960s and 1970s. We do not know the answer for sure, but if today's situation with Black youth and education is any indication, I would venture to say the results might very well have been different—and this time different likely means bad.

Like Grace, Reia did come to realize there were differences in education based on race as well as gender that she could identify.

And I really didn't see any blatant differences, to be truthfully honest with you, until I got to high school and it was really for the most part just one of my math teachers where there was a blatant difference in the way she treated Black students and the Whi[te students]. She was very prejudiced obviously. That wasn't very subtle with her. It was pretty obvious that she treated the White students [different] and she helped 'em out more. Like when they came up to her desk to ask questions or if they asked questions while she was standing at the board, she answered their questions and seemed that [she] really enjoyed answering. But like if we raised our hand [or] didn't understand something, she'd get an attitude and kinda like she made you feel dumb and stupid. . . . And the woman—this was God sent. But she got sick or something happened where she couldn't finish off the rest of the school year so we had to get transferred and I was transferred back to the Algebra teacher that I had and I ended up getting a 'B' in Geometry for that school year. But it's like I didn't even get the foundations. My foundation wasn't really established that well but I still got in there and did well and I know I woulda made straight As in Geometry. I would have liked Geometry a lot better if I'da had a teacher that wasn't like her— that wasn't prejudiced and thought we were all stupid and dumb.

Though educators and the like have debated the merit of the concept of self-fulfilling prophecy, the excerpt above would seem to support the notion that self-determination on the part of the teacher is significant in the education of children. Of course, race is significant as well. Despite proclamations by some that we are all now on a level playing field, there is an assumption that such teachers as the above no longer exist. Some Blacks even buy into this, which may threaten their resilience and self-efficacy. Educator Carla O'Connor reports the following in her study of educational resilience:

Only two youths outside of these resilient students [i.e., the six students that were the focus of her study in a group of 46 students total] made any reference to means by which social injustices might be redressed. Both of these youths, neither of whom were especially conscious of structural constraints, referenced the role of the courts. However, instead of emphasizing how legal action might be used to actively resist social injustice, they conveyed how Civil Rights laws have actually reduced Black peoples' need to fight. For example, on being asked to what extent she thought being Black would affect her chances of getting ahead in America, Lisa responded, "Well now not really as much as in my mother's day 'cause we got Civil Rights laws now that helps protect us against discrimination." Leroy explains, "If I am the best qualified for the job and I got the experience and degrees to prove it, they know that I can sue them if they don't hire me. So they not going to take that chance." (p. 621)

Yet, if equality and social justice truly ruled, then we would not expect to see the differences we do in the performance, resources, and outcomes between Blacks and Whites. Race does matter. It may not matter to everyone, but it matters to enough people to make a difference despite Civil Rights laws because though you can legislate people's actions you cannot legislate their beliefs. When a teacher thinks a student is stupid or dumb just because of the color of his or her skin, I do not see how that child can expect to survive, much less thrive. Fortunately, Reia was resilient enough and had enough confidence in herself to get past this one teacher. But what about the ones who were not resilient or confident or had the support Reia had, such as Grace? Who is the exception and who is the rule in this situation? So far, the odds are 2-to-1 against Reia as the rule.

Another reason this issue of integration of schools as a result of *Brown vs. Board of Education* seems significant in regard to Grace and Reia relates to the quotation from Wright's guest appearance on the Gordon Elliot television show cited in the previous chapter. Grace did not have to deal with this problem because school integration did not occur while she was a student even though she was still in school at the time of *Brown vs. Board of Education* decision; hence, all her teachers were Black. However, the enactment of *Brown vs. Board of Education* had occurred by the time Reia was in middle and high school. She did not have the burden of race while developing a strong self-identity, but we will see later that this is not the case for the remaining participants. Race is a heavy burden to bear for children; yet Black children have to do it everyday. During an activity I do in one of my classes, called a Fishbowl, there is an inner circle and outer circle made up of Black students and non-Black students, respectively; the Black students describe what the "Black Experience" is, as based on their own experiences but also in conjunction with course readings that label it as such and describe it. When I recently did this activity in my classes, one Black student said, "Being Black is never being neutral." It is heavy indeed.

As was the case with Grace, Reia does point out that everything is not rosy just because everyone in your world is Black. Both Grace and Reia mention the problem of favoritism. Though favoritism is not specific to Black or White teachers, the kind of favoritism Grace talks about is very color conscious—colorism in the Black community. In this colored world, "White is alright, Brown get out of town, and Black jump back." Though similar issues may be relevant to White teachers, overall, I do not think the shade of your complexion is as significant as the complexion itself for some, though I should note that Maya, Reia, and Sonja pass the brown paper bag test but neither Grace nor Deidra does. But, it does not matter how light-skinned you are (or how long your hair is) if all one can see is a Black person and not a person worth as much as the next person, regardless of race.

Another point Reia makes that Grace concurs with is that:

> Everybody's different, everybody's unique, everybody's different and it takes different things to help some people [or] to make people catch on or click and you just have to find out what it is. And I think that has a lot to do with the teaching, with the method of teaching and even parents—that's important too. To say somebody's a bad reader to me is to say that they weren't properly taught. The time and the patience weren't [there]. They didn't receive the time and patience that they required because they're different. They might not catch on to reading or what as quick as I did. Like Marcus and Johnny. They needed another method. They needed another way of helping them to catch on to some of those things. But you know, a lot of us was thrown in class together and you either sink or swim. I think that's ridiculous. I just think that's terrible.

The belief that some children are left behind because there is something about them that is different is not new, but it is unfortunate. More and more it seems that schools are for certain kinds of children and not others. If a child does not fit the image school is geared for, there is conflict. More often than not, the child ends up being the loser because if the child is unwilling or unable to change to fit the mold, school is certainly not going to change. Hence, you either sink or swim. However, I agree with the other women, as do most of you I'm sure, that all children should benefit from school and not just a few. And as President Clinton said, a brain scan can tell us if a child can learn, but we have to decide that we will actually teach that child to swim or let that child sink. At least with Reia, not all of her teachers were willing to let her sink or, as the case may be, to attempt to drown her. The boys, her brothers, were not so lucky.

Johnny and Marcus did not make it. They didn't have anybody. As is often the case with many African American boys, Johnny and Marcus did not fit the mold and, subsequently, they dropped out of school, or were pushed out. As Reia notes,

> *When I look back now I say obviously it was something wrong, but at the time I didn't necessarily pay attention then. Because, for example,* [look at] *Marcus and Johnny. Johnny dropped out about in tenth grade. He musta been about sixteen or something like that when he stopped going, when he dropped out. Marcus was going but his reading and spelling was very limited. And I guess I wasn't aware of it at first but later on I started* [to think]. *There was an obvious difference in the way I was excelling in school and the way they were* [and] *we were going to the same schools. . . . Felicia and I did well but the boys did not. The boys did not do the same. And I figure they was intelligent as well. I mean, my goodness, they were raised in the same house. I don't know if there were some things happening differently in the house, but I think the system had a lot to do with it. I realize now that the system has had a lot to do with it. There're real subtle things that were happening to Black men, with Black children, male children, in school obviously.* [The women had a better opportunity than the men did in school.]

For various reasons, African American males too often have problems with schools. I recently saw a conference paper at the annual meeting of the American Educational Research Association by educator Audrey Mc-Cray titled "There's Something about the Way He Walks." The paper addressed the problems African American males have in schools and how something as innocuous as the way they walk is enough to contribute to the conflict between them and school. (I would suggest you could do a similar study entitled, "There's Something about the Way He [or She] Talks"—though, of course, language is not innocuous.) Who do these boys then get to be as men? Not anyone the Reias in this world are interested in.

As I look back over my academic career, I am proud of myself. Through-out high school and college, I've received recognition and honor for my academic achievements. I was the first person in my family to have completed a Master's Degree. Education is one of the most valuable things anyone can do for themself and I strongly encourage my clients and family to go-for-it.

Oh, what a difference.

Sometimes I try to look deep within myself
Afraid of what I see and what I don't see.
Afraid to love or take the slightest chance at anything
Trying not to get hurt while trying out this love.
Yet longing to love and be loved
Feelings so deep they creep inside, swelling in my heart wanting to
    take control.
If only we could learn to love equally and see how wonderful it
    would be.
Reach out and touch me
Hold me near
Love me until of love I have no fear.

—"In Search Of," author unknown

• • •

OVERCOMING AND BECOMING

Like Grace, Deidra is in a time of conflict and struggle. Although Grace's writings were of great interest to me because she is a good storyteller, Deidra's writings were of interest because they were the saddest. Unlike Maya, who claims to have long since reconciled with her disappointments and past dreams, Deidra is just beginning to realize and address her struggle. She is still trying to define and configure her conflicts with language, literacy, and identity. She has hopes and dreams like everyone else, but she is beginning to see the difficulty of realizing them because she has a literacy problem. Most of her goals are connected to that particular problem in some way, as described in her narrative.

This is not to say that literacy plays such a crucial role in one's life that it is indispensable, as Reia proclaims. However, since literacy is a locus of concern for Deidra due to her realization of the role it has and will continue to play in her life until she can come to terms with it and effectively deal with it, it is no surprise that it weighs heavily on her thoughts and, therefore, her goals and possible selves.

Deidra has goals she wants to achieve and possible selves she hopes for and fears. Deidra lists eleven goals that fall into all but one goal domain, Friendship. This is the same goal domain not listed for Maya, Grace, or Reia. Below are Deidra's goals.

Educational Goals:
Get a degree in something
Family Goals:
Get married
Have children/have a family
Occupational Goals:
Become an R.N. nurse are become a psycholog[ist] *are social worker one day*
Personal Well-Being Goals:
Overcome my literacy [problem]
Physical Comfort Goals:
A nice house
Religious Goals:
Letting God be first in my life
Social Helping Goals:
Help another with there problem and understanding what the are going threw
Travel and Adventure Goals:
Travel

Several of these depend upon her literacy goal because she cannot see herself accomplishing them without getting past it. If she does not become literate, she will not be able to get a degree, become a nurse, or have children. Those goals are connected for her because she believes she must be literate and speak "standard" English to succeed. If she does not become literate, she will not be able to get a job that pays well enough for her to support the children she wants, nor will she be able to adequately help her children become literate if she herself is not literate. That is the rationale she gives in her narrative for several goals. She believes this to such an extent that those hoped-for possible selves could become dreaded possible selves if she is not able to achieve them. She could be on the verge of being where Grace is now, just as Grace may be on the verge of being where Maya is now. We might be able to extend this to the point that Maya is where Deidra may well be in forty years.

One thing Deidra has in her favor for achieving her goals is that she realizes what she needs to do in order to accomplish them. Her dilemma is whether she will be able to do those things necessary to achieve her goals. This is not something she can do on her own, which means she is not in complete control of the situation. A partial loss of control may be disconcerting if she knows what she needs to do but cannot find adequate support to do it. As she seems to indicate in her narrative, the help she has sought for her literacy problem may not be enough because of a lack of skills among the adult literacy workers. This may lead to frustration, which may lead to her not accomplishing her goals.

Her combined reading and writing possible selves along with the literacy possible selves present a mixed pattern. Deidra believes her reading is better than her writing at present, and she identifies with reading more. However, she thinks both will describe her in the future. Both reading and writing follow the pattern of a constant increase from "describes me now" to "will describe me in the future." This is not the case with literacy. She averages the same score for each perspective for literacy possible selves. In fact, "literate" as a possible self receives the same score as the "illiterate" possible self: 3 (between "not at all" and "somewhat"). Why are the scores the same and why are they so low? A clue to the former may be seen in Deidra's definition of literacy: *"It's when a person is having problem with reading and writing. Can read and write but scared."* (There is that relationship again between confidence and literacy.)

Deidra, like everyone else in the study, received questions about literacy and its definition before I answered any questions about it or provided a definition. I was interested in finding out what she thought it was instead of having a definition imposed upon her by me. During the interview, I asked her to define and contrast literacy and illiteracy. As you can see, her definition of literacy may be more appropriate as a definition of illiteracy.

Sonja: How do you define illiteracy?
Deidra: *A person who has a deficiency problem of reading and writing.*
Sonja: OK, then how do you define literacy?
Deidra: *A person who can read and write but can not explain it.*
Sonja: OK, tell me again. Distinguish for me between illiteracy and
    literacy.

Deidra: *I don't know. Like I say a person who has a deficiency problem with a reading uh comprehending problem. Some people can read and write but don't understand what they're writing, and some people can read and write and don't understand anything.*

She distinguishes the two by saying that "illiteracy" means someone cannot read or write or has trouble reading or writing, while "literacy" means a person can read the words on the page and physically write words but cannot understand what she reads and/or she cannot compose a paper. In that case, Deidra sees both as problematic. Her definitions fit Grace's problems with literacy. From Deidra's perspective, Grace has a literacy problem, but Grace is not illiterate whereas she herself (i.e., Deidra) is both literate and illiterate. So, if being literate means you do not understand what you read or write and being illiterate means you are unable to read and write, a difference in score would not be appropriate for her since she fits her own definitions of both terms. Despite the confusion, her response is in line with a key aspect that all but one participant has included in her definition thus far: comprehension. Whether or not one is literate, more than reading and writing are involved. If you do not understand what you are reading or writing, you are not literate.

In any case, the low scores across the board are difficult to understand, because her narrative says she has trouble reading, writing, and comprehending, but she's getting help and wants to do better. As such, a change from high to low would be expected. She has admitted she has a problem, literacy. The mere fact that she sees it as a problem should indicate higher scores for "describes me now"; however, she should have the lower scores she marks for "would like this to describe me in the future" and "will describe me in the future" since it is a goal she is trying to achieve. What her scores also do not explain are the high ratings for "value literacy." Since she completed the Possible Selves Inventory on her own, I do not know what she was thinking. However, I think I can safely assume that "literacy" meant something different from "literate" or "illiterate," maybe even the more traditional, "the ability to . . ." rather than the inability to do something. If that is the case, her response to the "value literacy" possible self is consistent with the majority of her data. For example, on her questionnaire her response to the question, "Is being literate important? How so?" was: *"Because it's important to me to know how to read and write without having to ask someone to read it and make sure what I'm writing is good to turn in and get a A or B on it."* If Deidra sees literacy as an ability instead of an inability, her string of 7s ("strongly agree") is understandable. She values literacy now, she would like to continue to value it, and she believes she will value literacy in the future. Those responses would correspond with her action of participating in an adult literacy program as well as her belief that literacy is connected to many of the goals she wants to achieve in her lifetime. In any event, we must keep her definitions in mind when reviewing any of her responses about literacy.

Another possibility for the confusion in Deidra's "literate," "illiterate," and "value literacy" possible selves scoring is that she did not understand the directions in the Possible Selves Inventory. She never told me she did not understand the directions while completing it, and I don't recall that she asked any questions about clarifying the instructions. (I do recall that after receiving it I was a bit confused by some things so I asked for clarification.) She completed the Possible Selves Inventory on her own as far as I know. However, it is quite possible she had trouble comprehending the instrument just as Maya did. I wrongly assumed she would ask for help if she did not understand something. It may be that she was embarrassed to do so. It may also be that she was just using the same strategies for completing the Possible Selves Inventory she uses every day of her life in handling text: she does the best she can with what she's got.

Deidra does not view "standard" English in the same light as literacy. While she indicates her high regard for literacy, she does not quite do the same for "standard" English. Of all the participants in the study, Deidra has the strongest ties to an African American English speech community. She identifies with that speech community above any other. That has caused her problems with Grace because Grace does not value the depth of Deidra's use of African American English as much as Deidra does and, therefore, she "corrects" or chastises Deidra when she uses certain African American English linguistic features.

Below is an excerpt from the Kitchen Talk audio taping that not only illustrates the correction that Deidra often receives from Grace, but also presents a good example of the variation in usage within African American English.[1] Both women are African American and both have several salient characteristics of African American English in their speech. Each identifies with her African American community. The primary difference between those communities is age group and perhaps to some extent socioeconomic status or class. So, though this is an exchange between a mother and daughter with strong ties to their African American communities and an identification and comfort with the language of those communities and the culture therein, they clearly have different opinions about what is and is not acceptable discourse despite those ties and despite the informal speech context. Again, there is a line that has been drawn that says, "This far and no farther."

The exchange is primarily between Grace and Deidra. The conversation took place at Grace's house when Deidra was visiting. They are in the kitchen preparing dinner while talking. This excerpt is from a discussion about television shows. (In the transcript, <xx> represents words I could not understand and, therefore, could not transcribe; @ represents laughing.)

> Grace: *I see they took Patti LaBelle's show off.*
> Deidra: *I know. I likeded that show.*
> Grace: *Now what you saying that fuh?*
> Sonja: It's supposed to be on next week.
> Grace: *That's <xx> talking bout I* likeded *that show.*
> Deidra: *I say I* likeded *that show.*
> Grace: *I liked. L-I-K-E-D.*
> Sonja: It's coming on today.
> Grace: *That—<xx> Don't you go down there changing—acting—*
> *hanging yo uh speech.*
> Deidra: @
> Grace: *That's two things—cause something else you said. Those tesses.*
> *Better be trying to tell them.*

Grace corrects Deidra and warns her not to return to Tiberius and revert to the bad language she used before living (and hopefully growing) in Picard. Grace does this correcting while using certain characteristics of African American English herself, such as zero copula and zero postvocalic /r/ (e.g., *"Now what you saying that fuh?"*). Apparently her African American English linguistic features are not as objectionable as Deidra's reduplicated past tense *-ed* (e.g., *"I likeded that show"*) and reduplicated plural *-s* (e.g., *"Those tesses"*). Grace "corrects" Deidra based on her perspective and knowledge of what "good" language use is. Interestingly enough, Deidra was not even aware of what was going on until Grace spelled it out for her. I, of course, was as oblivious as possible.

Deidra's response to Grace's rebuke and her possible selves data are not unexpected given her close ties to her African American community. She recognizes that she values African American English more than "standard" English. Though she also plans to continue to use African American English, she is a little ambivalent about claiming it. For example, she indicates she neither agrees nor disagrees for the "describes me now" and "would like this to describe me in the future" times for both the "speak African American English" and "speak 'standard' English" possible selves. Of course, again, this may be a matter of comprehension of the instrument. However, it may also be indicative of the discussion earlier based on sociolinguist William Labov's hypothesis about the nature of African American Vernacular English. If, for example, I report that Deidra uses consonant cluster reduction 40% of the time in her data, what is she using the other 60% of the time? According to Labov, she is accessing the GE component of African American Vernacular English instead of the AA component. However, if that is the case (i.e., AAVE is composed of AA and GE components and OAD is different), then African American Vernacular English speakers are always speaking African American English—it just sometimes looks as though they are speaking OAD because of the overlap from the GE component of AAVE.

In any event, Deidra is not very enthusiastic about "standard" English, but she intends to use it in the future possibly because of her goals connected with literacy and her strong belief that she must speak "standard" English in order to be successful. That is, she may believe it is inevitable and necessary that she learn "standard" English in the process of achieving her Educational, Occupational, and Personal Well-Being goals even though she prefers African American English. Still, she does not plan to give up African American English when she achieves her goals. That is something Grace seems either unable or unwilling to accept even though she herself would not give it up either—she would only better control when, where, and with whom she would choose to use African American English and "standard" English. As it stands, neither has as much control as she would like for switching from African American English to "standard" English and vice versa.

Everybody Doesn't Talk the Same

That statement is most certainly true. We all talk differently, but we can usually understand each other if we try. In the previous excerpt of the conversation between Grace and Deidra, Grace never claims she does not understand what Deidra is saying. (I find it interesting that comprehension is apparently not very important in language use but is considered an essential aspect of literacy by the participants.) It has nothing to do with what Deidra says but how Deidra says it. Some people view such differences as bad. They want to eradicate them. That is not likely to happen because, as writer Paule Marshall notes, "language [truly] is the only homeland" (p. 7). Such is evidenced every day in the continued use of African American English and its possible divergence from instead of convergence toward General American English, despite everything socially, economically, educationally, and otherwise that tells African Americans they should not use African American English.

Deidra says "[speaking African American English is] *knowing what your Black culture is about. And how they uses their English. What type of words they uses. And understand the Black world.*" She also says that just because you are Black does not mean you can speak only African American English or that you should. *"There are Black people who speak good English."* Deidra says she speaks African American English because she understands it better than "standard" English. In her speech samples, she clearly uses African American English. However, as with all the participants, she also uses what she refers to as "good" English because her speech does not consist totally of African American English linguistic features (and not that it would or could given Labov's coexisting systems construct) and because of a response she gives to a question I asked her during the interview that surprised me.

> *I talk the way that I talk because I'm trying to better myself. Sometime I might just say something and it might be like, "Now you know you wasn't supposed to say it. And look at the way you said it. You know that wasn't right. You 'pose to had said it this way."*

Her response indicates she is aware of her own speech differences. She sees "good" language as a vehicle for success and opportunity. She sees African American English as a means of identification with her community and family. She accepts the differences between the two and feels they each have a place. What I find interesting in all this is that she believes she speaks "correctly," at least sometimes. And she is right. She is quite capable of at least partially producing what she believes is "good" English at the very least because of the GE component in her language.

During the INT sample, she is fairly consistent in her use of African

American English linguistic features. She uses the morphological features 27% of the time possible and she uses the phonological and syntactic features 15% and 19% of the time possible, respectively. In other words, less than half of her speech contains African American English linguistic features in a somewhat formal setting. In the KT sample, she uses African American English phonological features 40% of the time, morphological features 60% of the time, and syntactic features 81% of the time.

Deidra's interview lasted 90 minutes and her total talk time comprised approximately 54 minutes of that. Her INT speech data consisted of 35 pages of transcription, of which 21 pages consisted solely of her own speech. She talked more during the first half of the interview than during the last half (i.e., for tape 1, side A, she talked 72% of the time). Of the 13,609 total words for the INT transcription, her own speech consisted of 8,332 words. Her KT speech sample consisted of 23 pages of her speech alone for a total of 5,515 words—the most for any participant. Her KT speech sample combined with her INT speech sample consists of 44 pages and 13,847 words of her alone—third highest of the participants.

Of the 18 African American English features I examined, Deidra uses all of them; but she does not use *they* possessive, completive *done,* and invariant *be* in her INT speech sample. Other than Maya, Deidra is the only person for whom all 18 features occur in the INT and KT speech samples. She is the only one for whom an entire category has a count in double digits for each African American English feature—KT phonology. Her speech yields the third highest total number of occurrences of African American English features (861, behind Grace [1,001] and Maya [976], with the next highest being Reia [311]) and the second highest percentage of African American English linguistic features for INT and KT combined (30%, second only to Maya's 45%, with the next highest being Grace's at 19%). However, she has more double-digit percentages for feature occurrence (23 of 36 possible) than any other participant (Grace is second with 21 of 36).

Despite the prominence of some African American English linguistic features in Deidra's INT and KT speech samples, not all three categories show a significant difference between her INT and KT speech. Phonology and syntax show a significant difference but morphology does not. As is consistent with the other participants thus far with the exception of Maya, morphology is the most likely African American English linguistic category not to show a significant difference in the use of African American English features between INT and KT speech; syntax is the most likely to show a significant difference in the use of African American English features between the two speech contexts. Ironically, Maya's African American English morphological features show the most significant difference between the two speech contexts.

I'm Scared I'm Going to Make a Mistake

Deidra hid for too many years. Correction: Deidra was allowed to hide for too many years. She has had several years of college. At over thirty years old, she is unable to construct an adequate middle-school-level text. She is also unable to read one with understanding. And although Grace has not had as much schooling as Deidra, her ability to produce a text is arguably better.

During the reading passage section of the interview, Deidra had more problems than any other participant with the exception of Maya. However, Maya would be expected to have a problem, given her grade-school education, but Deidra would not be expected to have such a problem since she has completed high school and has had some college experience. Nevertheless, all too often Deidra had to struggle just to say the words. As with each participant except Reia, I read the passages at some point after she read them with the hope that hearing the words might help her understand better. That was a mistake, because it only served to show a difference that did not need to be highlighted.

Despite her difficulties with the reading passages, Deidra did offer explanations for each passage she read. She had difficulty understanding them, but she did try to make some meaning of them. Still, it was difficult, for both of us. Our exchange during the first reading passage, a quotation from literacy scholar Johan Galtung, is a good example of the problems we both were having during this part of the interview. I also include Maya's reading of the same passage for comparison. In the transcript, the words enclosed in [ ] represent overlapping or simultaneous speech (usually my speech).

Deidra: *What would happen if the whole world became literated?*
Answer. Not so very much, for the world is not by and large structured in such a way that it is compali—no capalet—is that right? [capable] *capable of absolving the impact. But if the whole world considers of—that's right?* [consisted] *consists of litertry—literated?* [literate] *literate um, um, automoon?* [autonomous] *autonomous . . .*

mmm . . . siterous [critical] *critical OK um constructive?* [mmm
hmm] *people capable of translating ideas into action individuals—
individually or collectively the world would change.*
{Maya: *What would happen if the whole world became litery* [literate]
*literate. Answer: Not so very much, for the world is by and large
structured?* [mmm hmm] *in such a way that it is compalable*
[capable] *that is it capable of—of uh,* [absorbing] *absorbing the
impact* [umm hmm]. *But if the impact the world the whole world—
but if the whole world consistee* [consisted] *consisted of literacy* [liter-
ate] [autonomous] *autonomous c-r-i-t-i-c-a-l what that is,* [critical]
critical [constructive] *constructive people capable* [umm hmm] *of
translating?* [mmm hmm] *ideas into action. I—I individually?* [mmm
hmm] *or* [collectively] *collectively* [umm hmm] *the world—would
be—would change* [umm hmm].}

Sonja: OK. So what do you think Galtung is saying?

Deidra: *Um, I guess he's saying that if the whole world was liter—um
have a literacy problem um then I guess everybody understand one
another huh?*

Sonja: If the whole world had a literacy problem, they would understand every—they would understand everything?

Deidra: *I mean if they become literate—I mean—everybody—I guess
everybody would understand everybody because nobody would
know.*

Sonja: Nobody would know . . . ?

Deidra: *I mean nobody would know——no one would talk about anybody, no one would have anything to say because everybody was
literate.*

Sonja: OK, so it's not that they have a literacy problem, they don't
have a literacy problem?

Deidra: *Well, if if he said become literate. I mean if you become literate
everybody was literate, then um, then it's nothing. I mean nobody
can read or write so what are you going to do.*

Sonja: OK, uh what do you think about that? Do you agree with
that?

Deidra: *No because everybody's not literate.*

Sonja: But he's just saying what if they were.

Deidra: *I mean that's just his point of view what if they were then,
what would become of the world.*

Sonja: I mean, if you—do you believe—what do you believe, if everybody was—in the world was literate then what, what do you think would happen?

Deidra: *I don't know. I'm pretty sure somebody would start reading and trying to better themselves.*

Sonja: Well think about what literate—what you said literate was versus illiterate. Remember what the other thing we had. Literacy was the ability to read and write. So if literacy means they would be able to read and write.

Deidra: *Well they are capable—they you know capable of doing it but. He's saying what if.*

Sonja: What if everyone was because at this point everyone isn't literate apparently.

Deidra: *Yeah, everybody's not literate.*

Sonja: OK. Um, I can't remember what you said about your agreement or disagreement with that.

Deidra: *Oh I don't agree with that. Because I mean at some form—if everybody was had some—you know become that way, I'm pretty sure that um, somebody would try and know that—I mean somebody would have the you know the capability of learning—I mean somebody how to read I mean everybody didn't come into the world learning how to read. So I mean everybody did come here learning—you know I mean, well I would say the whole world came here like literacy, but they learn and they taught each other so I would think they would do it again.*

Sonja: Do what again?

Deidra: *Learn to—learn each other how to write read and you know overcome the literacy.*

I find it interesting and ironic that one of the very issues of this study—literacy—was so confusing and difficult to discuss. Deidra, the one participant who painfully admitted to having a literacy problem, could not reconcile the very meaning of the term. She continued to see "literacy" and "illiteracy" as sharing the idea of "not" something. On the other hand, for someone who claims to be literate and a reader of texts, I did not do a very good job of meeting Deidra where she was and understanding what she was trying to say. I was unable to read her text. Only now have I begun to understand what she was saying, or at least what she wasn't. Even more disheartening to me is my inability to redress

Deidra's plight while imagining what a teacher with possibly little training in reading instruction and, consequently, detecting and correcting reading problems could have done. I know I felt helpless and still do. I was only discussing five short reading passages. What happens when the task is a book chapter for social studies or biology or English? Someone had to know if it took only a small sampling such as the above for me to see the depth of the struggle Deidra faces everyday.

It was obviously difficult for both Maya and Deidra to read the passage. They had about the same number and kind of stumbling blocks in the passage: "capable," "consisted," "literate," "autonomous," "critical," etc. Neither understood the passage without some explanation or probing, and even then I am not sure either understood it. But again, we are, theoretically at least, comparing someone with a grade-school education with someone with minimally a high-school education. Practically, we are apparently comparing apples and apples instead of apples and oranges.

As difficult as it was for Deidra to read and comprehend a text, it was just as difficult for her to produce one. However, unlike Maya and Grace, Deidra did have writing samples to share. She gave me two papers she had written while in college that I used along with her written responses to Letters 1 and 2 and her information questionnaire for her writing samples for a total of 5,234 words. She wrote Letter 1 in cursive, but she wrote Letter 2 in print. Her handwriting is legible whether she prints or writes in cursive, but it often seems labored, though not nearly as labored as Maya's. Unfortunately, neither Letter 1 nor Letter 2 really responded to the questions I asked. That likely indicates she had a problem understanding the letters I wrote.

In the letters she produced for the study, Deidra demonstrated several features of African American English: *"scrip"* instead of "script"; *"stated"* instead of "started"; *"try to ignore put down . . ."* (i.e., no plural *-s* marker); *"I moved out of my mother house."* (i.e., no possessive *-s* marker); *"if what I'm writing sound good"* (i.e., no third-person singular *-s* marker); *"He than turn to me"* (i.e., no past tense marker); and *"children was pasting and I wasn't."* She shared several of the features Grace had in her writing, but she does not tend to have as many occurrences as Grace. There were several misspellings as well (e.g., *"there"* instead of "their" and *"your"* instead of "you're").

Deidra has a problem with punctuation. The punctuation of her handwritten documents is at Level 1. She has problems with capitalization, but her periods and commas were not as haphazard as Grace's. Still, 90% of her punctuation was problematic. Her somewhat sporadic use of capitalization for certain letters indicated to me she may not always mean a capital even though she uses the capital form and has lowercase versions of some letters. Some other items to note are that she consistently uses "another" for "other"; she consistently uses "are" instead of "or"; and she has trouble with verb tense.

Within a few months of completing this project, Deidra was no longer attending college or participating in the adult literacy program. She is at a standstill in her writing development. Even though she has been in school longer than she has not, she has been unable to master the skills of schooling. Still, she has been receptive to the promises and ideologies that schools supposedly teach alongside those skills. She believes there is a better life waiting for her if only she can conquer her "literacy."

Deidra may be clinging to the literacy myth, but she does not have as much faith in the myth of "standard" English. Her suspicions about "standard" English may be due to her identification with an African American community that strongly identifies with and uses African American English. Discord within our sociocultural and historical contexts is expected. When there is a clash, the stronger identification will usually win out. Since she would rather identify with a community of African American English speakers than a community of "standard" English speakers, she chooses to speak African American English. Her waning belief in the "standard" English myth may also be part of her ongoing struggle with what she has been schooled to believe and what she has learned by experience. After all, she has completed several years of college while struggling with her "literacy." Is literacy or "standard" English really important?

Only If You Believe It Is

The above is Deidra's response to the question, "Is speaking standard English important?" Much of what this study addressed was derived from that very question: what do you believe? Deidra identifies with the Ideologies of Opportunity, Progress, and Emancipation. She identifies most with the Ideology of Opportunity, though the Ideology of Emancipation is not far behind, and least with the Ideology of Progress.

The lowest score she gave any item was 4 ("neither agree nor disagree"), and this was mostly confined to the Ideology of Progress. Those items of uncertainty were: "political democracy," "a distinction between myth and history," "people who are less likely to commit a crime," "a lower birth rate," "liberal and humane social attitudes," and "better educational opportunities." I find the last one surprising given her struggles with education and the reasons she gives for those struggles: literacy. I also find it surprising since it is a key component of the Ideology of Opportunity, the ideology she identifies with the most. This is made more interesting when considered along with some of her Possible Selves Inventory responses. On her Possible Selves Inventory, she slightly agrees with the statement, "In order to succeed or function in this country, I (like everyone else) must be literate," and strongly agrees with the statement, "In order to succeed in this country, I (like everyone else) must speak standard, or 'good,' English." The lesser agreement with the former corresponds with her uncertainty about better educational opportunities but not with her language beliefs.

Deidra has maintained that though language may be more important to younger people than to older people like her grandparents, "standard" English is only important if you believe it is. When she talks about language she refers to it, in part, with respect to identification. She allows that an African American is not restricted to speaking African American English just to identify with the African American community, but she also sees language as a means for communication. Thus, language is both a cultural artifact and a means of communication outside her community. But when she talks about language she does not indicate that she believes that "standard" English is important for success or connected to intelligence. She actually gives a very interesting example in her narrative showing why she does not believe the latter to be true:

> For instance, like a young child can hear their parents talking correct English because that's the way they talk and they grow up talking like that. That doesn't mean that they know how to read or write. So therefore, it's not like it's a big deal to me because I might be a person that can read and write and might can't talk that well.

This is certainly in conflict with Reia's narrative where she says she judges intelligence by how someone talks. Deidra makes a good point in saying the opposite; i.e., just because you talk "good" does not mean you are intelligent—it just may be the way you learned how to talk because of the exposure to that talk from parents and/or others. Only in response to specific ideologies or during the Possible Selves Inventory does Deidra indicate something contrary to views she expresses elsewhere. Also, lack of clarity may be due to the wording of the lead statement in the ideologies section of the interview, which does not separate responses for literacy and "standard" English. She would have had to specifically make the distinction as part of her response. Since Deidra did not do that, it is difficult to resolve this issue of seeming contradictions in her beliefs about "standard" English and literacy.

It is easy to see how Deidra's identity is being shaped and is shaping who she is and who she may become by her sociocultural and historical contexts. Despite her strong ideological beliefs, she is able to question them more than Maya or Grace has thus far because she sees the contradictions and frail promises made by society and education in her life. Many of the gaps, inadequacies, and inequalities are becoming clearer to her as she reflects on her life, goals, and possible selves with an eye to the future. But given what she has been able to do so far, how much is in her control and how much is dependent on others?

She has tried to be brave, as indicated in her statement about her language, which I think can be applied to her situation overall: *"And far as other people talking, I mean I can't control their talking, but I can try to better myself on my language and everything."* In other words, she realizes she cannot change others but she can change herself (does it follow then that others cannot change her unless she wants to change?); however, she needs a little help. We all need a little help (and a little guidance) every now and then. I do not think Deidra has ever gotten that help— *"No one taught me anything. . . . I didn't have anybody to push me"*—and that is shameful and unacceptable.

I have talked about taking responsibility for your actions, yourself, your life, and your decisions. But there is a point at which you do not have the power or control to do what you would like or change what you do not want. Deidra is at that point. And I am sure she is not alone. She needs to and wants to do more than just get by. She has the ability and desire to dream. If those possible selves have no hope of becoming because no one ever helps her to rectify this unconscionable silencing or encourage and empower her David-sized hoped for possible selves that seem to be losing to her Goliath-sized reality, what will become of Deidra?

I Don't Like to Think about If . . .

[If I had it to do all over again] *I don't know* [what I would change
about my education or my educational experience]. *I don't like to think
about if when I was coming up would I have changed or what I woulda
did. But I can say now I'm in a program to help me more with that and
as of this point in my life I want to change it. But I can't speak for back
then because I didn't know and what you don't know you can't really
say I wanna change it. But if that was possible, I wish that I could
have been more open and said that I had a problem, but I didn't so
it's something that I have to deal with now and get the help that I
have to get.*

Are we really our mothers' daughters? This sounds so unlike Grace, and
it is hard to believe that one of Grace's children said such a thing. Deidra, of all the participants, was most cheated in her education—even
more so than Grace, in my opinion. Grace can read even though she
doesn't always understand all that she reads and she probably isn't reading at a twelfth-grade level, but she is a lot closer than Deidra. Yet the attitude displayed in the above excerpt is wonderful. This is very different
from Grace's narrative, where she dwells on what might have been or
should have been and she seems to be unable to get past her past. Deidra, on the other hand, says she is not going to dwell on the past because
she cannot change the past—she can only deal with where she is now
and go from there.

Nevertheless, as Deidra herself says, *"I just didn't get the education that
I needed."* That is a problem. Deidra should not have slipped through the
cracks because schools should strive to not have cracks. Yet, this is the
third participant in a row to mention that some children just don't make
it in school; they just get left behind or are left to sink instead of swim,
fall instead of fly. It is nice to see, though, that Deidra is not living in the
past, which I hope means she is not doomed to repeat it despite her
dropping out of the literacy program and essentially not living up to her
own words or her own expectations.

Deidra's situation is indicative yet again of the role of caregivers and
teachers in the lives of children. Deidra does not have much educational
resilience or a sense of self-efficacy given the problems she has and the
limited abilities she has to redress those problems. She did not have that
someone to support her and enable her to be educationally resilient.

[Your language and literacy compared to my language and literacy are] *totally totally different. Totally different. I couldn't even compare myself to your language and writing and stuff because I'm not on the level that you're on. I guess I can say you were interested in your writing and your language and how you felt and I wasn't because no one taught me anything. You had someone in school to really push you. I didn't have anybody to push me. One time I ask, you told me it was a lady who use to make y'all get the dictionary when you was in what, elementary school or something? It's some teachers help you when you at that level and I didn't get that part. So you and I are just, when it comes to that literacy or anything, we are totally the opposite. In that way you know more than me. I could know more than you in some other ways but in that way we're just totally different.*

Although I can agree with Deidra that I had people (and in the above the person was Mrs. Foudy) who seemed to care about me and who took an interest in me, knowing that does not tell me why it happened. Why does that happen for some children and not others? I raised this question to one noted Stanford educator, who responded (in my paraphrasing), "I don't think we know why. I don't think we can ever know why. Sometimes we don't even know how. I think it may just be that God sprinkles something around and it falls on some and not on others. How else can you explain why a family in India with 12 children has one child who's brilliant, who's special, who stands out from the other 11?" I cannot deny that some people are special, different, extraordinary. But this is not about the extraordinary, it's about the ordinary. There has to be some tangible reason why some are chosen and some are not.

SONJA
I Had a Positive Experience

I am ever mindful of the fact that the groups I belong to—African American people, women people—are still in the process of pulling the gags out of our mouths; that in speaking freely and publicly, in expressing our thoughts and feelings, we do so as much for our ancestors and foremothers as we do for ourselves.

—Marcia Ann Gillespie, in Johnson, *Proud Sisters*

• • •

BY THE GRACE OF GOD GO I

The funny thing is I do not think I could have made the statement in the subtitle of this chapter during the time I was going through grade school or even college. It is funny how things do not look as bad when there is time and experience to provide a little distance. *"Had I not had people who were supporting me and encouraging me and letting me know that I could do these things, I don't think I would be doing any of this right now."* At the time, I did not realize I had all that support. I can see it a lot better now. Recognizing that has helped me realize my possibilities and allowed me to dream a little more. Grace can attest to that:

> *You were in school when you were two months old. So all that played a big part. That could've had a big, big effect on you as you know by now. Because the school I had you in, those people were good to you and they just loved you. I remember that lady. She said, "I just love Sonja," she say, "And she's just so smart." And you were fat and she said, "Oh she's just so pretty." And people cater to people like that. So they probably was helping you and teaching you. . . . But you always had story books and you always liked to do stuff like that and we always helped you. You was always interested in stuff like that and we always helped you. Preparing children for an education is preparing yourself for your future.*

I think Grace is on to something. I think those early experiences did have a significant effect on me. I also think they help to explain a little bit about the chosen ones, so to speak. According to psychologist Albert Bandura, physical attractiveness and sociable temperamental qualities help to draw nurturing caretaking. As children develop positive attributes, they become more engaging to others and attract support from them. In other words, this is the positive effect of the self-fulfilling prophecy: cute children with good dispositions and personalities attract enabling adults and thereby establish a pattern of not only attracting these nurturing adults but also seeking them out as their confidence in themselves grows from these early experiences. That, at least in part, can explain how some children are made to stand out and are chosen by nurturing caretakers to learn to fly. As a result, early on some are picked while others are not. Reia and I were chosen to learn to fly; Maya, Grace, and Deidra were not.

My opportunity to fly and dream may be why I listed more goals (more than fifty) than any other participant. It could also be because I was more familiar with the instruments and measures and what I wanted from them. I listed goals and possible selves that could be categorized into every goal domain except one. My list of goals included the following:

Educational Goals:
> *Ph.D. in English*
> *M.A. in Linguistics*
> *B.S. in Math*
> *M.A. in Education or even a Ph.D. in Education*

Family Goals:
> *Good wife*
> *Good parent—if I were ever a parent*
> *A good homemaker*
> *Being joyously married to my husband for the rest of our lives*
> *Helping my mother, father, and maybe others in my family become (more) literate*

Occupational Goals:
> *A college professor*
> *Good teacher*
> *Good researcher in my field*
> *Good speaker (e.g., at conferences)*

Teaching at a major university

Submitting papers for publication and doing research

Groundbreaking research in language, language and uses of literacy, literacy, or something bigger—like incorporating goals, education, etc.

Tenure at the university I want to be at

A brilliant career

Personal Well-Being Goals:

A good writer

Writing a book

Self-confident

Positive/good self-esteem

Patience and love towards humankind

Loving, a good heart

Forgiving

A healthy body, mind, and soul

Physically fit

Good softball player

Good tennis player

Good singer

At a good weight

Speak and write several foreign languages

Could play the piano or some musical instrument

A good person

A computer whiz

A great cook

Physical Comfort Goals:

A good job with good benefits and good pay

Living in a house we are buying; home owner

Driving new cars

Power and Wealth Goals:

A post-doctoral fellowship

A beginning faculty fellowship/grant (e.g., Spenser Foundation)

A MacArthur Fellowship award

Financially secure

Religious Goals:

Doing God's will for my life

A Christian, saved

Salvation and peace and joy

> *A good spiritual relationship with God*
> *Spiritual, a heart for God*
> *Faithful to God*
> *Reading and understanding all of God's word (bible) that is intended*
> *Going to see my God in heaven*

Social Helping Goals:

> *A person who makes a positive difference in this life and in the lives*
> *of others*

Travel and Adventure Goals:

> *Go to all the major league baseball stadiums*

Like the other participants, I did not have any Friendship goals. My highest-ranked goals are in the Religious and Occupational goal domains. One Occupational goal in particular stands out and it should come as no surprise by now:

> *I couldn't really think of anything else despite my mother continually telling me throughout the course of my life that I wouldn't be a good teacher for various reasons. I think about it sometimes, after having taught that class* [i.e., my first experience as a graduate student teaching College Writing], [that] *she might have a point. But if I'm gonna have a first profession, I would like that to be it.*

My most feared possible selves are in the Religious and Personal Well-Being goal domains. My accomplishment and avoidance of the respective possible selves is fueled by conflict and contrariness. I know the right thing to do most often to attain or avoid the goal, but knowing does not always translate into doing. I am usually aware of the conflict and contradictions, but sometimes I am not. For example, one of my highest-ranked hoped-for possible selves is to be a good teacher. I think I work at that goal more than anyone I know, yet I sometimes do things that are contrary to that. Those times most often involve grading. I think I give good assignments, but I often have a hard time with assessment because I often have standards or goals that are too far beyond my students, or so they tell me. Still, I find it difficult to be flexible because I often believe—whether I admit it or not—that my students should be at least as devoted to being a good student as I was and still am. They should come to class every day and they should want to learn and grow. Although it may be a good thing to have high standards, this does not go well with inflexibility if the goal is to be a good teacher. So, I always have to have a check for my rigidity because I know if I did not, I would be doing a disservice to students and to the very idea of teaching and learning.

Though I do not list many goals specifically related to language and literacy, they are nevertheless important to what I do. I devote time to those issues in some way each and every day. I listen to what people say and how they say it. I think about how others might perceive their speech and question the possible ideologies behind them. One might normally suggest this is due to my level of education or my personal interest in language given my experiences; however, given Deidra's level of education and educational experiences, that suggestion is not very convincing. There are obviously other factors that have to be taken into account as I have indicated.

> I guess I can say you were interested in your writing and your language and how you felt and I wasn't because no one taught me anything. You had someone in school to really push you. I didn't have anybody to push me. One time I ask, you told me it was a lady who use to make y'all get the dictionary when you was in what, elementary school or something? It's some teachers help you when you at that level and I didn't get that part. So you and I are just, when it comes to that literacy or anything, we are totally the opposite.

I disagreed with her assessment at the time. Upon reflection and learning, I know she identified at least one of the factors. As I said, with time, experience, and reflection, I now know I had support and Deidra did not. I had a desire that in part was due to the early support I received and sought. Deidra, like Grace, did not have anyone to push her and give her that support.

When I was young, I sought approval through grades and my conduct at school. I was not born with the self-motivation to do well in school. I wanted to be liked by my teachers and I wanted to do well for them to show that I was a good person who deserved their attention. But that could be because I initially got their attention because, as Grace said in her interview, *"The school I had you in, those people were good to you and they just loved you. I remember that lady she said, "I just love Sonja," she say, "And she's just so smart. . . . "Oh she's just so pretty." And people cater to people like that."* Deidra did not get that part. She did not have those early experiences that I had and she did not have the early opportunity to develop a self-motivation for success in school or with language and literacy. She was taken care of by Grace until she was taken from Grace. At that point, she was at home with her paternal grandparents for the most part. Early experiences are crucial for self-efficacy, motivation, resilience, identity, education, language, literacy, goals, possible selves, and a host of other things. So, when in my interview I said my parents did not contribute to my language and literacy development, I was wrong. They did contribute even though they may not have known it at the time either. I am glad I know now.

EXPERIENCES: PROBABILITIES OF POSSIBILITIES

In the narratives of the five participants, certain differences in our experiences stand out as influential to our goals. Each had different experiences in school, each reached different levels of schooling, each is at a different point in her language and literacy development, and each woman deals with the issues discussed in this study in different ways. Maya never finished grade school, but she did pursue developing her language and literacy beyond her educational level, and I think she has been successful in doing that. Grace finished high school (a diploma, not a GED) as her self-described crowning educational achievement, but it was a somewhat hollow victory because of her language and literacy development (although I think she is better off than she believes). Reia earned a bachelor's and master's degree and is quite comfortable with her language and literacy development despite her continuing work on her writing skills. Deidra has had several years of college, but she is not literate at that level. I have earned a Ph.D. and have met with some success in my language and literacy development.

According to my Possible Selves Inventory data, my writing averages are close to my reading averages as I do not value writing more than reading, but I do see writing as more difficult for me than reading. Although there are many texts I have found difficult to comprehend in academia, my writing is more difficult in the sense that it is something I have to produce. My thoughts about the differences between my reading and writing are similar to Reia's. A text written by someone else that I read is easier to address than a text I have to write for others. As Reia indicated, the complete construction of such texts—from scratch, from your own knowledge and understanding, from your own abilities and creativity—is a daunting task that seems to ever evolve and mature differently from my reading. This distinction between reading and writing follows the trend of most of the other participants. I can say though that my reading greatly informs my writing and, as a result, the two are certainly interrelated. The more I read, the better reader *and* writer I become.

I also agree with the other participants that comprehension is an important aspect of literacy, but I would add that one's ability and desire to make a text meaningful to oneself are important as well. Still, literacy is more than the sum of its parts. It is not something you finally achieve but rather something you continue to do or become, as indicated in the passage I wrote (the fifth reading passage) and used in the interview, unbeknownst to the participants.

> Literacy is a social construction. While literacy may be said to begin with the introduction of writing systems, literacy is not the same thing as writing. If a person is only able to read the words on a page or write letters on a page that form words, that does not make the person literate. Just because one can read and write does not mean that one is literate. We can perhaps more usefully think of literacy as the focus of a changing and complicated dialectic between talk and inscription. It is multidimensional. Literacy is the process by which one learns to read and/or write and grows to understand and (critically) think about a text in a way most meaningful for the individual in the environment and culture of the individual. Literacy, therefore, can vary from society to society and possibly from individual to individual in a given context and the meaning one chooses to make in that context.

As such, I do not think I have reached my full capabilities. I still have room for learning and growing in this area, just as is the case for Maya, Grace, Reia, and Deidra. It is simply that we are each at different places.

Although I concede that I speak "standard" English and I probably will continue to do so, I value it less than African American English regardless of my ability to speak either. The issue of ability is more important to my assessment of my possible selves than is my desire. That might account for why my scores follow the same pattern as Maya's—a higher "would like to describe me in the future" score than "will describe me in the future." For example, I would like to be both a "good writer" and a "good reader," but the chances of my becoming a "good reader" seem more promising than my becoming a "good writer." I desire them equally but realistically I see the results differently because of my views about what a "good reader" and a "good writer" are.

That might be an acceptable assessment for "standard" English and language as well. It is more difficult to see language or "standard" English as something one has finally achieved when change is a viable part of a language's existence. Also, since language is inseparable from one's identity and since we all speak a language collage, or idiolect, it is easy to imagine that the language picture is bigger than whether our subjects agree with our verbs (according to Oprah Winfrey's definition of "good" English in 1987) or whether *periplus* has a Latin or Greek etymology. This seems clear when looking at what makes up one's language. In this study, I charted particular features of African American English. As with the others, I have features from both African American English and "standard" English. My language—our language—consists of elements from wherever we choose to get them and use them. So, I can at least provisionally understand and articulate the notion of an African American component and a General English component of my African American English as coexisting systems and as a means of explaining what we all do anyway: style shift.

My INT speech sample is slightly different from everyone else's in two ways. Although my entire interview lasted approximately 127 minutes with approximately 121 minutes of my speech alone, I analyzed only the first 45-minute segment of my interview, for which approximately 43 minutes was my speech alone. Also, since I could not interview myself, my husband interviewed me. He did an excellent job in that of the 18 pages for that 45-minute segment, 17 pages consisted of my speech alone. Of the 8,678 total words, 8,315 were my words alone. These statistics exceed those of Maya's full interview transcription and compare favorably to Deidra's. Part of the reason I chose to only use the first 45 minutes of my interview for my INT speech sample is because I had originally chosen to do that for everyone. However, I decided to analyze the entire interview for everyone in the study in part because there were some differences in use beyond the first 45-minute segment of the interview. In my case, however, there were no differences in the kind and type of features present. So, I stayed with the original 45-minute segment, which I believe to be comparable to the other participants.

My KT sample consists of 16 pages of my speech alone (second lowest of the participants) and 3,959 words of my speech alone (lowest of the participants). I think my totals are lower because I tried to elicit as much data as I could from everyone else without dominating conversations. I wanted to get more data from the other participants than from myself. So, my total number of pages for the INT and KT speech samples is 33 (lowest of the participants) and my total number of words is 12,274 (second lowest of the participants). (Of course, had I analyzed my entire interview, I would have been in the top three for highest totals instead of the bottom two for lowest totals.)

For the INT sample, I used only three African American English linguistic features of the 18 analyzed: final consonant cluster reduction, zero plural -s, and zero past tense -ed. The number of African American English features used rose to 15 of the 18 for the KT sample. Only three African American English linguistic features were not present at all in my speech for the INT or KT samples: labialization of /θ/ > /f/, lowering of /ɪ/ > /æ/ before /ŋ/, and completive *done*. My data follows the same pattern as everyone else's—there is an increase in the percentage of African American English features used from phonology (the lowest), to morphology, to syntax (the highest) in the KT context. The INT context presents a slightly different picture. African American English morphological feature use tends to be the highest there, except for Maya (morphology is the lowest and syntax is the highest) and Reia (phonology is the lowest and syntax is the highest). So, Grace, Deidra, and I control the use of our African American English syntax more than our morphology use whereas Maya and Reia control their morphology use more than their syntax use.

Even though my speech has the fewest African American English linguistic features of any other participant in total or within the INT and KT contexts, its importance is greater than its presence in my speech. Apparently I am more comfortable and more able using African American English syntactic features than morphological or phonological features in the KT context and more conscious of not using them in the INT context. However, there is a significant difference between my speech for the INT and KT contexts for all three African American English linguistic categories I analyzed. So, despite my minimal usage, African American English is present nonetheless.

I do admit that there was something afoot during the Kitchen Talk audio taping. Most researchers are concerned about the "observer's paradox" when doing data collection such as mine. As a researcher of language, you want to get as much "natural" speech as possible, but how much "natural" speech can you get if you are there (referred to by sociolinguists as the observer's paradox)? My situation was a little different in that I was a normal part of the environment, an insider, since the participants were members of my family who were used to talking to me though not on a daily basis. Also, the subjects of our conversations did not generally focus on (their) language. We talked about the same things we would normally talk about. My participants had only to overcome the presence of the microphone and not the microphone, artificial conversations about (their) language, and me, the researcher. That was quite easy to do when it was not just the participant and me in the room, which occurred more often than not. This naturalistic, participant-observer type data collection made the observer's paradox irrelevant. As such, the speech of Maya, Grace, Reia, and Deidra is quite "natural." My speech on the one hand was affected. I feel I often tried to use African American English during the KT audio taping because I, the researcher, knew I wanted to find African American English linguistic features. On the other hand, as I had indicated earlier, I had already begun to try to use more African American English than I had in the past because of my desire to identify more with the community I grew up in and am a part of. So, at the very least, my INT and KT samples show that I know and can use African American English such that it does not seem "unnatural" or out of the ordinary to the other participants who use it on a more regular basis since no one ever said anything about my language at any point during or after the project, though they have in the past.

I remember there was an instance where this was maybe a couple of years ago, or maybe last year when I may have been talking to them and you may have come into the room, and then they'll say, "Oh look at her talking all proper now," or something like that. So I know my parents or people in my family have made comments about my language. So they must notice a distinction between the two, but they don't say something like that.

Still, even with my increased use, my language did not contain as much African American English as the others, but it did contain some.

As a group, the participants in the study show they do talk differently in informal and formal contexts. Our speech combined differs between INT and KT for all three categories of African American English linguistic features I examined. Individually, only three (one in each linguistic category analyzed) of the 18 features analyzed did not show a significant difference: labialization of /θ/ (i.e., /θ/ > /fɪ/), zero possessive -*s,* and completive *been.* Labialization of /θ/ should not be a surprise since it is a feature that did not occur at all for three of the five participants. Although zero possessive -*s* and completive *been* are features that do not tend to occur in speech in quantities high enough to reach significance, especially with only five participants, the lack of significance is also due to there really not being much of a distinction between the two contexts for at least three of the five participants. Both were features that seemed to be used regardless of context. We could extrapolate that zero possessive -*s* and completive *been* are the least stigmatized features for this group of African American English speakers and that labialization of /θ/ is the most stigmatized feature for this group of speakers.

I WRITE

Just as my language stands out compared to Maya, Grace, and Deidra, so do my reading and writing. How well I do either is debatable. During my interview, I read the passages and discussed them with my interviewer just as the others did during theirs. I did not have difficulties with the passages as the others did, but, then again, I picked them and wrote one of them.

My writing stands out compared to Maya, Grace, and Deidra because I have so much more of it. I could have provided numerous writing samples, but I chose five in addition to my letter and information questionnaire for a total of 18,637 words partly because that is how many Reia provided. Two African American English features I analyzed were present in my writing samples—zero third-person singular -*s* and zero copula. Both were also present in my speech samples. Of all the participants, I had the least number of African American English linguistic features in my writing (2) and the least number of misspelled words (5, e.g., *"form"* instead of "from" and *"gaberdine"* instead of "gabardine"). Zero third-person singular -*s* (e.g., *"The high number of evaluative and emotive adjectives contribute to the . . ."*) occurred once in a class paper and zero copula (e.g., *"I'm not sure if this the last book I read"*) occurred once in my information questionnaire. Maya had the second fewest African American English features in her writing (5), but then she only had 127 words for her one writing sample (Grace had the most with 88 occurrences of African American English features and Deidra had the second most with 49). Based upon Shaughnessy's five levels of punctuation, my punctuation is at level 5. So, Reia's assessment that my writing is more advanced than hers is correct with respect to Shaughnessy's levels of punctuation since she is at level 4 and I am at level 5. That may account for the difference in the number of African American English features present in our writing: 22 occurrences for Reia and 2 for me.

My writing practices are different from the other participants because writing is a large part of my profession. The others do not have as high a demand for writing as I do, especially in the form that I do, though Reia's job requires quite a bit of writing and she does a lot of personal writing outside of her job. None of this reflects how well I write, only how much I write. Although I have developed a personal stake in my writing, I do not do much personal writing. However, the whole development of this study is a personal writing that I chose to share. In any event, I do a good deal of reading and writing as part of my daily life. I would like to do both better, but they serve me well for now.

PROMISES AND LIES

Although I speak "good" English and am highly literate according to the other participants, my criticisms about both are harsh, especially compared to the others. The average scores for my level of agreement with the statements about the Ideologies of Opportunity, Progress, and Emancipation are clearly lower than everyone else's. It would appear that I do not agree with the ideologies. Even though I have been in school the longest, the extra time seems to have made me the most cynical about the ideological indoctrination of schooling. That seems to be a pattern for the participants: the longer a participant was schooled, the more likely they are to have lower scores within a category than someone schooled for a shorter time. At only two points is the pattern interrupted: for the Ideology of Emancipation, Grace's average score is higher than Maya's and Deidra's is higher than Reia's. Obviously Grace strongly identifies with that ideology. Again, I can only offer the reasons I did in Reia's chapter for why her score is lower here when one would expect a higher score given the theme of self-esteem in her narrative. Also, she does not conform to the less-acceptance-with-longer-schooling idea I suggest above when comparing her overall average score for the combined categories to Maya, Grace, Deidra, me, or the group average.

It is quite obvious that I am the outlier, so to speak, since, everyone's average score for the ideologies matches or exceeds the average scores for the group with, again, the exception of Reia's low average score for the Ideology of Emancipation. However, even though I have the lowest average score for each ideology, I have the highest standard deviation (i.e., they vary more) for two of the three categories: the Ideology of Opportunity and the Ideology of Emancipation. Hence, the others are more consistent in their agreement than I am in my disagreement with the ideologies. I had seven scores at 4.5 (neither agree nor disagree) or higher in response to the thirty statements: "greater success in school" (Ideology of Opportunity), "transformed" (Ideology of Emancipation), "empowered" (Ideology of Emancipation), "better educational opportunities" (Ideology of Opportunity), "more likely to take education seriously" (Ideology of Opportunity), "emancipated" (Ideology of Emancipation), and "critical thinkers" (Ideology of Emancipation). Not one of my scores was above 4 for the Ideology of Progress.

The Ideology of Emancipation was the most accepted ideology among the participants and the least varied in agreement. The Ideology of Progress was the most varied and the least accepted of the ideologies. The Ideology of Progress pushed the limits of the participants' acceptance of the ideological indoctrination of school and society.

I should make a disclaimer about my responses to the ideology statements during the interview:

> I want to clarify something too. I don't think "standard" English has much to do with any of these and I will say now that I'm mostly focusing on literacy. Speaking "standard" English isn't really doing much for you in any particular case except in the education thing since that's what they want you to do. And maybe job opportunities because people judge you based on that. I felt I had to say that.

I was the only participant to verbally separate "standard" English and literacy during the interview, which is why I say my ideological beliefs differ for language and literacy even though I realize the two are connected by similar ideologies.

My animosity toward the "standard" English myth is reflected in my narrative:

> Given my beliefs about language and knowing what I know about the way people speak, and the way some people think about how others speak, I talk the way I naturally do because the more that I read and

the more that I think about it, the more that I get angry. I feel the injustice of judging people on the way that they speak and just trying to judge their intelligence, their abilities. It bothers me and I think that's why I make a conscious effort to not use standard English a lot more now.

Some people assume that those who talk "well" are smart even though they may not be and that those who don't talk "well"—African American English speakers, Southern English speakers, etc.—are stupid even though they may be smart. The problem is that they (the latter group) are often not given much of a chance to show their intelligence. On an episode of "Who Wants to Be a Millionaire?" one of the contestants who won the fastest-finger round and made it to the hot seat was a Southerner who spoke Southern English, spoke slowly and deliberately, and wore thick glasses that loosely hung on his nose. For several questions of the contestant's appearance, the host, Regis Philbin, as well as many audience members, continually laughed at the contestant in some way. Philbin at one point had to say he was going to control himself. Philbin never said why he was laughing, nor did he venture to ask the audience why it was laughing. I knew why they were laughing. All I could think about was what a fine example of linguistic bigotry was being shown on national television on the highest-rated show on television. They were laughing because they were thinking, "What a hick. How did a doofus like him get on this show?" As you can see, once I realized what was peculiar to my mind, there was no turning back.

My antagonism towards both the "standard" English myth and the literacy myth is also reflected in my response to the two statements in the Possible Selves Inventory that address this issue.

> In order to succeed in this country, I (like everyone else) must speak standard, or "good", English.
> In order to succeed or function in this country, I (like everyone else) must be literate.

On a scale from 1 ("strongly disagree") to 7 ("strongly agree"), I marked 2 for the former and 3 for the latter. Again, I give "standard" English the edge because we more often encounter people's speech before their literacy. That makes speech more vulnerable in some ways than literacy. Again, Grace's story about Byron's ability to get over is a good example.

That may also be why I spent more time while I was growing up on my speech than on my literacy. Be that as it may, both have my attention now.

Can You Help Me Figure This Out?

In comparing the participants and considering my education, I felt that my life was most like Reia's and Deidra's was most like Grace's. That is ironic since Deidra did not live with Grace past the age of two until she was an adult and I am the one who did live with Grace, and I am not Reia's child or Maya's child, nor did I live with either for more than two months at a time during some summers during my childhood. How can that be? Like Reia, I outgrew my parents' education.

> *Because it seemed at some point in my schooling, I had actually out-done them in a way. I mean I would be the one that would go around correcting them in their language or something like that. By the time I reached high school, I was the one that they would ask questions of. I didn't go to my parents and say, "Would you help me with my home-work," or "Can you help me figure this out." That wasn't the sort of situation that my parents were in because neither one of them I don't think felt particularly confident in their language and literacy capabilities.*

My parents did all they could. I sought out others who could provide what they could not. I had some teachers who wanted to see me fly and did what they could to help me. Why didn't Grace and Deidra get that? Did I really fit the school mold? I cannot deny that I did. But that does not erase the fact that Grace and Deidra did not fit the mold but should have had teachers and others who did everything they could to help them fly. In "Applying Linguistic Knowledge of African American English to Help Students Learn and Teachers Teach," Baugh uses the analogy of a three-legged stool as representative of the relationship between parents, educators, and students for school success. If one or more legs is not functional, the stool cannot stand. Someone (or something) has to fill the void. Someone has to help. Some parents or caregivers do not have the confidence to meet with teachers when they know their child needs help. Some parents do not have the skills or the experience to know what to do when they see their child struggling because sometimes they cannot help themselves or sometimes they just didn't get that part when they were in school and they don't know anything different. Some parents do not care, just like some teachers do not care, just like some students do not care, but I have to believe that is not how it's supposed to be. We just have to figure this thang out.

One has the feeling that nights are becoming sleepless in some quarters, and it seems to me obvious that the recoil of traditional "humanists" and some post-modern theorists to this particular aspect of the debate, the "race" aspect, is as severe as it is because the claims for attention come from that segment of scholarly and artistic labor in which the mention of "race" is either inevitable or elaborately, painstakingly masked; and if all of the ramifications that the term demands are taken seriously, the bases of Western civilization will require re-thinking. Thus, in spite of its implicit and explicit acknowledgment, "race" is still a virtually unspeakable thing, as can be seen in the apologies, notes of "special use" and cir-cumscribed definitions that accompany it—not least of which is my own deference in surrounding it with quotation marks. Suddenly (for our purposes, suddenly) "race" does not exist. For three hun-dred years black Americans insisted that "race" was no usefully dis-tinguishing factor in human relationships. During those same three centuries every academic discipline, including theology, history, and natural science, insisted "race" was *the* determining factor in human development. When blacks discovered they had shaped or become a culturally formed race, and that it had specific and revered dif-ference, suddenly they were told there is no such thing as "race," biological or cultural, that matters and that genuinely intellectual exchange cannot accommodate it. In trying to come to some terms about "race" and writing, I am tempted to throw my hands up. It always seemed to me that the people who invented the hierarchy of "race" when it was convenient for them ought not to be the ones to explain it away, now that it does not suit their purposes for it to exist. But there *is* culture and both gender and "race" inform and are informed by it. Afro-American culture exists and though it is clear (and becoming clearer) how it has responded to Western cul-ture, the instances where and means by which it has shaped West-ern culture are poorly recognized or understood.

—Toni Morrison, "Unspeakable Things Unspoken"

• • •

As I was going through the data one day after being overwhelmed by all the work I had done for this project and all the possibilities it held, I suddenly realized there were no easy answers. It was not as simple as asking a question and then fitting it perfectly into some slot. Some of the questions I asked did not fit neatly into the categories I delineated. Some questions—and some answers—were bigger than that. I could not easily separate language issues from literacy issues just to get back to my argument that language and literacy were connected in important ways and here is why. I was going about this wrong, and doing it in a way I had argued against. Yes, we can talk about language apart from literacy and vice versa. But what would be the point here? In my context, they *are* together. They are together because I am interested in something bigger than language, bigger than literacy. I am interested in those aspects as they relate to a bigger picture, a better picture—a holistic picture in the issues surrounding why I do what I do.

I began this book by talking about the need to deconstruct ourselves in order to (re)construct our lost selves. It is a move from "me" to "you and me" to "me" to "us" to something that makes "you and me" separate and together. We all have journeys to make. It can be called "life." We learn and grow and change during this journey, and it is not easy. We become. Whatever it is we become, it connects us to others. I think that is why stories are so important. In an episode of *Star Trek: Voyager,* there was a society that treasured stories above all other possessions. Stories were special; they were invaluable. Stories have value because they can contribute to our learning and growing. We can often find something personally beneficial in them. We can see things in them that we may not have seen otherwise. They can make evident our connections and our reality. They are our lives, and they can shape and reveal us for who we are and who we can become as well as our connection to others.

I recently read a manuscript about African American women who were returning to college to complete their bachelor's, master's, or other advanced degrees. The author called them "re-entry" women. Even though I am not a re-entry woman, the stories those women had to tell resonated with me because I saw not only myself in them at times, but also Grace and other women (in my family) I know. I saw how we can come back from turns our lives took that we may not have wanted but that we needed to follow in order to prepare us for other roads to come. We don't always get what we want, but sometimes we get what we need. That is where the possibilities are, and the vision we need can emerge and grow and let us know that we can do it.

MAYA

I don't expect too many changes to be made in my life in the next year. You know what I'm saying? I 'spect to remember more, that's for one thing. I expect to remember more and I expect to be healthy like I am the next year.

[In five years from now, I see myself doing the] *same thing I'm doing now. Going to church, doing my housework, doing what I got to do. Still going to church that's for sure. I feel like five years from today though, I wouldn't be too much different in my action. And my health. I don't be looking to be in bad health like some people.*

[Working on this project] *makes me want to keep trying and cope with life better. If I could keep it in mind, it's a help to me. It's a help to me to try to do the things I want to do more, think more and read more. All that thinking. At least it'll help my mind or something, to study it maybe. I enjoyed doing that. Cause that is a help to me now. In a way it's a help to me.*

In the more than five years since Maya made the above remarks, her overall physical health has been good, but she has been diagnosed with Alzheimer's disease. She does not drive anymore, which means she does not go to nursing homes anymore to help others. She and John will not be taking a vacation together. Sadly, in March 2001, she lost John when he died in his sleep. She does not like to travel anymore and she is afraid to fly. She seems to be getting tired and looks for a little more rest than she used to. Part of that is due to the medication, but it is also because she does not have enough people to interact with on a daily basis who make her life a little more enjoyable and a little fuller. Since she just stays at home (she doesn't even go to the beauty shop anymore), she is essentially alone and lonely. She still goes to church every Sunday and is the "church mother," a fact which she, the church, and her family celebrated for her eightieth birthday. She can still read her Bible and cook and clean a little, but she needs help more and more, and she needs someone to spend some quality time with her. The Alzheimer's may be slowly taking away the strong mind she wanted, but it is not taking away her humanity.

GRACE

The changes I expect to be making in the next year for myself is practicing more on my literacy, such as my reading and my writing, and trying to understand more of what I read and write. And just becoming a better reader and a better writer. And becoming literate—not just reading and writing and not understanding what I'm reading.

[In] *5 years* [from now], *if I stay with Jesse, I can't see myself doing anything but what I am doing now and that is nothing because Jesse is one of those people who thinks life and marriage is going to work, coming home, eating. But, if I am by myself I feel I would take the time that I devote taking care of him* [and] *turn that time into something positive by getting into a reading, writing & spelling class. I feel in the next five years I will be able to take control of my life; start durning something positive for myself like working toward so*[me] *type of degree. Like I said, knowledge is success, power & wealth. "A mine is a terrible thing to waste."*

[Working on this project] *has made me think a lot. That I really need to read more, I really need to write more. That I can do better really than what I'm doing. I need to get a project or something, something that I can do constantly and keep it going. And, like you say, get in a book club or something and start reading books, start writing more, start understanding, start doing more things to help me to better myself. And maybe one day I will, in the next few years, think about taking some classes and stuff like that to get me some type of degree. Because it really did help me by doing the papers and answering the questions and stuff like that. It helped me to realize that I can pick up a dictionary and pick up a book and read it and learn the meaning of words and sorta put together a paper, whether it was just done right. But at least I did the writing.*

And it kinda made me feel real good to write that when I was doing my life story and different stuff like that. It made me feel good. And I enjoyed getting the dictionary and looking up words and learning about words and stuff like that. And it just made me feel if I continue this I could do a lot better. So it really helped me. I may not have did my sentences or my punctuations and stuff like that just right, but I did write it and I felt I wrote it in a way where you could read it and understand it.

Grace has made some major changes in her personal life in the more than five years since she said the above, but she is still concerned about her language and literacy and still not very confident in her abilities. She did leave Jesse and she is now on her own, but she has yet to *"take the time that I devote taking care of him* [and] *turn that time into something positive by getting into a reading, writing & spelling class."* And she certainly has not *"start durning something positive for myself like working toward so*[me] *type of degree."* The divorce was not kind to her financially (she did not get any settlement for the house, and she retained responsibility for all the bills), but she will tell you anytime that she is better off mentally and spiritually because a heavy burden was lifted from her. She lives in an apartment by herself and she still has her friends and family for a support network, but sometimes she does get a little lonely. She plans on retiring from her job soon so she can get two incomes to make ends meet and do something different that she might like better, but she may postpone her retirement till 2003 because she would get almost twice as much. She still talks about her literacy and language issues, but that talk does not include what she can do for herself to accomplish what she wants. She is too afraid. She still needs confidence. Maybe that book on re-entry women can be a start for her—practice, practice, practice. Maybe resilience and self-efficacy can still have a chance to blossom when one is no longer a child but an adult still looking for answers and support and encouragement.

REIA

In the next year I'm gonna take one day at a time. I'm gonna continue to work on my spiritual and emotional growth. That's probably my biggest goal right there. That's the most significant, the most important to me. There are some other things as far as like my job or as far as my field, psychology. Like [I'm] *planning on starting these substance abuse groups. That's an opportunity that's presented itself where I'm going to make some effort in learning more about drugs and alcohol. As a mat-*

ter fact, starting next month, I'ma take a college course on substance abuse. So that'll help me and I'll probably be working toward drug and alcohol certification.

Those are just opportunities that are presenting themselves. It's not like something that I just gotta do or gotta have. It's just that here's an opportunity and I'm taking opportunities as they come, as they present themselves to me. I'm not putting a whole lotta energy in trying to make stuff happen. I'm not making any definite plans about anything. I'm just kinda trying to take life as it comes. But at the same time I'm not being passive about it. I'm seizing the opportunities when they present themselves. I jump into it, I get into it, I put all I got into it.

In five years, I see myself married with a child or two. I plan to eventually enroll in a Ph.D. program to further my studies and do the research that will lead to my future books.

I think one of the biggest things that [working on your project] *made me think about is it's made me look at some of the good stuff that Maya has instilled in me and tried to teach me although she's only had this third-grade education. She's encouraged literacy in us and she's wanted us to go further than what she did. It's made me think more about that than I think I ever had; kinda made me see some good qualities in that aspect that she possesses and that she's tried to give to us.*

Reia seems to have changed the most of all the other participants in the more than five years since the completion of the project. She moved back to Tiberius and has had a couple of different jobs. She continues to work in public service, but that has not always been easy. Her first big job upon returning to Tiberius went out of business after it seemed she was finally getting on her feet. She later got another job that also went out of business but later found a new direction. Making your way in the public welfare domain is not always kind and is too often dependent on the kindness of strangers that may not come through. She moved into her first home just in time to prepare it for her first child, Elijah. She now has a son and daughter (the two children she wanted) but not a husband (something she also wanted but has not obtained). She is a single parent who does not seem as idealistic and motivated and confident as she was during the project over five years ago. That is a shame. But she is still resilient and still thinking of ways to achieve her goals albeit differently from how she may have originally planned.

Hopefully, in the next year, [I can] *get into some type of program for* [nursing]. *Hopefully my literacy will be much better as I go through these programs within this year here and next year so within the year ahead I can kind of concentrate on becoming a RN.*

My goal in life two are three years from now is to become either a Registered Nurse or a Social Worker. I always wanted to be a nurse. I always wanted to be a nurse. I went to the hospital with my grandmother one day and I just seen all these people round and these nurses in these white uniforms and I always wanted to be a nurse. I always wanted to wear a white uniform.

Oh [working on your project] *brought up so much. I learned a little more about myself. I mean I'm aware of it but it kind of brought it out of me to talk about it and it inspire me to get some help; to really get the help that I need. You know as I was doing it, I realize that even though I might write a little better now, it just really not where it's supposed to be. I mean cause writing, trying to think and write and put all that down on paper, it's sort of complicated for me because I hadn't did it in a long time. So it made me realize that I really do need that program and I need to stay in it and not just go a couple of times and leave and decide that I don't wanta do it anymore.*

I don't know how to put [what I have gotten out of this project] *into words because it have gave me self-esteem to continue to say that I can do it. It made my mind kind of at ease once I wrote everything and did everything and I said, "Well, one day," I said, "I can do this." If I can sit down and write and go over and look through the dictionary and do this and that for* [this project], *then I can do what I need to do.*

Deidra stopped going to the Adult Literacy Program not long after the project in part because she felt it was not helping her progress well enough or fast enough. As a result, she is not getting any help. She has since married and had the daughter she always wanted. She also recently moved into her first home. However, she is in no better shape now to help her child or herself with respect to literacy than she was before. She has gone back to college to get a degree, but I somehow think that if she does manage to get through college with a degree, it will be a hollow victory because she may not even be able to read it. (It was difficult to write that sentence, but the reality of it is just as painful.)

SONJA

As I look ahead in my life in the next year, we need to decide about all kinds of stuff in terms of relating to where we're gonna be living and where we're gonna be working. I think we change everyday and I certainly know that I'm changing and I hope at some juncture within this next year that I'll be mentally and physically healthier than I am right now.

Working on this project sometimes made me feel really competent and excited that I'm learning a lot of stuff. Other times I felt pretty anxious and stressed out because of deadlines that I've had for various things. I feel that I'm learning and I'm growing in this particular area. I feel I've also taken on a particular burden because I see from reading certain texts and some of the writing that I've done and some of the positions that I've taken, I feel I have like this burden because I see positions that people in my family are in and I feel obligated in some way to help them and I'm not sure that I can cause I don't know if I've reached that level where I can actually do something like that. Maybe that just isn't my line. Maybe it would take someone who deals with adult literacy problems everyday to help them and that may not be something I can do. So it's made me see a burden that I'm not sure that I can overcome. It's made me see problems like that with other people (i.e., am I gonna help them or am I able to help them).

Given the time and energy I have invested in this project, I want to get a Ph.D. That's what I want. I want it done and I want it over with. I want to move on to a job. I want to actually see where I've actually helped the people in my study and not just taken something from the people in my study and I wanta try to find a way that I can do that. But that's certainly the two accomplishments that I want: that I finish the doctoral program and I graduate. Then I want to get my job and find some way to help the people that have helped me. That's what I want to get out of it.

I have not done all that I wanted to do, but I am making progress. I did earn my Ph.D., bought a new car, and bought our first home, and I am now also the proud mother of a beautiful, healthy son. My life has changed quite a bit, but I am continuing to learn and grow and become. I am still trying to make connections and find more pieces to this puzzle of identity along a road I have chosen to take and a journey I have chosen to travel. The other participants still have views about language and literacy that are troubling to me, but then so do a lot of people. When I was moving to our new home and would tell people I was in English, they would usually make some response that had to do with a need for improvement in the language of "those Southerners." Even though I am from the South, I apparently do not sound like a Southerner to them. I am, therefore, somehow qualified to correct the "bad" language of those that do. I guess I cannot expect more from others when my own family feels the same way.

The above vignettes are responses to the questions asked in the last section of the interview. They show where the participants were at the conclusion of the project more than five years ago. As you can see, that is not necessarily where they are now or where they wanted to be.

At this point I am probably the participant in the study most optimistic about my own goals and possible selves, but I am the most pessimistic about the language and literacy ideologies that I grew up with. I was once where Grace and Deidra are now. I bought into the ideologies hook, line, and sinker. When I started college, I began to question my assumptions about language. Like the others, I have seen the unfulfilled promises and blatant contradictions. The more I have learned about language and literacy, the more I see the problems inherent in the ideologies and our society. I accept the contradictions for what they are: smoke screens. So why can't Maya, Grace, Reia, and Deidra see them for what they are?

Grace has often told me that it is easy for me to say, because I already speak "good" English, that how you talk should not matter as long as you are understood. She has said that I would not be a good teacher because I expect others to know what I already know. She is not sure I could teach someone to read or write or speak "good" English because I already know how and I would not be able to see how others do not. She has a point. It is easier for the rich to say to the poor that money does not buy happiness and that it is not important, because they have it and they know it. The poor person often would at least like the chance to know it. As long as I can speak what Grace and the others consider "good" English and as long as I am literate, it may be difficult for me to really understand their struggle with realizing the contradictions in the ideologies they hold onto and to accept their counterargument that how you talk matters whether I think it should or not.

The quantity and quality of educational experiences I have had greatly influenced the ideologies I have held onto. The longer I am in education, the more pessimistic I become about these ideologies that affect our lives whether or not we live by them since they can be and are so readily thrust upon us like when a drug dealer is trying to get someone hooked. Even though Grace is no longer attending school, she is around people who are. She sees what they do and she hears them talk. She has great respect for those who seek an education and she is very supportive of their efforts, but she does not extend that to herself. Deidra is still not literate in a meaningful way, but she is still plagued with the notion of getting an education for better opportunities. They are alike in that respect because their circumstances force them to address sensitive issues. I fear their dilemma with these issues may make them more powerless rather than empowered because of their lack of confidence and too few victories to push them in another direction.

I also cannot help but notice the similar statements Grace and Deidra made about working on this project and the eerie echo it had for me because I now know how fleeting the feeling was and that it will take more than this one project to make a difference, even in the lives of those so close to me. Grace said:

> *It helped me to realize that I can pick up a dictionary and pick up a book and read it and learn the meaning of words and sorta put together a paper, whether it was just done right. But at least I did the writing. And it kinda made me feel real good to write that when I was doing my life story and different stuff like that. It made me feel good. And I enjoyed getting the dictionary and looking up words and learning about words and stuff like that. And it just made me feel if I continue this I could do a lot better.*

Deidra said:

> *It have gave me self-esteem to continue to say that I can do it. It made my mind kind of at ease once I wrote everything and did everything and I said, "Well, one day," I said, "I can do this." If I can sit down and write and go over and look through the dictionary and do this and that for* [this project], *then I can do what I need to do.*

We are our mothers' daughters. Neither had the early experiences I had that I now know I benefited from, but at some point they are going to have to let that go and take a leap of faith. We may not be what we want to be, but we do not have to remain where we are and we do not have to be who we used to be. It is time for Grace and Deidra to get unstuck, to become—to learn to fly.

Despite our differences, language and literacy have been and continue to be important to us. We have all held similar language and literacy ideologies at some point in our lives, but our different experiences while holding onto those ideologies have brought each of us to different points and have left us somewhere between being stronger believers and greater skeptics.

In asking about beliefs while observing practices, I often found contradictions. This was no surprise, for we all hold contradictory beliefs. Sometimes we recognize them and sometimes we do not. In a conversation about her narrative, Grace steadfastly insisted she did not use the word "stuff" and she did not say "kinda" but instead used "kind of," the "correct" phrase. The taped speech samples indicate otherwise. Still, that is what she believes. Pointing out contradictions in someone's beliefs or practices does not ensure such things will be changed. It may only serve to indicate a discrepancy that will be forgotten as soon as the discussion is over. I hope the participants will ponder and reconcile their contradictions in a meaningful way. I do not know if that has happened for them yet or if it will happen, but it might. That possibility is enough to cause me to try to make a difference. I think the second poem that Deidra felt compelled to share is appropriate for all the women who participated in this very personal project.

> The biggest people with the biggest ideas can be shot down by the
>   smallest people with the smallest minds.
>   Think big anyway.
> People favor underdogs, but follow only top dogs.
>   Fight for some underdogs anyway.
> What you spend years building may be destroyed overnight.
>   Build anyway.
> Give the world the best you have and you'll get kicked in the teeth.
>   Give the world the best you've got anyway.

SMOKE SCREENS, INTERSECTIONS, AND DIRECTIONS

Our language and literacy identities are important to our lives, as demonstrated by the women in this study. It should be clear that the sociocultural and historical contexts of these women greatly contributed to their language and literacy identities. How else can you account for the fact that someone who has had more than fifteen years of schooling is not literate? or that someone who has had more than twelve years of schooling is afraid to write a memo or a letter on her own? or that someone saw others working at the age of thirteen instead of going to school without much chance for salvaging those lost years?

Despite our similarities, we each had different goals and possible selves that were products of our sociocultural and historical contexts and how and to what extent we interacted with and identified with our transactions in those contexts. Education more so than age or generation seems to be a dominant variable in the patterns I have discussed for language, literacy, identity, and goals. The order of these narratives could have flowed just as well not by age, but by education. I would venture to say that generation and education are linked because of the role sociocultural and historical contexts played and the environment of their lives. Maya indicated she did what she saw the others around her doing: drop out of school around thirteen, get a job, work, and have a family. She grew up in a society that legally discriminated against and oppressed Blacks just because they were not White. She was denied opportunities.

Grace did what she saw others in her family doing as well as not doing: she got married after becoming pregnant, she finished high school because none of her other siblings had accomplished that, she took care of her family, and she worked in service jobs because that is what she thought life was all about. She broke the pattern and found a nice, stable job as a clerk—a blessing from God, as she describes it. She grew up during a time when Blacks were segregated and oppressed. She came of age in a society and a nation on the verge of legal change.

Reia had an older sister whom she admired and looked up to and who inspired her to go to college—something no one before Felicia had done. She was able to participate in Head Start and make Felicia's reality of going to college and then graduate school a realized possible self, surpassing that of her very inspiration. She grew up during a time of more opportunities for Blacks; in a nation and society in transition from what it once was to the promise of what it might become.

Deidra discovered a profession she wanted to pursue, but there was a mismatch between that long-term goal and the subgoals (e.g., literacy and "standard" English) needed to accomplish it. She believed she should be literate and she might need to speak and write "standard" English, but her behavior did not match her beliefs. The most likely entities involved in this mismatch were education, community, and family. She strongly identified with her family and community, but not with education. Even though her grandparents encouraged her to go to college to become a nurse, her lack of identification with education at that point made her goal of becoming a registered nurse problematic. She, like Reia, grew up during a time of early transition for a people and a nation. She is now living in a time of unfulfilled hopes, dreams, and possible selves.

My contexts often changed as I went from staying with Maya and her children in Tiberius to living with my parents in a working-class neighborhood in Picard, or as I went to a predominantly non-White or White school. As my contexts changed, so did I. I was influenced by and identified with various contextual entities depending on the different sociocultural contexts I was in. Although I, like Deidra, did not always know what was necessary to achieve my long-term goals and my commitment wavered over the years, I did continue to pursue subgoals (e.g., literacy and "standard" English) that complemented my long-term goals. I grew up during a time of transition and increased opportunities for Blacks and in a system that allowed me a better chance to make the most of the new frontier.

The participants' situations are not unusual when put into context. I have focused only on a small sample, but there are many more like them. Maya was not the only one who dropped out of school to work. Her husband did the same thing. So did Deidra's grandfather. That is just the way it was for them. They had to work to survive at a time when African Americans had very few choices. Grace finished school during a time when there were more opportunities for her than Maya had had. She remembers the struggles of her mother and her peers as well as her own to make those opportunities possible. Reia had opportunities to go farther than anyone in her family had gone before, and she did. She is part of a group of first-generation college graduates. Deidra did not have the opportunities she needed to go farther than her predecessors, and so she has not done so (even though she exceeded her grandparents and parents in the amount of schooling she received). I had opportunities Deidra did not have and, as a result, my identification with education and the support I received were much stronger than hers. I did more with what—and whom—I had to work with and I was able to become the first person in my family to earn a Ph.D.

Maya made more of her opportunities later in life because they were there, unlike before, and because she chose to challenge herself to continue learning as a means of increasing her faith and understanding of God's will for her life. Grace did better than many by finishing high school, in spite of becoming pregnant, and then going to vocational school to develop a trade. Reia has used her education in an area in which she is interested, but her accomplishments seem limited and puzzling. There is a lack of stability and success in her life, which seems to have had more promise than has been realized. Deidra, unfortunately, got lost in a system that did not seem to care if she learned or not. Apparently it was more important to matriculate than to educate.

Deidra is neither the first nor the last student who is afraid to speak up in class. She is also not alone in choosing silence over a fear of public recognition of her failure to learn to read and write or her inadequacies in language use as judged by her family and others. She has tried to get by for most of her life with smoke and mirrors because in her eyes she had little choice and even less hope. I do not think she is a poster child for "illiteracy," nor do I think she can be considered a martyr in this matter. She is responsible for her actions just as the school and her caregivers are responsible for their (in)actions. Still, there must be something wrong. We all need a little help from someone, but we obviously do not always get it. Maybe we get it when we need it most and hers just has not arrived yet.

Today, more often than not students are told they must finish high school in order to get a better job. They must go to college in order to get a better job. They must be literate in order to get a better job. They must _____ (fill in the blank) in order to get a better job. All is said and done in order to get a better job. Better than what? Unlike the model proposed by critical literacy educator Paulo Freire in much of his work, in which the result is believed to be not outside yourself or in spite of yourself but rather because of yourself, society proposes a model in which the result is a better job. If you do what you are told, you will get a better job. Grace and Deidra did what they were told. They both have jobs, but neither of them is quite satisfied with their options. The same might be said for Reia. The Ideology of Opportunity may have sounded good to them, but in the end, it is the Ideology of Emancipation that may be the least of three evils.

Even though Maya did not finish grade school and both Grace and Deidra had post-secondary schooling, she may be the most literate—if such a modifier can be used—of the three. She is pleased with her life. Her life includes being able to read and engage the Bible as part of her relationship with God. It is part of her prayer routine in the morning and her daily life. She reads the Bible everyday, and she understands it and interacts with it. In actuality, it is her life's work. She can knowledgeably engage you on most topics that relate to the Bible; yet this is the same woman who could not read and complete the instruments for this study. Grace and Deidra had more success with completing the paperwork for this project and would probably be considered more literate than Maya by most people's standards. However, that is where the dilemma is: Who determines the worth of one's literacy? As with "standard" English, the likely answer is: the individual.

While schools have chosen to be adjuncts to the employment process, the worth of one's schooling or education or growth or, yes, language and literacy, is neglected. Literacy can be empowering, and it is for Maya. But as Deidra says in her narrative, she didn't get that part, and neither did Grace. Instead of being independent thinkers with confidence in their abilities they are dependent, fearful, and dissatisfied, as are too many others, as indicated by literacy scholar Ruth Finnegan:

Some would . . . interpret this [literacy] myth not just as a misleading and incomplete picture but as a smoke screen masking past and present inequalities. The myth can be seen as playing an essential ideological function for the governing social, political, or educational order, whether manifested by earlier imperial expansion or by current national or international inequalities. So, when people might want, for example, houses or jobs or economic reform, they are instead given literacy programs. They can even be blamed for their own poverty, presented by the dominant myth as the result not of social inequalities but of their failure to become literate. This may be an extreme view, more applicable in some cases than in others—but it may indeed have some grain of truth.

Finnegan says her point of view may be harsh, but it may also be true. It is not that literacy and "standard" English are inherently evil; they are social constructions subject to the same maladies and imperfections as those who constructed them. The rhetorical ideologies I defined and described are disseminated by institutions. Unfortunately, they are misused to the detriment of "minorities," the poor, and the disinherited. Quite a few people who are not of the White middle class want to take part in the benefits of being in the White middle class. They want equal chances, but they may not want to give up who they are to get them. We, as educators, as society, as individuals, must recognize and value the languages others possess and we must know that it is an integral part of identity.

CONCLUSIONS

I set out to determine the language and literacy identities of my grandmother, my mother, my aunt, my sister, and myself. I found one entangled by her hopes and fears; one remorseful but content with life as it is now because that is all we have anyway; one seemingly confident but unfulfilled and confused by the contradiction; one struggling with the selves she has constructed and the journey she has undertaken to understand them; and one who is a typical African American woman of the South trying to solve the riddle of whether she is a product of her environment or a woman of independent means. You may be able to figure out who they all are, but you would be way ahead of most of them. Whether or not they know it, they all at various points in their lives chose what was peculiar to their minds, just like so many of us do.

I see the intersections between literacy and "standard" English in my life and in that of my mother's. My mother and I often have disagreements about her reading and writing and my impatience with helping her complete certain tasks. I have often felt my mother is quite capable of writing the notes she wants me to dictate to her in "good" English or reading the passages she asks me to "translate" for her. I tell her she just does not have confidence, that she is quite capable of doing it on her own. I think we are both partially right. My mother does not have confidence, but she is also unable to satisfactorily read a text and compose a written text of her own—in her eyes. She is not literate in a way she wants to be. Her struggle continues.

My mother can write—she is perfectly capable of transcribing what

I dictate to her. Sometimes she does not know how to spell a word, so she asks. My Ph.D. husband does that. But she knows all the letters of the alphabet and is quite capable of writing them—much better than I can. Reading is a little more difficult for her. She does not understand the meaning of some words and she cannot pronounce some words without help, though I could say the same about myself on occasion.

She is also capable of communicating her thoughts verbally and expressing herself. She does not feel she speaks "good" English—and she wants to—but I wonder what she feels she is doing every time she talks to me. So what if she speaks a less prestigious variety of English. Is that any less of a language? Are the people who speak less prestigious varieties less human? Less intelligent? Less significant? What if she is not literate? Is she less human or intelligent or significant for that also? No. In fact, my mother is typical of many people. She speaks a variety of English that is not valued—sometimes even within her own community but most often outside that community of speakers.

An example of this private (covert) prestige but public scorn is the Ebonics controversy of 1996–1997. When it occurred, there were not only Whites lamenting the supposed acceptance of African American Vernacular English in the schools, but also many noted and notable African Americans who spoke out with conviction against the Oakland Unified School Board's Ebonics Resolution, including African Americans who unquestionably use African American English. It is similar to California's passage of the controversial denunciation of bilingual education in a state that has more multilingual people than does any other in the United States. As such, some of the very people who may have benefited from bilingual education voted against it. W. E. B. DuBois' discussion of what he termed "double consciousness" for African Americans is alive and well not only in the African American community but in most, if not all, "other" communities. We just can't seem to let go of who we know we are—culturally and linguistically rich—how we are seen by the majority not like us—dumb, ignorant, lazy, shiftless—how we are treated socially, politically, and educationally—disenfranchised, dispossessed, disinherited—nor can we embrace who we want to be or should be—acknowledged, respected, valued, and vindicated—just because we are all human no matter what our cultural, ethnic, and linguistic differences are.

All of the women presented are not only typical of many African American women, but also typical of many of the dispossessed. Their stories are reflections of ourselves and glaring reminders of our educational and social needs as a nation and as a community. Their stories resonate not only with speakers of African American English, but also with speakers of Spanglish, Southern White Vernacular English, New York City English, Gullah, Appalachian English, and any other variety of American English. These varieties are disrespected and unacknowledged as the viable, vibrant languages they are, and will continue to be so as long as their speakers are also marked as such. Linguistic bigotry is not constrained by race (as also illustrated by the Southern television contestant who evoked laughter when he spoke). I know this because even though we are criticized for our language and told that if we assimilate, thereby obscuring our differences, then we can take our place in that seemingly color-blind society, it is not true. I know what I know, and others know it too. In my book, *Sociocultural and Historical Contexts of African American English,* sociolinguist John Baugh relates the following thought experiment he has used across the country:

Imagine a different history for the United States, one in which there are no citizens of color. Under this scenario, Columbus would have crossed the Atlantic and encountered no indigenous populations and all ensuing immigrants would have come from Europe such that they did not exhibit any significant racial differences. This imaginary history is one in which there would have been no African slave trade, nor would there have been Chinese immigrants imported to build the railroads, and there would have been no internment of Japanese Americans during World War II. All citizens would be White. (pp.320–321)

He then asks the following question: "Would linguistic prejudice still exist in an 'all White' United States and, if so, what would that prejudice be based upon?" (p. 321). Invariably the answer is yes: no one has denied that linguistic prejudice would prevail in this imaginary world on the grounds of region, sex, class, education, and occupation, among others—just like it does right now in the real world.

The problem is that not only do linguistically diverse groups— whether bilingual or bidialectal—suffer, but so does everybody else. The irony is that there are more people who are bidialectal than would care to admit it. Unfortunately, the continued belief of many that only the poor and "dark" peoples have this problem (because everyone knows that middle-class White people use only "proper" grammar) only reaffirms the ever-present linguistic bigotry and elitism that are contributing factors to why we have such glaring educational needs. Until the people of the United States confront their linguistic bigotry and acknowledge that linguistic diversity comes in varying shades of language and dialect, until they confront their linguistic elitism and acknowledge that there is no such thing as "proper" grammar (as opposed to the "slang" that young people, people of color, and the generally dim-witted try to even call a language or something grammatical), and until the United States government and its citizens legally, politically, and educationally acknowledge that dialect differences matter and need to be accounted for—just as bilingual differences matter and need to be accounted for, if we really want one nation, under God, indivisible, with liberty and justice for all, and if we want its citizens to be literate and confident and strong—then we will always have the Mayas, Graces, Reias, Deidras, and Sonjas with us—just like the poor.

APPENDIX 1

Participants' Possible Selves Data

	Maya	Grace	Reia	Deidra	Sonja
Language and Uses of Literacy					
Describes me now	4.6	3.7	6	4.1	5.7
Would like to describe future	6.1	5.6	6.4	5.1	6.4
Will describe me in the future	4.6	5.9	6.4	6.2	6.2
Reading					
Describes me now	5.4	3.8	7	4.3	6
Would like to describe future	6.6	6.3	7	5.8	7
Will describe me in the future	5.4	6.8	7	6	6.8
Writing					
Describes me now	2.5	2.8	6	3.3	6.3
Would like to describe future	4.8	5.3	6.5	4.8	7
Will describe me in the future	2.5	5.5	6.8	6.8	6.5
Literacy					
Describes me now	5	5.5	7	5	6
Would like to describe future	7	7	7	5	7
Will describe me in the future	5	7	7	5	7
African American English					
Describes me now	7	4	4	5.5	5.5
Would like to describe future	6	3.5	4	5.5	5.5
Will describe me in the future	7	3.5	4	7	5.5
"Standard" English					
Describes me now	4.5	3.5	5	3.5	4
Would like to describe future	7	5.5	6.5	4	4
Will describe me in the future	4.5	6	6	6	4.5

APPENDIX 2

Participants' Speech Samples Data

	IT Mean	IT SD	KT Mean	KT SD	t	p	r^2
Maya							
Phonology	33.80	30.73	45.80	39.54	2.10	<.10	.52
Morphology	41.50	18.32	75.17	35.69	3.06	<.05	.65
Syntax (1–5)	55.80	27.09	79.20	4.76	1.97	<.10	.49
Syntax (6–7)	8.00	9.90	23.50	10.61	NA	NA	NA
Grace							
Phonology	8.00	9.82	15.00	17.23	2.06	<.10	.51
Morphology	32.33	14.76	53.50	34.39	1.48	NS	.30
Syntax (1–5)	36.80	35.63	77.40	19.35	2.76	<.05	.66
Syntax (6–7)	3.50	3.54	9.50	7.78	NA	NA	NA
Reia							
Phonology	0.86	1.76	12.00	9.25	3.11	<.05	.71
Morphology	10.33	15.57	18.00	17.91	1.45	NS	.30
Syntax (1–5)	13.20	7.19	46.00	12.00	7.83	<.001	.94
Syntax (6–7)	1.00	0.00	3.00	0.00	NA	NA	NA
Deidra							
Phonology	17.20	15.04	35.60	19.09	2.09	<.10	.52
Morphology	35.83	35.23	64.00	33.18	1.46	NS	.30
Syntax (1–5)	36.00	36.70	82.60	18.27	3.74	<.01	.78
Syntax (6–7)	0	0	24.00	9.90	NA	NA	NA
Sonja							
Phonology	0.80	1.79	3.20	4.09	2.14	<.05	.53
Morphology	0.40	0.80	35.17	38.91	2.17	<.05	.49
Syntax (1–5)	0	0	32.80	12.50	5.87	<.01	.90
Syntax (6–7)	0	0	6.50	9.19	NA	NA	NA
Group							
Phonology	11.67	12.52	27.20	19.18	4.26	<.01	.82
Morphology	18.80	13.72	38.20	20.63	4.10	<.01	.81
Syntax (1–5)	20.60	17.79	63.60	20.27	5.90	<.01	.90
Comp. *Done*	0.60	0.55	8.00	7.91	2.08	<.10	.52
Inv. *Be*	4.40	6.43	18.60	12.20	2.95	<.05	.69

APPENDIX 3

Participants' Language and Literacy Ideologies Data

	Maya	Grace	Reia	Deidra	Sonja	Group
Ideology of Opportunity						
Mean	6.60	6.50	6.13	5.75	3.56	5.70
Standard Deviation	0.32	0.76	0.83	0.89	1.64	1.46
Ideology of Progress						
Mean	6.36	5.80	5.80	5.10	2.40	5.10
Standard Deviation	0.40	2.02	1.42	0.99	0.99	1.89
Ideology of Emancipation						
Mean	6.28	7.00	5.42	5.71	4.28	5.74
Standard Deviation	0.27	0.00	0.98	0.76	1.04	1.15
All Ideologies Combined						
Mean	6.43	6.27	5.80	5.43	3.17	5.42
Standard Deviation	0.36	1.54	1.19	0.94	1.41	1.65

NOTES

DEDICATION

The Julie Dash quotation and the Johnnetta B. Cole quotation are from Diane J. Johnson, ed., *Proud Sisters: The Wisdom and Wit of African-American Women* (White Plains, N.Y.: Peter Pauper Press, 1995), pp. 15 and 25, respectively.

INTRODUCTION

1. *Sista, Speak!* centers on a primary question: "What are the language and literacy attitudes, practices, and ideologies of my participants?" To answer that question, I conducted a multidiscipline, mixed-methods research project encompassing four dimensions—education, language, literacy, and goals (including possible selves)—and two aspects of these dimensions—practices (e.g., linguistic repertoire) and beliefs (e.g., literacy ideologies). The participants were five African American women in one family, my own.

To collect oral data, my first step in this study, I participated in activities as I normally would while also observing and recording the participants' speech in various contexts, both public (e.g., at a mall or a restaurant) and private (e.g., in their home), particularly noting and charting their use of eighteen linguistic features of African American English as recognized by sociolinguists John Baugh, John Rickford, Walt Wolfram, Guy Bailey, and Geneva Smitherman:

Phonological Features	*Examples*
Final consonant cluster reduction	mind [maɪn]
Vocalization of or zero postvocalic /r/	after [æftə]; your [jo]
Deletion or reduction of postvocalic /l/	help [hɛp]; he'll [hiə]
Labialization of /θ/ (/θ/ > /f/)	fifth [fɪf]
Lowering of /ɪ/ > /æ/ before /ŋ/	singular [sæɲjələ]; thinking [θæŋkɪn]

•

Morphological Features	*Examples*
Zero plural -*s*	This five *pound* of shrimp.
Zero possessive -*s*	This *Kathy* boy.
Zero 3rd-person singular -*s*	At least he *know* you have a phone.
Zero past tense and past participle -*ed*	I probably woulda *end* up keeping it.
They possessive	They had *they* own area.
Generalization of *is* and *was*	Some people *is* worser than me.
	You *was* determined.

Syntactic Features	*Examples*
Zero copula	She know she doing wrong.
Negative concord	I *don't want nobody* doing that.
Existential *it* and *they*	*It's* a lot of it in there.
Demonstrative *them*	*Them* people are terrible.
Completive *been*	It *been* so long.
Completive *done*	He *done* sold all that.
Invariant (or immutable) *be*	I don't *be* eating that stuff.

When an African American English linguistic feature occurred in the oral data, I marked the presence of the feature (F) in the transcript, tallied all the occurrences of the feature, and then counted all possible occurrences of the feature (P). So, the formula for computing the frequency of a linguistic feature was: F / F + P.

The next step was to write a letter to the women requesting specific information about literacy (open to their interpretations) and education, and reminding them about the study. This first formal written contact asked them for information about their literacy practices. Throughout all phases of the study I encouraged the participants to contemplate and define literacy for themselves, but especially initially. Literacy practices and experiences were therefore negotiated with each participant. Each could decide on her own what to share with me; however, I specifically asked for writing samples (e.g., letters, essays, creative writing, and oral presentations) spanning a period of time to be determined by the individual. Since I knew Maya would have trouble writing a letter, Felicia helped her respond to the letters and tape-record her responses. Nevertheless, Maya wrote a brief letter in response to my first letter in addition to providing a recorded response with Felicia's help. This first written contact with the participants also included two goals questions: "Think about all you would like to achieve, obtain, and/or experience during your life. List as many as you can"; and "What do you see yourself doing five years from now?"

I later wrote the women a follow-up letter requesting both clarification and missing information as well as writing samples. The primary dimensions covered in both letters, as listed above, were education, literacy, and language use; the key aspects were beliefs and practices. Concerning education, sample items in the letters included: "[Tell me] as much information about your schooling as you can remember" and "[Tell me about] key moments in your life that pertain to education and your attitudes about them."

The second letter also included an information questionnaire and a Possible Selves Inventory. The Possible Selves Inventory, developed by Hazel Markus and revised by me for my purposes, was divided into two sections: twenty-nine possible selves and fifteen statements to be rated. Participants used a 7-point scale ranging from 1 ("not at all") to 7 ("very much") to rate the possible selves. For the statements, participants used a 7-point scale ranging from 1 ("strongly disagree") to 7 ("strongly agree"). In the information questionnaire, questions pertaining to education included: "What were your favorite subjects in school?" and "What were your grades like in school?"; and in the Possible Selves Inventory were such entries as: "I was a good student in school" and "Uneducated." Concerning language, sample items on the information questionnaire included: "Given your beliefs, please define 'standard,' or 'good,' English, in your own words. That is, what do you mean when you say someone 'talks good' or 'speaks well'?" and "Is speaking Black English important? How so?"; in the Possible Selves Inventory entries were: "Value Black English," "Speak Black English," "Value standard English," and "Speak standard English."

The three questions applying to the twenty-nine possible selves were: "How much does this possible self describe you now?"; "How much would you like this to be a possible self for you?"; and "For you, how likely is this possible self?" Entries for rating under "writing" possible selves included: "write on a regular basis," "enjoy writing," "good writer," "and value writing"; for "reading" possible selves: "enjoy reading," "value reading," "good reader," and "read on a regular basis"; for "literacy" possible selves: "value literacy" and "literate"; for "African American English" possible selves: "speak Black English" and "value Black English"; for "'standard' English" possible selves: "value standard, or 'good,' English" and "speak standard, or 'good,' English." All of the aforementioned were also listed for "language" and "uses of literacy" possible selves. Entries for negative possible selves included: "occupationally burned out," "unemployed," "underemployed," "uneducated," "stupid," "illiterate," "incompetent," "a failure or underachiever," and "speak 'bad' English." Entries for positive possible selves included: "self-confident," "admired," "successful," "ambitious," "intelligent," and "motivated." There was also a section where participants were to list and answer questions about their "hoped-for" possible selves and "feared" possible selves, but that section was not completed by everyone and, thus, I excluded it from most analyses.

The fifteen statements to be rated were: "I was a good student in school"; "I feel I do not have much to be proud of because of my language and literacy"; "When I read, I usually underline passages and make notes in the margins"; "I speak up for myself"; "When I do a job, I do it well"; "In order to succeed in this country, I, like everyone else, must speak standard, or 'good,' English"; "I like most things about myself"; "I keep quiet more than I speak out"; "I argue with others when I think I'm right"; "I became what I dreamed of becoming when I was younger"; "I think I have good ideas"; "I sometimes don't like myself that much because of my language and literacy"; "I am happy with the way I am"; "In order to succeed or function in this country, I (like everyone else) must be literate"; and "I think I am an important person."

With the speech samples and written materials collected and partially analyzed, I next audiotaped individual interviews with each woman. Though the interview was tailored for each participant, the two handouts I used were the same for everyone. The first interview handout contained thirty statements on literacy and "standard" English ideologies (the lead-in statement for each was "Literacy, in the traditional sense of 'the ability to write and read,' and/or standard English, in the traditional sense of 'the correct or proper way to speak,' lead to . . ."): eight representing the Ideology of Opportunity ("a society with a better economic development"; "a society of wealth and productivity"; "a society and people with greater social equity"; "a society and people who are achievement oriented"; "people who have better educational opportunities"; "people who have better job opportunities"; "people who have greater success in school"; and "people who are more likely to take education seriously"); fifteen representing the Ideology of Progress (" a society with a lower birth rate"; "a society with political democracy"; "a society with political stability"; "a society with urbanization"; "a society and people who make a distinction between myth and history"; "people who have a skeptical and questioning attitude"; "people who are more capable of general and abstract uses of language"; "people who are more capable of logical, analytic, and rational thinking"; "people who are innovative"; "people who are less likely to commit a crime"; "people who are politically aware"; "people who are more globally—nationally and internationally—and less locally oriented"; "people who have more liberal and humane social attitudes"; "people who overcome the adversities of a deprived or deficient culture"; and "people who are productive"); and seven representing the Ideology of Emancipation ("people who are transformed"; "people who are autonomous"; "people who are capable of translating ideas into social action"; "people who are critical thinkers"; "people who are emancipated, real or symbolic"; "people who are personally empowered"; "and people who are social revolutionaries").

The second handout consisted of five quotations from the work of various scholars that directly or indirectly addressed literacy and "standard" English ideologies. The first passage was by literacy scholar Johan Galtung:

> What would happen if the whole world became literate? Answer: not so very much, for the world is by and large structured in such a way that it is capable of absorbing the impact. But if the whole world consisted of literate, autonomous, critical, constructive people, capable of translating ideas into action, individually or collectively—the world would change.

The second passage was by John Baugh:

J: O. K., so what happened?

DJ: Oh, yeah, now, check it out. I'm riding down the street, all right? I got me a blue Monza, and my lady by my side. We pull up to a stop sign, you know, and I stop. Y'know? I look both ways and then I starts to go. Well, midway up the next block, up slides this policeman who tells me, "Pull over!" Y'know, like, he pulls up along side me and then parks his bike in front of my car.

J: Uh huh.

DJ: So, he gets off the ol' bike and starts walkin' back to my car, and I'm sayin' to myself, "Why me?" So, he tell me, "You ran the stop sign back there and your brake light's out." I said, "I ain't run the stop sign," and he said, "You ran it!" So he take my license and proceeds to start writin' up this ticket when it dawns on me what's happenin.' I said, "Well, wait a minute man; if I didn't stop at the stop sign and you came from 'round the corner, then you've never seen the back of my car; you pulled in front of me. So how can you tell me my brake light is out 'less I stepped on the brake for the stop sign?" (Imitating the officer's voice) "Well, you just a smart [@#$!] ain't ya kid?"

The third passage was by literacy scholar Ruth Finnegan:

Some would interpret this literacy myth not just as a misleading and incomplete picture but a smoke screen masking past and present inequalities. The myth can be seen as playing an essential ideological function for the governing social, political or educational order, whether the earlier imperial expansion or current national or international inequalities: so when people might want, say, houses or jobs or economic reform they are instead given literacy programs, even blamed for their own poverty which the dominant myth can present as the result not of social inequalities but of their illiteracy. This may be an extreme view, more applicable in some cases than in others— but it may indeed have some grain of truth.

The fourth passage was by Creole linguist Robert Le Page:

People create their linguistic systems (and we all have more than one) so as to resemble those of the groups with which from time to time they wish to identify. Both the groups and their linguistic attributes exist solely in the mind of each individual. When we talk we project the universe as we see it on to others as on to a cinema screen in our own images, expressed in the language we consider appropriate at that moment, and we invite others by these acts to share our universe.

The fifth passage was my own, but I labeled the author "anonymous" so as not to bias the participants:

Literacy is a social construction. While literacy may be said to begin with the introduction of writing systems, literacy is not the same thing as writing. If a person is only able to read the words on a page or write letters on a page that form words, that does not make the person literate. Just because one can read and write does not mean that one is literate. We can perhaps more usefully think of literacy as the focus of a changing and complicated dialectic between talk and inscription. It is multidimensional. Literacy is the process by which one learns to read and/or write and grows to understand and (critically) think about a text in a way most meaningful for the individual in the environment and culture of the individual. Literacy, therefore, can vary from society to society and possibly from individual to individual in a given context and the meaning one chooses to make in that context.

The interview was valuable not only because of its scope but also because it provided one of the two speech contexts to be analyzed and it provided a reading sample. The interviews averaged about two hours and focused on attitudes and beliefs, but also included questions about behavior. All four of the primary dimensions of the study were accounted for in the interview schedule since I wanted the interview to integrate all the information I had collected up to that point. Sample items from the interview schedule about language included: "Do you talk differently to women than you do to men?" and "How are standard English and Black English different to you?" Sample items about literacy included: "In your opinion, what does being able to read mean?" and "What does being able to write mean?" Sample items about education included: "Do you believe your race and/or gender had an affect on your education and your life?" and "In your opinion, what is the purpose of education?" The interview schedule provided information about goals both retrospectively and in the near future. Sample items included: "What did you dream of becoming when you were young?" and "As you look ahead to your life in the next year, what are the decisions or changes you expect to be making in your life?"

To compensate the participants for their participation in the project, I gave each of them a gift that related to language and uses of literacy (e.g., a book). Each gift was chosen specifically for the individual. None received the same gift and no one refused her gift (possibly because it was given during Christmas). The gifts ranged in value from $20 to $35. I also gave additional materials to Grace and Deidra to assist them in their language and literacy development.

2. The narratives are composed of both spoken and written pieces in order to make a quilt unique to each voice and each experience. Casual conversations in various contexts (e.g., the mall, the kitchen, workplace, etc.) provided the informal speech data, or what I call "Kitchen Talk,"

and an interview provided the formal speech data, or what I call "Interview Talk." The written data comes from responses to the information questionnaire, the possible selves inventory, letters the women wrote to me in response to particular questions, and other writings voluntarily given to me by the women to include as typical samples of their literacy practices.

1. OUR LANGUAGE, OUR SELVES

1. Though most works do not define African American English, I think it is important to do so or at least to propose a working definition. African American English can simply be defined as the language spoken by or among African Americans. As is the case with any language or variety, it is systematic and rule-governed. It is also referred to as African American Vernacular English, African American Language, U.S. Ebonics, Black English Vernacular, Black Vernacular English, and Black English. It is not "bad" English, imperfect English, or bastardized English, just as Australian English and American English are not. Not all African Americans speak African American English and not all people who use African American English need be African American. However, by and large, it is indicative of language use in the African American community. For more information see Salikoko Mufwene's "What Is African American English?" (in *Sociocultural and Historical Contexts of African American English*, ed. Sonja L. Lanehart [Amsterdam: John Benjamins, 2001]), Arthur Spears' "Black American English" (in *Anthropology for the Nineties*, ed. Johnnetta B. Cole, 96–113 [New York: Free Press, 1988]), and William Labov's "The Logic of Nonstandard English" (a chapter in his *Language in the Inner City* [Philadelphia: University of Pennsylvania Press, 1972], 201–240).

2. As for the discussion on identity and goals, according to educational psychologist Paul Schutz's "Goals in Self-Directed Behavior" (*Educational Psychologist* 2 [1991]: 55–67), the study of motivation involves looking for answers to two basic questions: "What influences our engagement in some activities over other activities?" and "What influences sustaining or discontinuing those activities?" "Goals" are one answer to those questions. In other words, goals act as points of comparison for determining where we are in relationship to where we want to be. Goals are important for understanding not only what behavior is directed to-

ward but also what is attended to in the environment and what and how we recall the experiences we have in the environment.

PART 2. THE ANALYSES: SURREALITY

1. Surreality is our subjective view of the world, a view that is limited by our experiences and then edited and reorganized by us for manageability and the perceived importance of the experiences, according to philosopher Robert Solomon. As educational psychologist Paul Schutz put it, it is reality from a point of view—*mine*.

7. "I'M COMFORTABLE LIKE I AM"

1. To help analyze the data on goals, I used a classification system identifying ten interdependent goal domains—Educational, Family, Friendship, Occupational, Personal Well-Being, Physical Comfort, Power and Wealth, Religious, Social Helping, and Travel and Adventure. For more information see Paul Schutz's "Goals as the Transactive Point between Motivation and Cognition" (in *Perspectives on Student Motivation, Cognition, and Learning: Essays in Honor of Wilbert J. McKeachie,* eds. Paul R. Pintrich, D. Brown, and Claire E. Weinstein [Hillsdale, N.J.: Erlbaum], 113–133) and "Goals in Self-Directed Behavior" (*Educational Psychologist* 2 [1991]: 55–67).

2. Responses to questions on the Possible Selves Inventory for all the participants can be found in Appendix 1. The responses are presented as averages of particular categories, such as "Literacy Possible Selves" or "African American English Possible Selves," instead of responses to individual items, such as "Enjoy reading" or "Value African American English." For information on which possible selves items are in each category as listed in Appendix 1, see note 1 in the Introduction.

3. Since Maya could not complete the Possible Selves Inventory by herself and did not seem to fully grasp the Likert scale, I usually had to assign a number for her possible selves based on the words she used to express her level of agreement and disagreement with the possible selves for her life.

4. All speech samples were typed double-spaced, with 1-inch margins all around and using 12-point Times font in Microsoft Word on a Macintosh computer.

5. I used one-tailed correlated t tests to determine significance for each participant's use of African American English linguistic features between Kitchen Talk and Interview Talk speech samples. See Appendix 2 for all statistical data on the speech samples for all the participants.

6. Any speech data represented by a percentage does not include the two syntactic features that could not be computed as such, completive *done* and invariant *be*. Hence, those two features are not represented in the figures unless otherwise stated. All references to statistical significance for speech data were determined by one-tailed, correlated t tests with p-values < 0.05. Since the amount of variance accounted for in most cases is quite high, I used the one-tailed t test.

7. In her *Errors and Expectations: A Guide for Teachers of Basic Writing* (New York: Oxford University Press, 1977), Mina Shaughnessy distinguishes five levels of punctuation by means of the different types of punctuation a writer uses. Those five levels are: Level 1: use of the period, the comma, and the capital; Level 2: questions marks, exclamation marks, and quotation marks; Level 3: semicolons and colons; Level 4: parentheses, hyphens, and dashes; and Level 5: ellipsis dots, brackets, and underlining.

10. "I WAS HIDING. I DIDN'T KNOW. I WAS SCARED"

1. In the interview transcript excerpt between Grace and Deidra, the words in italics are examples of reduplicated *-ed*. I did not include this feature for analysis here. Keep in mind then that the participants did use other African American English linguistic features that I did not analyze here because it was not possible to analyze all the features discussed in the research literature. However, this study does include more linguistic features than are analyzed in most other studies of African American English. There are other linguistic features of African American English in the text as well, such as copula deletion, but I highlighted reduplicated *-ed* because that is the focus of the dispute.

BIBLIOGRAPHY

Andersen, Margaret. *Thinking about Women: Sociological Perspectives on Sex and Gender.* 2nd ed. New York: Macmillan, 1988.

Ash, Sharon, and John Myhill. "Linguistic Correlates of Interethnic Contact." Paper presented at the Twelfth Annual Conference of New Ways of Analyzing Variation, Montreal, 1983.

Bailey, Guy, and Erik Thomas. "Some Aspects of African-American Vernacular English Phonology." In *African-American English: Structure, History, and Use,* eds. Salikoko Mufwene, John Rickford, Guy Bailey, and John Baugh, 85–109. London: Routledge, 1998.

Bandura, Albert. *Self-Efficacy: The Exercise of Control.* New York: W. H. Freeman, 1997.

Bassard, Katherine Clay. "Gender and Genre: Black Women's Autobiography and the Ideology of Literacy." *African American Review* 26 (1992): 119–129.

Baugh, John. "Applying Linguistic Knowledge of African American English to Help Students Learn and Teachers Teach." In *Sociocultural and Historical Contexts of African American English,* ed. Sonja L. Lanehart, 319–330. Amsterdam: John Benjamins, 2001.

———. *Beyond Ebonics: Linguistic Pride and Racial Prejudice.* Oxford: Oxford University Press, 2000.

———. *Black Street Speech: Its History, Structure, and Survival.* Austin: University of Texas Press, 1983.

———. "Language and Race: Some Implications for Linguistic Science." In *Linguistics: The Cambridge Survey,* vol. 4, ed. Frederick J. Newmeyer, 64–74. Cambridge: Cambridge University Press, 1988.

———. "Review of *Twice As Less.*" *Harvard Educational Review* 58 (1988): 395–403.

Deutsch, Martin, Irwin Katz, and Arthur Jensen, eds. *Social Class, Race, and Psychological Development.* New York: Holt, Rinehart & Winston, 1968.

DuBois, W. E. B. *The Souls of Black Folk.* New York: Bantam Books, 1989 (1903).

Erez, Miriam, and Isaac Zidon. "Effect of Goal Acceptance on the Relationship of Goal Difficulty to Performance." *Journal of Applied Psychology* 69 (1984): 69–78.

Etter-Lewis, Gwendolyn. *My Soul Is My Own: Oral Narratives of African American Women in the Professions.* New York: Routledge, 1993.

Farr, Marcia. "Language, Culture, and Writing: Sociolinguistic Foundation on Research on Writing." *Review of Research in Education* 13 (1988): 195–223.

Finnegan, Ruth. "Literacy as Mythical Charter." In *Literacy: Interdisciplinary Conversations,* ed. Deborah Keller-Cohen, 31–47. Cresskill, N.J.: Hampton Press, 1994.

Freire, Paulo. *Pedagogy of the Oppressed.* Trans. Myra Bergman Ramos. New York: Continuum, 1989.

———. *The Politics of Education: Culture, Power, and Liberation.* Trans. Donaldo Macedo. South Hadley, Mass.: Bergin and Garvey, 1985.

Freire, Paulo, and Donaldo Macedo. *Literacy: Reading the Word and the World.* South Hadley, Mass.: Bergin and Garvey, 1987.

Galtung, Johan. "Literacy, Education, and Schooling—For What?" In *A Turning Point for Literacy: Adult Education for Development. The Spirit and Declaration of Persepolis. Proceedings of the International Symposium for Literacy, Persepolis, Iran, 3 to 8 September 1975,* ed. Leon Bataille, 93–105. Oxford: Pergamon, 1976.

Giddings, Paula. *When and Where I Enter: The Impact of Black Women on Race and Sex in America.* New York: Bantam Books, 1984.

Goody, Jack, and Ian Watt. "The Consequences of Literacy." *Comparative Studies in Society and History* 5 (1963): 304–345.

Graff, Harvey J. *The Labyrinths of Literacy: Reflections on Literacy Past and Present.* London: Falmer Press, 1987.

———. *The Legacies of Literacy: Continuities and Contradictions in Western Culture and Society.* Bloomington: Indiana University Press, 1987.

———. *The Literacy Myth: Literacy and Social Structure in the Nineteenth-Century City.* New York: Academic Press, 1979.

Hugo, Richard. *The Triggering Town.* New York: W. W. Norton, 1979.

Jensen, Arthur R. "How Much Can We Boost IQ and Scholastic Achievement?" *Harvard Educational Review* 39 (1969):1–23.

Johnson, Diane J., ed. *Proud Sisters: The Wisdom and Wit of African-American Women.* New York: Peter Pauper Press, 1995.

Kaestle, Carl F., Helen Damon-Moore, Lawrence C. Stedman, Katherine Tinsley, and William Vance Trollinger Jr. *Literacy in the United States: Readers and Reading since 1880.* New Haven: Yale University Press, 1991.

Labov, William. "Co-existent Systems in African-American Vernacular English." In *African-American English: Structure, History, and Use,* eds.

Salikoko Mufwene, John Rickford, Guy Bailey, and John Baugh, 110–153. London: Routledge, 1998.

———. *Language in the Inner City: Studies in the Black English Vernacular.* Philadelphia: University of Pennsylvania Press, 1972.

———. *The Social Stratification of English in New York City.* Washington, D.C.: Center for Applied Linguistics, 1966.

Labov, William, and Wendell Harris. "DeFacto Segregation of Black and White Vernaculars." Paper presented at the Twelfth Annual Conference of New Ways of Analyzing Variation, Montreal, 1983.

LeClair, Thomas. "A Conversation with Toni Morrison. 'The language must not sweat.'" *New Republic,* March 21, 1981: 25–29.

LePage, Robert B. "Acts of Identity." *English Today* 8 (1986): 21–24.

LePage, Robert B., and Andrée Tabouret-Keller. *Acts of Identity: Creole-Based Approaches to Language and Ethnicity.* Cambridge: Cambridge University Press, 1985.

Lippi-Green, Rosina. *English with an Accent: Language, Ideology, and Discrimination in the United States.* London: Routledge, 1997.

Locke, Edwin A., and Gary P. Latham. *A Theory of Goal Setting and Task Performance.* Englewood Cliffs, N.J.: Prentice-Hall, 1990.

Markus, Hazel, and Paula Nurius. "Possible Selves." *American Psychologist* 41 (1986): 954–969.

Marshall, Paule. *Reena and Other Stories.* New York: The Feminist Press, 1983.

Marvin, Carolyn. "Constructed and Reconstructed Discourse: Inscription and Talk in the History of Literacy." *Communication Research* 11 (1984): 563–594.

Mezzacappa, Dale. "Summit Pushes for Higher Standards, Salaries for Teachers." *Athens Daily New/Athens Banner-Herald,* October 3, 1999, p. 3A.

Milroy, James, and Lesley Milroy. *Authority in Language: Investigating Language Prescription and Standardization.* 2nd ed. London: Routledge & Kegan Paul, 1991.

Morrison, Toni. *Song of Solomon.* New York: Plume, 1977.

———. "Unspeakable Things Unspoken: The Afro-American Presence in American Literature." *Michigan Quarterly Review* 28 (1989): 1–34.

Mufwene, Salikoko. "What Is African American English?" In *Sociocultural and Historical Contexts of African American English,* ed. Sonja L. Lanehart, 221–251. Amsterdam: John Benjamins, 2001.

Mura, David. "Strangers in the Village." In *Race, Class, and Gender: An An-*

thology, eds. Margaret L. Andersen and Patricia Hill Collins, 11–20. Belmont, Calif.: Wadsworth, 1992.

Naylor, Gloria. *Mama Day.* New York: Ticknor & Fields, 1988.

O'Barr, William M. "Professional Varieties: The Case of Language and Law." In *American Dialect Research,* ed. Dennis Preston, 319–330. Philadelphia: John Benjamins, 1993.

O'Connor, Carla. "Dispositions toward (Collective) Struggle and Educational Resilience in the Inner City: A Case Analysis of Six African-American High School Students." *American Educational Research Journal* 34 (1997): 593–629.

Orr, Eleanor Wilson. *Twice as Less.* New York: Norton, 1987.

Rickford, John. *African American Vernacular English: Features, Evolution, and Educational Implications.* Oxford: Blackwell, 1999.

Rickford, John, and Angela Rickford. "Dialect Readers Revisited." *Linguistics and Education* 7 (1995): 107–128.

Rickford, John Russell, and Russell John Rickford. *Spoken Soul: The Story of Black English.* New York: John Wiley & Sons, 2000.

Schutz, Paul A. *An Interactive Process Ontology for the Self-Regulating Aspects of Knowing, Learning, and Emoting: The Relationship between Goals and Feedback in Learning.* Unpublished dissertation. University of Texas, 1989.

———. "Goals as the Transactive Point between Motivation and Cognition." *Perspectives on Student Motivation, Cognition, and Learning: Essays in Honor of Wilbert J. McKeachie,* eds. Paul R. Pintrich, D. Brown, and Claire E. Weinstein, 113–133. Hillsdale, N.J.: Erlbaum, 1994.

———. "Goals in Self-Directed Behavior." *Educational Psychologist* 2 (1991): 55–67.

Scribner, Sylvia, and Michael Cole. *The Psychology of Literacy.* Cambridge: Harvard University Press, 1981.

Shaughnessy, Mina. *Errors and Expectations: A Guide for the Teacher of Basic Writing.* New York: Oxford University Press, 1977.

Sledd, James H. "Bi-Dialectalism: The Linguistics of White Supremacy." *Contemporary English,* ed. David L. Shores, 319–330. Philadelphia: Lippincott, 1972.

Smitherman, Geneva. *Black Talk: Words and Phrases from the Hood to the Amen Corner.* Boston: Houghton Mifflin, 1994.

———. *Talkin and Testifyin: The Language of Black America.* Detroit: Wayne State University Press, 1977.

————. *Talkin That Talk: Language, Culture, and Education in African America.* New York: Routledge, 2000.

Solomon, Robert C. *The Passions: Myth and Nature of Human Emotion.* Notre Dame, Ind.: University of Notre Dame Press, 1976.

Spears, Arthur K. "Black American English." *Anthropology for the Nineties,* ed. Johnnetta B. Cole, 96–113. New York: The Free Press, 1988.

Stuckey, J. Elspeth. *The Violence of Literacy.* Portsmouth, N.H.: Boynton/Cook, 1991.

Walker, Alice. *The Color Purple.* New York: Harcourt Brace Jovanovich, 1982.

————. *You Can't Keep a Good Woman Down.* San Diego: Harvest/Harcourt Brace Jovanovich, 1981.

Wiley, Ralph. *Why Black People Tend to Shout.* New York: Penguin Books, 1992.

Wolfram, Walt. *A Sociolinguistic Description of Detroit Negro Speech.* Washington, D.C.: Center for Applied Linguistics, 1969.

INDEX